PHILOSOPHY OF INDIAN MUSIC
Contribution of the Trinity

PHILOSOPHY OF INDIAN MUSIC
Contribution of the Trinity

Dr. John Christopher Kommalapudi

AKANSHA PUBLISHING HOUSE
NEW DELHI-110002 (INDIA)

AKANSHA PUBLISHING HOUSE
4649-B/21, Ansari Road
Darya Ganj, New Delhi - 110 002
Ph.: 23263193 / 9811582579 / 09435116718
Fax: 011-23263193
Email: ektabooks@yahoo.com
visit us: www.akanshapublishinghouse.com

Philosophy of Indian Music: Contribution of the Trinity

First Published 2010

ISBN 978-81-8370-206-5

PRINTED IN INDIA

Published by Akansha Publishing House, New Delhi and Printed at Mehra Offset, Delhi.

Dedicated to
My beloved Father
Late JOHN VICTOR KOMMALAPUDI,
the sole master of my being
and
My loving Mother
Mrs. DEEVENAMMA,
With deepest love, respect and regard.

Contents

Foreword

Music has been defined as a way to attain the *puruṣārthās* of life. In the ancient world it was always connected with a philosophical or ethical choice. The philosophy of Indian music was part of the analysis of Sound or *Nāda,* which included in its ambit, music and dance, grammar, language and meaning. All the systems of philosophy have accepted the concept of *Nāda.* The total philosophy of Indian music was not contained in one text or series. Since the *Vedic* times onwards the ethical, aesthetic and spiritual use of music has been clearly evident. India, more than any other culture, has emphasized the role of music in attaining transcendence.

This book is casting its light on emerging ideas and interests in philosophy in general and in philosophy of music in particular. The foundational concept of this book, that the values of music are gained through direct experiences with its meaningful sounds, remains intact, is explained and applied in broader, more inclusive in scope, with a philosophical stance as the basis. In addition, it clarifies and updates for readers the explanations of musical feeling, musical creativity, and musical meaning that are at its core.

Dr. K. John Christopher has spared no pains in culling the material from more than 300 publications in preparing this valuable conspectus-"Philosophy of Indian Music: Contribution of the Trinity." This work will be an outstanding contribution besides being a boon to scholars and students of music.

Dr. John Christopher's wide range historical study of Indian music covers from the earliest historical traces of our music to the present day. What I feel that he is the most authoritative in this realm as he examined early texts and authorities in detail. The philosophical values of Indian music must be brought to match with modernity. Dr John Christopher has both the requisite musicianship and the scholarship for such a task. "Philosophy of Indian Music: Contribution of the Trinity" is both an admirable work of art and a real contribution to the movement towards greater understanding of philosophy of Indian Music, ushering new horizons in analyzing this art in a philosophical way.

The present book is one of the most important contributions to the study and understanding of philosophy of music and I commend it to the reader whole heartedly. I congratulate the author for his zeal and wish him that he will contribute his spirit in philosophy of music.

L.K. Mohana Rao
Principal College of Arts and Commerce
Andhra University
Visakhapatnam

Prefatory Note

In Indian culture it is the belief that all forms of arts have a divine origin. Music is also believed to have originated from the Gods. Some ancient treatises describe the connection of the origin of *swarās* to the sounds of animals and birds. Man, with his keen sense of observation and perception, tried to simulate these sounds. His ability to distinguish between sounds of different frequencies, qualities and timbre would have been an important factor in the evolution of music.

It is generally accepted that the *Veda*s are a probable source of Indian music, which has developed over the centuries into the sophisticated system that it is today. The word "*Veda*" means knowledge. Thousands of hymns in the *Vedas*, which are dedicated to the Gods and Hindu rituals, in the form of chants were passed down by oral tradition from generation to other. There are four Vedas: Ṛg, *Yajus*, *Sāma* and *Atharvaṇa*. Of these, the *Sāma Veda* is said to have laid the foundation for Indian music. *Sāma Veda* consists mostly of *Ṛg Vedic* hymns, set to musical tunes. These are used to be sung during *Vedic* sacrifices, sometimes accompanied by a musical instrument.

Apart from the *Sāma Veda*, there are references to music and musical instruments in the *Upaniṣads*, *Brahmaṇās* and *Purāṇās*. In Epics like *Rāmāyaṇa* and *Mahābhārata* there are some references to music. The music system in practice during Bharata's period must have been similar in some respects to the present day Carnatic system. Bharata's *Nātya Śāstra* mentions many musical concepts that continue to be relevant to Carnatic music today.

In India mythology has a very important place and its influence on the art and culture of the country is phenomenal and music is no exception. Owing to its spiritual and devotional aspects, music is associated with Hinduism, the dominant religion of India. The origin of this art has been attributed to the Gods and Goddesses. Moreover, individual deities are associated with different kinds of musical instruments, *Kṛṣṇa* with the flute or *Saraswati* with the *Vīṇa*. The literary sources such as the epics and mythological anthologies also mention the close association of music with divinity.

Apart from these sources, many saints and scholars believe that music is the greatest form of *tapasya* (penance) and the easiest way to reach godhead or to attain salvation. Most of the musical compositions are either philosophical in content or describe the various deities or incidents from Hindu mythology. There are others who believe that music itself is divine and that the perfect synchronisation of the performer with the musical sound, *Nāda*, the real divine bliss. This practice is called *Nādopasāna*. Many musicians and music lovers visualise divine forms in the *Rāgas* or the melodic entities of music.

Dr. John Christopher has done a meticulous study in the field of Indian music and in his book, "Philosophy of Indian Music: Contribution of the Trinity." He opens to the reader a pleasant vista of the musings of the philosophy of music. The book is both an introduction to philosophy of music generally and an introduction to philosophy of Indian music in particular. This book that reminds the connoisseur's mind why philosophy matters, especially as applied to the things we love most. This book provides new and distinctive outlines of philosophy of music, especially, the devotional music of South India.

Music is divine. "*Advaita siddhi ki Amarathva Labdhiki Gānamē Sōpānamu*" (Music or song is the way through which one can attain *Advaita Siddhi* and attain *Amaralōka*.)

S.D.A. Joga Rao

Acknowledgements

In this age of rising aspirations and national progress Indian Music has become so much of national pride and the veneration for it has been cultivated in every town and the cities of India. In this context, the 'book' is intended to expound the reasons for the same, so that it is to be known and understood by everybody.

Indian music gives solace to the heart as well as the mind and goes deeper down into realms where emotion and intellect coalesce into intuition. Its appeal is primarily to the emotion; but it sublimates these emotions into impersonal experiences where the dualities merge into a great synthesis, where joy and sorrow merge into ineffable bliss. Indian music never loses sight of high purpose, the realization of Divine Bliss through beauty of sound. Indian music is not meant just to give a pleasurable sensation to the ear and stop there. It pleases the ear, but that is only the first step. The vibrations in the air which cause this titillation in the ear set up corresponding vibrations in our nature; our emotions are affected; our mind is also influenced; even the vital currents in our body are affected by these vibrations.

Selina Thielemann, in *'The Spirituality of Music'*, says:

> "Spiritual union is the creative union of progenitive forces whose coalescence acts as the prime cause of universal progression. It is the union whose core reality is truth, hence sweetness, for else the vibrations of the cosmic energies could not find their response in creation. It is the union whose inner substance is music, for music

> is the supreme expression of transcendental sweetness. It is the union whose actuality, whose definiteness defies all pain and distress on the way towards this ultimate goal."

Devotional poets, saints, saint-composers and mystics brought the wisdom of the ancients, the *Ṛṣis* and the *Āchāryas*, to the common people. They adopted the local language and used the medium of song in their mission. They were pilgrims, all the time moving among the people. They came from all classes and strata of the society, which in itself were the outcome of the universality and the basic oneness of men that they proclaimed.

They might have risen in diverse schools of religion or philosophy, but all of them emphasized the fundamental truth and the eternal values from music to music through music. Their plea was for sincerity of faith in God, fellowship of beings and integration of the whole man. It is these philosophical positions that have inspired me to undertake this research work. Rabindranath Tagore, in *Gitanjali*, expresses his feelings towards Divine Music.

> "I know not how thou singest, my master. I ever listen in silent amazement. The light of thy music illumines the world. The life breath of thy music runs from sky to sky. The holy stream of the music breaks through all stony obstacles and rushes on. My heart long to join in thy song, but vainly struggles for a voice. I would speak, but speech breaks not into song, and I cry out baffled. Ah, thou hast made my heart captive in the endless meshes of thy music, my master!"

I am aware of the magnitude of the concept; Indian music and therefore I have limited my endeavour only to a study with special reference to devotional music of South India. I have made an attempt to incorporate the philosophy of Indian Music in a broad perspective.

I express my deep sense of gratitude to Professor G. Veerraju, Chairman, Board of Studies, Department of Philosophy and Religious Studies, Andhra University, Visakhapatnam, for all the necessary academic help and intellectual guidance that he rendered to me during my book.

I express my sincere thanks to Prof. L.K.Mohana Rao, Principal, College of Arts and Commerce, Andhra University, for having kindly consented to write the Foreword.

I am deeply indebted to Prof. S.D.A. Joga Rao, Head of the Department of Philosophy and Religious Studies, Andhra University, Visakhapatnam, who is my great inspiration in all my endeavours and also who has kindly accepted to write a word of appreciation for the book.

I offer my heartfelt thanks to Prof. P. George Victor, Prof. S. Satyanarayana, Prof.Y.V. Satyanarayana, Dr.S.C. Suguna Kumari, Associate Professor, Dr. B.V.S. Banusree, Associate Professor and Dr. B. Ravi Babu, Assistant Professor, Dr. Ch. Prema Kumar, Guest Faculty, Department of Philosophy, Andhra University for their academic guidance and cooperation.

I cannot adequately express my gratitude to my brothers Dr. M.P.N. Vijaya Kumar, Faculty, Department of Library and Information Science, Andhra University, Visakhapatnam, Dr. B. Mohan Rao, Faculty, Department of Sociology, Andhra University, Visakhapatnam, for helping me in so many aspects not only in academic work but also in my personal life.

I express my loving gratitude to my beloved mother Deevena Victor, my sisters, Mrs. J. Mary Prabhakar, Mrs. K. Vinolia, Mrs. P. Jasmin, my brother, Mr. K. John Lincoln, my brothers-in-law, Mr. J.D. Prabhakar, Mr. K. Sampath Kumar Bhashyam, Mr. P. Jaya Prasad, my sister-in-Law, Mrs. K. Phebe, my wife Mrs. Vijaya Christopher, my daughter, Sharon Christopher, my son, James Rahul, my father-in-law, V. paul, my mother-in-law, Rosemond Paul, who have not only inspired me but also stood behind me.

I also express my sincere gratitude and thanks to Akansha Publishing House, New Delhi, who showed keen interest in publishing this book.

K. J. CHRISTOPHER

1

Introduction

Music is a spiritual art and science of harmony. It is the divine art, considered by philosophers, seers, musicologists and poets. It bestows absolute bliss and happiness upon mankind, which are permanent and everlasting. Music melts the hearts of the human being and draws every living being with its magical notes, transporting the listeners to the unknown region of enchanting sound harmonies. The purest form of *Sādhanā* can raise the musician to the mystic truth of philosophy and in that stage the musician could be in direct communion with the heavenly bliss and could achieve an immediate awareness of the absolute truth and tranquility.

The word music comes from the Greek 'mousike' and is derived from 'Muse'. The Muses were supposed to have been entities responsible for all the arts and for being the mysterious suppliers of artistic inspiration to humans. Historians suggest that use of the word mousike implies a relationship between music and poetry which continues to survive to the present day.

Aristotle pointed out that it is not easy to determine the nature of music or why anyone should have knowledge of it. In the modern times there has been a rational attempt to distinguish between music and noise. A musical tone accepts to have a uniformity of vibration that grants it a fixed tone. Tone is only one component of music.

There are also, rhythm, timbre (or tone colour - i.e. a note played on a flute has a different timbre to exactly the same note played on a trumpet, etc.) and texture.

The ability of music to have a profound effect on humans has been recognised from the earliest references recorded in history. It has been regularly applied in the service of religions since the time of the Vediç hymns in ancient India. For the Greek philosopher Pythagoras, music was regarded as a department of mathematics. He laid the foundations of acoustics, which led to recognize the relationship between pitch and the length of a string.

Plato considered music to be a part of ethics and was anxious to regulate the use of modes (arrangements of notes into scales) because of their various effects on humans. Plato saw a relationship established between the character of a man and the music that represented him. He argued that rhythmic and melodic complexity should be avoided that could lead to depression and disorder. Plato advocated simplicity. Music, in its perfect form, would echo divine harmony; rhythm and melody would imitate the movements of heavenly bodies (the origin of the idea of music of the spheres) and reflect the moral order of the universe. Plato distrusted the emotional power of earthly music. He argued that certain sensuous modes were dangerous and advocated a strong censorship of music. He approved of music in only accepted ethical forms, which he valued. For Plato then, music was a psycho-sociological phenomenon. Even though Plato's attitude towards Music saw it as a shadow of the Ideal, it accepted a symbolic significance of the art.

Aristotle developed the concept of art as imitation, but argued that music could also express the universal. His idea that works of art could contain a measure of the truth within themselves strengthened the symbolic view. Aristotle fell on line with Plato with the view that music could mould the human character. He admitted that all the modes recognize the happiness and pleasure which could be of value to both individual and the state. He advocated a rich musical diet. Aristotle also stated that those with only theoretical knowledge of music could not be good judges with regard to performance as those who could perform it. Aristotle's pupil Aristoxenus gave considerable credit to the powers of perception of the listener to music. According to Aristoxenus music has got to play a functional and emotional role that requires hearing and intellectual abilities by the listener.

Throughout the 17th and 18th centuries, as new schools of philosophy emerged, attempts were made to re-evaluate music. Kepler was a new Pythagorean, who argued for followed by planetary movement, the harmony of the spheres etc, while Descartes saw it as an arm of mathematics and followed Plato in the matter of demanding moderate rhythms and simple melodies that would not excite and perhaps cause immoral outcomes. Leibniz argued music that mirrored a universal rhythm and reality that was constructed from mathematical relationships. Music was a means by which this could be experienced in the subconscious mind. Kant ranked music as the lowest of the arts, distrusting its wordlessness, but gave it some value when combined with the word. Hegel acknowledged the power of music like Kant and preferred vocal music. Hegel made a new observation, that music had no independent existence in space and was not therefore objective. Hegel prognosticated that music was of value only in subjective form to any individual appreciating it. For Hegel the essence of music was rhythm and its counterpart was found in man's innermost self.

The 18th century sprouted contextual explanations of music. Although there was a general agreement that music connected to emotional life, much time was given to explain contexts, such as ritual, religious, nationalistic, military, funerary etc. all of which related music only to various aspects of the human environment and experiences within it.

Modern musical educators have universally agreed that most human ears can be "educated", and that an audience so educated is in fact endowed with musicianship in terms of its ability to listen to and appreciate music of high art. Access to this "stronger, quicker, more necessary and infallible," is therefore an ability that might in some require some initial effort and training. Conversely, some forms of music, by no means lowly, appear to be immediately accessible and seemingly 'universal' or 'fundamental'.

Such a discussion of music, which is far from exhaustive from a philosophical point of view, and in terms of the question, "What is Music?" would be incomplete without at least a brief mention of Darwinism. Darwinism has undergone many transitions, particularly in today's postmodern world. In its approach to music, it cited birdsong as an example of an advantage in natural selection. Human tonality began, like birdsong, with the voice, its use for natural selection advantage by the group etc. Darwinism has held a largely defensive position against the argument that nature does not over-engineer, with the consequent difficulty in finding a Darwinist explanation for the human mind to have been engineered by natural selection to the degree that an individual like Beethoven can compose a symphony of such high art and that in addition there is a human audience to appreciate it.

Post-modernist Darwinism, however, has become focused on the microscopic, and upon genes, memes, and cells. Cells, made up of genes, each containing DNA supposedly contain memes, pieces of code that determine the behaviour of the cell and the behaviour of the brain which in turn controls the entire organism. Each of these components is bent upon only its survival and upon, collectively, the reproduction of the organism, and therefore the survival of the meme. This reductionalism, arguably the usage of modern scientific discoveries for the purpose of defence of the Darwinist theory has, however, occured in parallel with tantalising scientific glimpses into the vibratory nature of cells — i.e. like all matter; they have their own frequency and are affected by other external frequencies.

While adding to the mystery of music and its meaning, these observations do little to enhance the Darwinist approach, generally, because that approach in the context of music is defensive and nominalist. Such nominalism, in the case of music, would require faith in a human-infallibility of the Darwinist juxtaposed against an overall failure by humanity to discover a universal mechanism to explain music as a phenomenon in objective terms, when at the same time as observed by modern science the relationships within tonalities (frequencies) within music (harmonics) are mirrored in the electromagnetic harmonics of the universe. Thus, while man can explore variations and complexities of music, the essence of music (harmonics + rhythms) is neither man's creation nor invention and exists externally from him.

Therefore, while Darwinist observations, on the fringe of an attempt by humanity to grapple with a Quantum Theory of the Universe, are interesting, the conclusions derived by Darwinism require us to accept, within that much wider context, that not only is man a machine, but that the whole Cosmos is such and that it is governed by a program not unlike the code delivering these words and graphics to the human screen. In the absence of a true Quantum Theory of the Universe, Darwinism can only be a subsidiary in the debate of Music, but it has value in the sense that it suggests, without intending to, a need for synthesis within the sciences, in which music as a phenomenon has a place in the search for an answer to the puzzle of existence.

In India, the idea of the worship of God through words and tune originated in the Vedic age (1500 B.C), with the coming of the Aryans. The Vedas contained hymns in Sanskrit which were meant to propitiate the forces of nature, each one symbolizing the reigning deity. These hymns were sung in tune and may be called the precursor of *bhajans* or devotional songs.

The musical activity is needed to establish and reestablish the contact with the divinity. Searching the Supreme bliss and attaining the spiritual climax in union with God is a continuous process. The idea of music as a divine art can be understood as an invention of divinities or as a general principle of divine creation. It may be interpreted as image, imitation, or anticipation of divine or heavenly music. It can be understood as a means of influencing divinities.

From the ancient *Vedic* times to the modern times, the term '*Brahman*' has been the most important unified concept of *Hindu* religion and Indian philosophy. In India through out the ages, the saints, seers, *yogis* and poets feel that the *Brahman* has always remained above all descriptions and beyond all words.

According to *Śhrīmad Bhagavad Gītā*, the Imperishable and Immutable is the Supreme *Brahman* The *Brahman* state is that of the Supreme existence, supremely aware of itself, namely *Svayamprakāşa*. It is *Saccidānanda* (*Sat, Cit, Ānanda*). Existence-Consciousness-Bliss. The *Taittirīya Upanişad* defined *Brahman* as the Self of all beings, the Reality that is One and all pervading principle. In the *Ŗgveda, Sāmaveda*, and *Yajurveda*, it is said that every thing in this whole Universe is God-made, God-protected and God-pervaded. The *Upanişads* describe the phenomenon of happiness as the Bliss of *Brahman*. In the essence of *Vedānta* and *Upanişadic* philosophy, *Nāda-Brahma-Vada* or Philosophy of Music was conceived. In India Vedic Philosophy refers to the concept of *Nāda Brahma* ('sound god') as the source of all vibrations, audible or inaudible in the cosmos. The sacred syllable *Om* is the oral representation of this sound genesis and in its written form it has had at least a thousand-year history. Repetition of a syllable such as *Om* or verse consisting of such syllables is an ancient meditation practice based on a belief in the efficacy of controlling vibration within the body.

Indian civilization has given prime significance to the oral tradition; hearing sacred sound is reflected in the name given to the most ancient sacred scriptures, *Śriti* (that which is heard), believed to be divine revelation. In India the musicologists, emphasized that *Nāda*, the Causal Music, being the source of all forms of *Vāk* is called *Śabda Brahman* or *Nāda Brahman*. In this process *Śabda* or *Nāda–tattva* has been completely identified with *Brahman-tattva*. Devoted musicians have regarded *Nāda* as *Parama Vidya* (Ultimate knowledge). *Vāk*, the vital force of the ultimate is the source of expressive sound. One can attain *Brahman* itself, by worshipping *Śakti* of *Brahman*. *Nāda* is the *Śakthi* of *Brahman*, synonymous with *Para Vāk*. Therefore, *Nāda Brahman* stands for the Ultimate Principle of Causal Sound or Cosmic Music, which is causative, creative and dynamic energy of the Supreme Being. Philosophers, musicologists and *Tantriks* regard *Nāda* as the material cause of the universe and identify it with the *Brahman* of the *Upaniṣads.*

The sages and *Ṛṣis* of India described *Sangīta* and *Sāhitya* as two limbs of the Goddess *Saraswathi.* According to Indian Musical tradition, *Brahma* first created music from the *Sāmaveda*. The bard-priest composed hymns, in praise of the gods, to be sung or chanted at the time of performing sacrifices. This tradition was continued in the Aryans new home in the northern India until a sizable body of oral religious poetry had been composed. This body of chanted poetry grew in massive proportions, and the best of the poems were compiled as an anthology called *Ṛgveda*. The name '*Veda*' (knowledge) stands for the *Mantras* and the *Brāhmaṇas*. *Mantra* means a hymn addressed to God or Goddess. The collection of the *Mantras* is called *'Samhitā'*. These *Samhitas* are *Ṛg, Sāma, Yajuh* and *Atharva.*

The *Ṛgveda*, the oldest *Veda*, is addressed to the elements of nature personified as deities, which are prayers for protection from calamities for attainment of prosperity - material as well as spiritual. It was not committed to writing, but the text and the chanting formula were carefully handed down by word of mouth from one generation to the next generation, up to the present period. The verses in the *Ṛgveda* are arranged according to the priestly families who used and, presumably, had composed the hymns These *Vedas* have several ancillary texts, called the *Brāhmaṇas, Āraṇyakas*, and *Upaniṣads,* which are also regarded as part of the *Vedas*. The *Vedas* are still chanted by *Brahmin* priests at occasions such as weddings, funerals, and also during their daily worship.

The *Vedic* hymns which were meant for *yajñas* were called *Yajur-veda* and the hymns that were meant for singing were called *Sāmaveda.* Music was evolved out of stanzas of *Ṛgveda* set to tunes and tones in the form of *Sāmagānas,* inspired with a religious motive and a spiritual purpose. *Vedic* music is the earliest instance of the deep relationship between religion and music in India. The *Ṛgveda* relied on recited hymns (*richa*). The musical chanting of the *Sāmaveda* employed more notes (finally settling on seven notes), and it is said to be the source of the later secular and classical music. In fact, the word *Sāma* itself is a compound expression which includes two entities: the first component '*Sa*' refers to hymns, i.e. *richa*, and the second component, '*Ma*' refers to the musical notes. The basic source of the spirit of music is *Ātman*, as per the description of the philosophy. The spiritual *Sādhana* is inseparable from the eternal spirit of music. The purest form of *Sādhana* can raise the musician to the truth of philosophy and direct communion with the heavenly bliss and could achieve an immediate awareness of the absolute truth and tranquility. Music in India occupies an important place in the spiritual *Sādhana*. Musical method and music took the first place in the order of any ritual connected with Gods.

In Hindu Mythology each God or Goddess is inevitably associated with some kind of musical instrument or legend. Goddess *Saraswati* is always shown with a *Veeṇā* in her hands, *Lord Śiva* with a *Damaru*, *Lord Viṣṇu* with a conch, *Brahma* with the *Mṛdangam*, *Lord Kṛṣṇa* with the Flute and *Nārada* with an *Ektāra* or Lute. Among the important landmarks of literature on music are the *Mārkandeya Purāṇa*, *Viṣṇu Purāṇa*, the *Brahma Sūtrās* and other *Purāṇa* and epics of the early period. Vocal music was prevalent, even from the *Vedic* times down to the present day as a continuous tradition. The sage *Vālmiki* composed the first Indian epic, the *Rāmāyaṇa*, written in *slokas* form. The word '*sloka*' refers to particular kind of metrical composition known for its brevity, easy tempo and rhyme. It is evident that precise concept of music or *Sangīt* had been established and appreciated from the various uses of musical metaphors in the epic. *Rāma* was an expert in *Gandharva*, the 'Classical Music' of the time. The term *Mārga Sangīt*, which was created and propagated by *Brahma* and other deities, was also used in the epic. *Mārga Sangīt* was not meant for entertainment and it was presented before the Gods to please them. *Rāvaṇa* the demon-leader and *Sugreeva*, the monkey-leader were well trained musicians. Occasions of festival music were known as *Samaj*.

The *Rāmāyaṇa* was also propagated, as an oral epic, according to the musical norms of oral tradition. This was the *pathya* mode of music making, ideal for narration, which was employed by *Rāma's* sons *Kuṣa* and *Lava* at *Rāma's* court when they sang a narrative song in praise of *Rāma*. The use of technical terms in popular literature signifies that knowledge in the concerned field of study is widespread in society.

Mahābhārata used the term *Gandharva*; a specific kind of music was referred in the epic. Musicology or the science of music was called *Gandharvaśāstra*. The expert practitioners of this particular music were called *Gandharvas* (Super beings). *Arjuna*, one of the heroes in the *Mahābhārata* learnt these musical arts from *Chitrasen*, a *Gandharva*. The names of the seven basic musical notes have been clearly mentioned in the *Mahābhārata*. The Epic bears testimony to the long living tradition of Indian Classical music.

The use of music in festivals and other social occasions brings out the importance given to music in human life. The stories of *Purāṇas* highlight the Divine Musical Knowledge. The music of *Vāyu Purāṇa* (300 AD) dealt with the rituals performed during a sacrifice. The *Mārkandeya Purāṇa* (400 and 500 AD) offers interesting insight into music. *Saraswathi* offers a boon to the King, *Aśvatāra*, a king of *Nāgas* or Serpents, nothing but the knowledge of the musical notes or svaras. The *Harivamśa* and *Bhāgavata Purāṇas* are rich of musical reference. The *Viṣṇudharmottara Purāṇa*, (400-500 AD) devotes one chapter each to *Gīt* and *Vādya*.

Indian music is predominantly melodic in nature and the unique *rāga* system, born of the various combinations of microtones and different embellishments produce sweet and soft impressions in the minds of listeners. The *rāgas* create a consoling and transcending attitude of the mind, and purify the knots of the mind through submission and devotion. The Indian *Rāga* System was originated in the *Vedic* period (*Ṛgvedic Period*). Indian tradition had a great intuition about the power of sound and intonation. The science of sound was very important for use in every condition of life in healing, in teaching, in evolving and accomplishment. It is only from this *Sāmagāna*, that seven notes were evolved which formed the basis not only for the *rāga* system of India, but also for what is known as world music. The formalized regional or *Dēśī* music enriched the treasury of Indian classical music in the form of *rāgas*. The present system of *rāga* music is somewhat a different approach followed in more systematic and scientific manner by seventy two *mēlakarta* scheme (Heptatonic Scales) devised by *Venkatāmakhi* with various permutations and combinations of *svaras* under *mēlakarta* and *janya* classifications in South Indian music and ten basic *thātus* or *mēlas* in North Indian Music (*Pandit Bhākthande*) contributing to the *rāga* composition and *rāga* development. Music is highly regarded as one of the channels for the development of an intimate relationship between God and Man in religio-cultural circumstances in India. The relationship established between music and religion, paved the way for devotional music or *Bhakthi-Sangīt*, and ultimately it became the way of life.

Vaiṣṇava Bhakthi spread all over the country in praise of *Lord Viṣṇu*, and thousands of songs were composed which created abundant musical forms. In Indian devotional music, '*Yoga Sādhana*' was the highest and noblest path, in which yogic path of *Gāna* which means *Sangīta* was prescribed to be the best and it has been further emphasized that there is nothing beyond music. The saint-composers like, *Kālidāsa, Bharata, Matanga, Nārada, Jayadeva, Śārangadēva, Purnandaradasa, Annamāchārya, Meerābāi, Surdās, Kabir, Bhadrāchala Rāmadas, Kṣetrayya,* and the Trinity of South Indian Classical music, namely, *Tyāgarāja, Muthuswāmi Dikshitār, Śyāma Śāstri* and other saint-composers followed the devotional path.

Indian music possesses a special character of its own and differs from music of other countries in its structure, temperament and method of improvisation. It has the most striking feature of being a synthesis between philosophy and religion. Thus in Indian tradition, music, religion and philosophy are interlinked.

In South India devotional music (*Bhakti Sangīt*) furnished a powerful stimulus to the rejuvenation of Hinduism. Groups of devotees headed by some prominent religious leaders moved from place to place and shrine to shrine, singing the hymns they composed in the course of the pilgrimages. The result was the use of simple diction and catchy tunes. The devotional hymns of the *Vaiṣṇava* and *Śaiva* saints not only stirred the hearts of the people of all stratas of society, of this region, but their activity of composing devotional hymns and singing them from shrine to shrine and temple to temple gave a new turn to the cult of *Bhakti.* This movement gave real impetus to the composition of devotional music which even to this day forms an important part of the music of India.

The first chapter deals with the relationship between music and religion and how music as one of the channels, influenced the religious activity throughout the ages. In India music is not an abstract concept that exists outside the concrete reality of being. It is indwelled by the cosmic principles whose dynamics make the universal mechanism function. Music is energy, but at the same time it is the expression of that energy, the definite manifestation of an unmanifested force. Music penetrates the cosmos as an invisible, inaudible vibration of bliss. Music is the elemental manifestation of cosmic harmony because music evokes harmony, accomplishes the union of opposing entities and thereby fulfils the primal ambition of all beings to become one with the Supreme. It is its mysteriousness - the mysteriousness of the musical sound that absorbs the mystery of the human soul and conveys it to the ear through the medium of sonic waves. Once the river of emotional waves merges into the ocean of sounding vibrations, their union becomes audible and the unspoken secret of the heart reveals itself in music.

Music is a spiritual experience whose perceptibility remains out of the reach of most sense organs: music is neither visible nor touchable, nor can it be tasted or smelt. Yet the phenomenon of music is not immaterial and it can be perceived by the only sense (hearing), which is alert at all times: music as a spiritual reality represents the very cause for that experience. Music is the object of the emotional experience. Unlike mere sound, music prompts an emotional response in any case. Music is sensual and emotional experience both in one. Through its vibrations, music exists as a material reality, which is perceived by the senses but accessed and apprehended emotionally.

Music instigates the highest form of communication, which is worship. Worship, dedicated service enlivened by the spirit of devotion is the primary way for the loving soul to communicate her emotional appeal to the beloved.

Devotion is not itself prayer or worship, but it is the invigorative quality of devotion that makes religious pursuits meaningful. In the Indian tradition, the term to denote devotion is *Bhakti*. 'Devotion' and 'music' are joined together by a common verbal basis, and their conjunction implies more than a mere linguistic stratagem. Music is devotional in any case, for devotion represents the vital essence of music, and there would be no music without the life-giving current of devotion.

The second chapter deals with the origin of *Nāda*, and its relationship with *Brahman*, the Supreme Being. In the *Vedic* tradition, sound is identified with the supreme reality, *Śabda Brahman*, the prime object of worship and meditation. Being given concrete shape in the chanted syllable, sound acts as the principal vehicle of communication between man and the forces of the universe. Reciting and chanting of sacred formulae has been the fundamental element of ritual and divine worship since Vedic times. The early Indian conception of musical sound as emerging vital substance is a remarkable synthesis of a number of ideas.

1. The divine origin of sound
2. The notion of a transpersonal world soul
3. The breath as living substance and agent of universal process
4. The special nature of the medium of *Ākāśa*
5. The efficacy of ritual action.
6. Utterance as an act of worship and means of knowledge
7. The metaphoric identification of thought, breathe, sound, and semen as means by which we act upon the world.
8. The mythical association of sound and speech (*Vāk*).

The evolution of Indian music has since early times been responsive to this cluster of cultural values.

The third chapter is on *Vedic* Chant, Intonation and Vedic music and the evolution of music since Vedic period. Indian theory of music was not developed as a separate science; but it emerged directly from the *Vedas*, the ancient treasure of hymns, conceived by *Ṛṣis* (seers) through divine vision. The evolution from the chanted syllable to the sung melody progressed in a gradual process and always in close association with the development of the religious thought.

According to its underlying spirit, the music of today represents a direct continuation of the practice of ritual service through the medium of sound that originated from *Vedic* chant. The four primary *Vedas* are the oldest and greatest of India's literary treasures as well as scriptural sources for later religious traditions. The most important is the *Ṛgveda,* a collection of 1028 hymns (in more than ten thousand verses) addressed to the principal *Indo-Aryan* deities personifying the various forces of nature. The *Sāma-Veda* is a much smaller collection of hymns, mostly from the *Ṛgveda*, set to melodies (*samans)* and rearranged for liturgical use. The hymns of the *Sāma-Veda* are conceived and rendered in specifically musical terms in pitch compass that extends at times to a full diatonic heptads. The instruction manuals pertaining to the *Sāmaveda* would contain some of the most informative material on the early musical system, both in theory and practice. The 'inherent sound vibrations' will be among the main concerns in this study, along with the means devised to capture the exact nature and structure of these vibrations, both in thought and practice.

The fourth Chapter deals with the spiritual inspiration of the origin of *Svaras* and *Rāgas.* Devotion associated with ambrosia of *Svara* and *Rāga* is salvation. The evolution of *Svara* and *Rāga* in Indian Music has its origin in *Vedas*, which gave unquestionable significance to music. *Vedic* music evolved as an undeniable essence of spirituality and each *Svara* has its own importance in its evolution. It is in the seven notes that the Lord lives and moves and has His being. If one can manifest the *Svaras* precisely, each one of them would form a veritable ornament to God. The *Rāga* constitutes the greatest glory of Indian music. Saint-composers rendered various *rāgas*, which have distinct form, a personality of its own, and anybody singing it should make the full personality of that *rāga* stand before the listener's mind. Music has played in this country an effective role as the handmaid of religion. The best sort of music is what it should be sacred. The conception of music has been spiritual and it is in the temples as part of *Sādhana* that music has flourished.

The fifth chapter presents the origin of devotional music in South India and how different poets and saint-composers propounded their religious and philosophical thoughts in their composition, taking music as a means to attain salvation. Religion in India is more a direct experience than a code of conduct. From an early age, different systems or *mārgas* (paths) have been prescribed for attaining the goal, variously called as liberation, bliss and heaven. However, the different *mārgas* were not contradictory and in some respects they supplemented each other. For example proficiency in *Jñāna-yoga, Rāja-yoga* and *Bhakthi yoga* are demanded from the highest *sādhakas* (devotees). Total surrender to the Almighty is signal on the path of devotion. Based on the *Upaniṣads, the Purāṇas* and personal experience, the builders of the path of devotion have chosen to reach God by their master-servant mother-child, preceptor-disciple (*Guru-Śiṣya*), *vātsalya* (friendly) and *madhura* (love) relationship. Love and devotion lead one to release from the trammels of worldly sufferings.

The royal road starts with the directions in *Bhāgavatha Purāṇa* and the *Gītā*. Liberation is devotion slave. Such a concept and understanding of spiritual motivation inspired many saint-composers to take up music as a means to propagate their philosophical and religious thoughts in attaining salvation. The birth of the *Bhakti* tradition in South India towards the end of the Gupta Period was the first and most significant move on the religious plane. *Saint-composers propagated bhakti*, the earliest of whom are known as *Ālvārs* from Tamil Nadu in South India who spread their message of devotion and love from the 6th century A.D. onwards.

The *bhakti* movement gave rise to an enormous amount of devotional poetry and song, which had an essential impact in the shape of Indian classical music. An important element of Carnatic music in South India is its devotional content. The lyrics of the traditional compositions, whether mythological or social in nature, are set entirely against a devotional or philosophical background.

The sixth chapter presents the devotional music of *Tyāgarāja, Muthu Swāmi Dikṣitār* and *Śyāma Śāstri,* the Trinity of South Indian Classical music in their devotional path. *Tyāgarāja* was a devotee of Sri *Rāma* and his devotional songs addressed to this deity are incomparable, in their depth of devotion and expression of yearnings of a soul for the vision and union with Lord *Rāma. Tyāgarāja* came from the line of the cult of reciting the Lord's name (*Nāmjapa).* He went about singing the glory of the Lord and spent his time worshipping and composing songs of Lord *Rāma. Śyāma Śāstri* composed all his beautiful compositions during his inspired moments when his mind and senses were completely lost to this world and he was at the heights of devotion and blissful state of consciousness. He was a devotee of *Kāmākṣi* and it is supposed that he had *Devi's darśan. Muthu Swāmi Dikṣitārs* compositions have a lot of literary significance. His compositions are mostly invocations to various deities, which have a deeper significance.

The seventh chapter presents the summary and conclusion of all the chapters of the book. All the aspects of Indian music have been covered after a thorough study and careful examination in the context of philosophical and religious perspective. Music and practice (*sādhana*) are not children's play. It is not a mere exhibition of tones, tunes and words, but it is living and dynamic in its form and nature. It is means to the human goal of salvation. Some of the ancient masters have proved this great truth of music-*sādhana*. The *Sāmagānas* of the Vedic period are the living example of this truth. Many years have passed through the medieval and present periods and replaced the ancient one. The age-long glorious tradition of philosophy of music in the spiritual India is still living, and will continue to live from generation to generation.

2

The Philosophic and Religious Roots of Indian Music

In the primitive society, men and women used to sing and dance as a part of pastime and pleasure in their everyday life, but they never enquired about the cause behind music and dance. With the gradual development of culture and civilization, there was an awakening in the intellectual and intuitional pursuits of men, and they began to seek and dive deep into the real significance of music and dance. Philosophy and science of music disclose the fact that sound is the cause and also the foundation of music. Sound is known in Sanskrit as *Nāda*. The vibrations of the sweet and soothing sound-units produce sound. *Rāgas, varnās, mūrcchanās, tānas, alamkāras*, etc, are also the outcome of the sweet and agreeable vibrations of the sound. From the science of music we know that a *Rāga* is a psycho-material object, and it is constructed out of man's innermost feelings and sensibilities. together with material ingredients of tones and tunes.

> "Because of the alliance with 'mathematics' music figured prominently in cosmology, astrology, and number mysticism. Speculations about the harmony of the universe were often inspired by musical facts, as in Plato's *Timaeus* (31-39), or as in the theory that the planets were governed in their motions by ratios of the consonances and therefore produced an unheard music (*Republic*.X). Greek writers

credited Pythagoras (582-07 B.C.) with the earliest acoustical observations.[1]

The main material of music consists of tones or sounds, and philosophical concept of music centers round the sound theory. In India seers of music found out this truth and idea long before. The intuitive authors on music of India discovered the mystery of sound (causal sound or *Nāda),* which forms the background of the grand structure of music, and philosophy of music is absolutely concerned with the theory and value of the causal sound (*Nāda)*. It is also called *Sphota* or *Śabda -Brahman* as expounded by *Patañjali* in his *Mahābhāṣya* and *Bhatṛhari* in the *Vākyapādiya.* [2]

> "Religious believers have heard music as the voices of gods and the cacophony of devils, praised it as the purest form of spirituality, and condemned it as the ultimate in sensual depravity; with equal enthusiasm they have promoted its use in worship and sought to eradicate it from both religious and secular life. Seldom has a neutral phenomenon, music had a high positive or negative value that reflects its near-universal importance in the religious sphere."[3]

Music is an Art par excellence, the highest among 14 *Vidyās* and 64 *Kalās* 'enumerated in Holy scriptures. *Vidyā* means the knowledge of God, which helps human being to lead a good and happy life. In the oriental conception of music, it has two complementary aspects, viz., the Spiritual and Aesthetic, which, in fact are like two sides of a coin. There is no question that both are inseparable and interdependent. Consequently music is included both under *Vidya* and *Kalā* as *Gandharva Vidyā* and *Sangīta Kalā*. Before understanding the exact significance of the famous and peremptory dictum available in *Hindu* scriptures, '*Na Vidya Sangīta para'* (there is no knowledge beyond the knowledge of music), one may like to ponder and perceive that the demonstration between *Vidya* and *kalā* is somewhat arbitrary in as much as 'all knowledge must in the ultimate lead to the realisation of the great mystery of God, man and the universe. Holy scriptures speak of *'parā vidyā'* (transcendental knowledge), and '*apara vidyā*' (immanent knowledge). In almost all branches of knowledge, we have this duality; the direct and the indirect, the inductive and deductive, the rational and the intuitional and so on. Ultimate realization can not be only along one path.[4]

Definition of Music

Music is a term too widely known to need any definition or explanation. It is quite clear that music has to do with hearing and is only a sound or a combination or succession of sounds just as painting has to do with sight and a combination of colours. But all sounds or combinations or successions of them, are not music; the rattling of a carriage is not music, nor the hubbub in a crowd, nor the barking of a dog, and so there is an infinite number of sounds which are not music. If it lies externally it must be in sounds themselves or their succession and arrangements, i.e., in matter or form. Upon considering several instances it appears to be in both of these. Matter as well as form is peculiar in a musical tone. If either is defective there will be no music. The notes of a nightingale are musical while the screaming of a kite quite the opposite of that, not only because pleasant successions proceed from the throat of the former and not from that of the latter, but also because the noise made by this is altogether unwelcome.

The establishment of musical forms and arrangements will be carried out by the science of music, which alone will be able to explain what combinations and successions will be musical and what not, and to put down various principles for distinction between them. However, as music exists and is composed and appreciated independently of any such philosophy or science we must be able to understand it without the help of any of them. It is universally admitted that all musical sounds effect us with pleasure, and on the contrary that unmusical sounds give us pain, though in other cases they may be said to produce no effect at all. The definition of music comes to this that music is a sound or a combination or succession of sounds so arranged as to affect us with pleasure.

> "A single agreeable sound of the same quality is not called music proper though there is no reason why it should not be. Similarly a mere combination of sounds without any succession will seldom be understood by the term of music; it has a peculiar designation for itself; viz. chord or harmony. Curtailing the definition so as to mean by it what is commonly understood, it becomes 'music is a succession of sounds so arranged as to effect us with pleasure".[5]

The word 'sound' is very general and not quite clear. Speech is also a sound or a succession of sounds and speech is able to please us in different ways, for instance, by humour, sublimity or elegance; but then it will not be called music. In this case, what pleases is not sound, but the subject of speech, which has nothing to do with music.

The term 'music' applies only to those sounds, which please us by themselves, independently of any other thing. Again, sounds may be taken to mean various kinds of sounds, as those of the letters of alphabet. An agreeable succession of such sounds is certainly a kind of music, but it is not music in its ordinary sense. To produce such succession is one of the objects of poetry and there it has a special designation, via, melody, and not music. Poetry aims at a good arrangement of various kinds of sounds; music at a good arrangements of various degrees (not kinds) of sounds, Poetry has to do with long and short, hard and soft, mute and liquid sounds; music with high and low ones.

B.N. Prasad says:

> "Music is a succession of various degrees of sounds so arranged as to affect us with pleasure by themselves and independently of anything else; in other words music is an agreeable succession of various degrees of sounds which independently, and by themselves, please the ear. Music does something more than simply pleasing us. It acts upon our imagination and raises various emotions. Hence to get a complete definition, the words 'and affect us with certain

> emotions' should be added at the end of the last definition. It should be carefully borne in the mind that 'music' is very often used so as to mean the art of music."[6]

> "One common definition of music as 'humanly patterned sound' conflicts with widely held religious beliefs that music is not humanly, but rather, divinely patterned."[7]

The philosophy of music, like many other high branches of knowledge, claims attention on intellectual grounds than on utilitarian grounds.

The Philosophy of Music

Dr. William Pole tried to explain the philosophy of music. He says that a philosophy of music shall contain the enquiries into various musical problems like, the musical sounds; the nature of the simplest elementary modes in which the material is arranged or prepared for use; the distinction between two varieties of music, known as melody and harmony, along with other musical materials like counterpoint, time measure, rhythm and form of music. We assume that the principles, which have determined or influenced them, may be classed under two distinct heads, namely, physical principles and aesthetical principles. By physical principles are meant such principles as can be deduced according to the laws of natural science, from the physical nature of musical sounds and from their known physiological effects on the human ear. By aesthetical principles are meant such principles as have resulted from the free action of the human mind, independently of any physical consideration. The philosophical investigation of music will show that the truth lies between these two extreme principles.[8]

"Swāmi Prajñānanda, elaborating the idea, says:

> "The philosoohy of music deals with the wisdom or essence of music it imparts to men a faculty of judgment and intuitive knowledge that make them analyse and understand music as the means to an end. Therefore by theory of music, we must not think only of the grammar of music, but also understand that the word conveys all

> the phases of grammar, science, literature, history, iconography, psychology and philosophy. Only by the practice of these phases of theory or *Śāstra*, men may attain excellence in music. The duty of the *Śāstra* is to lead to the genuine path of spiritual *Sādhana*, and when *Sādhana* gets fruition, men attain in their lives, immortality and everlasting bliss." [9]

C.E.M. Joad takes the broader aims of philosophy in general and remarks:

> "Philosophy is concerned not with phenomena, but with their meaning; not with facts, but with values; not with what is, but with what ought to be; not with means, but with ends."[10]

End or value is the prime achievement in philosophy, and that end or value is to be realized in one's experience. It is an undeniable fact that a man seeks happiness or pleasure in his life, and tries to avoid pain and sorrow, living in this world of cause and sequence. But the question is what sort of happiness or pleasure he seeks. Generally it is found that he seeks happiness or pleasure in his life as a result of his actions and aspirations and enjoys that happiness or pleasure to mitigate his selfish motive only. But, he fails to get and enjoy it all the time in all actions, because happiness and pleasure (*sukha)* are always mixed up with unhappiness and sorrow (*duhkha*) like the co-presence of light and darkness. Music is not meant only for material gains. It has higher purpose and goals.

Swāmi Prajñānanda states:

> "In regards to music, man generally cultures music in order to enable him to get material gains and worldly pleasures. The philosophy of music states that music is the highest art because it confers upon man absolute bliss and happiness, which are permanent and persisting all the time." [11]

Further he explains:

> "From the philosophical analysis of problem and mystery of the universe it is found that everything material is based on its subtle form, and everything subtle, upon its causal one. The cycle of cause and effect forms the world of appearance. Man's intellectual pursuit begins with an enquiry into the cause of everything around him, and with this act of enquiry, metaphysics begin as a theoretical aspect of philosophy of being and becoming. The philosophy of music is also concerned with an enquiry into the ultimate cause of the manifestation of music, and helps men to get into the core of its mystery and offers them the everlasting bliss and happiness even in this life on the earth.[12]

Indian music is intertwined with the structure of Indian culture and philosophy. Dr. Arnold Bake rightly observes:

> "It is impossible to divorce Indian music from the whole structure of Indian culture and philosophy with which it is interwoven in a number of ways from the earliest times of which we have records."[13]

> "The idea of music as a divine art implies that music is not considered on its merits alone, but points beyond itself and man to the divine. Thus music can be understood as an invention of divinities or as a general principle of divine creation. It may be interpreted as an image, imitation, or anticipation of divine or heavenly music. It can be understood as a means of influencing divinities. And, finally, the meaning and mission of music can be realized in cultic praise of the divinity."[14]

Music as Communication

Music appeals to the emotional faculties of man and is therefore able to articulate what words, as the instruments of rationality could never express. Music, through its spiritual essence, ties the communicative bond, while at the same time music remain accessible to man on the phenomenal level through its very own phenomenology of sound. The supreme transcendental reality is omnipresent in the nature, but it is not discernible by rational means because of its non-material essence. Man is a rational animal who will apprehend only that which can be perceived by the senses as well. Therefore, in order to arrive at his spiritual aim, man requires a medium that can act as a link between his rational understanding and the transcendental reality. This connecting medium is music with its dual capacity to appeal to both the emotional and the rational spheres: spiritual in its essence, music manifests itself as a physical reality to be sensually perceived.[15] Music is a general term for many modes of human communication using movements that produce and reproduce sounds. The term designates not only 'knowledge of moving well' but also the exercise of such knowledge. Musicians are human beings who communicate by 'moving well' to produce and reproduce sounds, and each instance of such communication is a performance. "Music has the character of communication. Sound spontaneously uttered by an individual serves as a contact sound, as a first step toward a call or a shout, or as a decoy, wooing, or warning call. Both speech and music develop symbols. Speech evolves ideas, which lead to thinking and logic. Music begins with emotional sounds."[16] Rabindranath Tagore emphasizes that the speech of his heart will be carried on in murmurings of a song because the communicative power of music exceeds the eloquence of speech.

> "No more noisy, loud words from me - such is my master's will. Henceforth I deal in whispers. The speech of my heart will be carried on in murmurings of a song." [17]

Selina Thielemann says, "Music instigates the highest form of communication, which is worship. Worship, dedicated service enlivened by the spirit of devotion is the primary way for the loving soul to communicate her emotional appeal to the beloved. Again among all forms of worship, music represents the mode par excellence, because music is nourished in its very substance by the spirit of devotion, and every act of music making is nourished in its very substance by the spirit of devotion, and every act of music making is essentially a statement of love, all worship, all music."[18]

Music as Devotion

"Music has always been considered divine in origin. Great *ṛṣis* and *Dēvas* have been associated with music. The authorship of some standard treatises on music, dance, and aesthetics and so on, has been attributed to great *ṛṣis*. In ancient *Sanskrit* literature there are descriptions of music concerts in which Great Ones like *Brahma, Indira, Prahlada, Nārada*, and the Great *Kumāras* have taken part and the sage *Śuka* acted as interpreter of the performance. Music is intimately connected with Divinity."[119]

Devotion is the life-giving energy that emancipates the human soul from the bonds of finitude, because devotion motivates the vital flow of emotion that melts together the opposite forces of the universe and fuses them in an all-unifying instant of love. The substance that forms the emotional fluid is music as the sounding manifestation of cosmic sweetness, as the melodious revelation of universal love, as the prime vocalization of the devotional quest. It is a devotion coupled with readiness for complete self-sacrifice, a devotion that reaches out beyond even the conception of self only to lead the devoted soul to full mergence with the cosmic stream of love.

Music is the motivating energy that inspires devotion, and at the same time it is the expressive force, which is inspired by devotion. Devotion is not a neutral quality; its arousal calls for the presence of an object towards which devotion turns. Being the principal simulative potency of devotion as well as the primary manifestation of devotional sentiments, music is obviously tied to the same object out of whose spirit devotion is born.

Music as Bliss

Music is more than merely a harmoniously structured arrangement of sounds. It has all the intrinsic qualities of a cosmic reality, and can incite that which is never to be achieved by ordinary human faculties.

Selina Thielemann observes:

"Music is a cosmic energy. Music is energy of bliss, of

> love, of joy - energy sent out by the supreme transcendental reality from which emanates all being, all life, and all existence. This transcendental reality is the formless source of all form, the nameless root of all names, and the soundless essence of all music. He is the omnipresent force of motion, the all-pervading radiation of light, and the inexhaustible flow of sweetness that fills the universe with bliss. He is the core inspirer of life on all planes of cosmic existence, who instigates and sustains the universal play of creation — the play in which the infinite and the finite, the formless and the form, the perennial and the fugitive continuously unite as playmates in the game of love."[20]

Music is not an abstract concept that exists outside the concrete reality of being, yet music is indwelled by the cosmic principles whose dynamics makes the universal mechanism function. Music is energy, but at the same time it is the expression of that energy, the definite manifestation of an unmanifest force. Music penetrates the cosmos as an invisible, inaudible vibration of bliss. In music, we come to confluence all opposite currents to mingle into the great ocean of harmoniousness, of sweetness, of bliss. In music, the infinite meets the finite, the timeless meets the momentary, the divine meets the human. Music melts dualities; music fuses the disconnected fragments of reality in order to establish the eternal truth of unity.

Prof. Josef Kuckertz says, "It is music that sets the personages on stage in motion, and that gives life to them as it is passed on to the spectator in the form of intense and profound experience. Bliss, received from the stage, becomes thus inspiration to act in the right spirit. Music is the vivifying emotional force that enlivens the rational facts on the universal drama-stage and adds the spiritual meaning to them: When there is no visible scenic action, sound becomes even more important to vitalize the contents of the words. Music is accomplishment, and music comes true through accomplishment: the perfect tune possesses the power of leading the soul to fulfillment of the aspired goal, hence 'the correct intonation becomes the essential medium to convey the thoughts and to evoke the object of desire. But perfectness must be paired with beauty, with the concrete manifestation of love, in order to turn into bliss, in order to make the soul truly blissful: if the tonal figures are moreover appealing, even beautiful, then listeners become enjoyed, even excited. The state of bliss is the ultimate quest of all beings, and whenever music is capable of evoking this state, in India, one speaks of a divine art."[21]

Confucius (551-478 B.C), the ancient sage of China propounded that the dual role of music is to produce a harmonious life in the individual and at the same time to establish a harmonious unity in society. He further says it is by the odes that the man is aroused. It is by the rules of propriety that the character is established. It is from music that the finish is received. He further says, when music and courtesy are better understood and appreciated, there will be no war. Speculations about the harmony of the universe were often inspired by musical facts, as in the theory that the planets were governed in their motions by ratios of the consonances and therefore produced an unheard music.[22]

Greek writers credited Pythagoras (582-07B.C.), with the earliest acoustical observations. He taught that the human soul was basically formed of Harmony and that music could restore this pre-existing Harmony to a mind tormented by contacts with the lower world. According to Plato, "the life of man in every part has need of harmony and rhythm. (Plato Laws) The man who has music in his soul will be most in love with the loveliest. We shall never become musicians unless we understand the ideals of temperance, fortitude, liberality and magnificence. The business of music should in some measure lead to the love of the beautiful."[23]

Music acts as the unifying agent that enforces their fusion, while at the same time music is in it the quest for union. Music is the elemental manifestation of cosmic harmony, because music evokes harmoniousness— because music accomplishes the union of opposing entities and thereby fulfils the primal ambition of all beings: to become with the supreme truth of existence.

Music as Emotion

As expressing human emotions, there is no other aspect of art or philosophy, which can excel music. Human emotions, while they can in general be grouped under several heads, are beyond clear-cut definition. We can only deal with certain broad divergences. Some of these emotions are very difficult to express either by words or by action; but such emotions can be expressed by music. Emotions like *Śhanti* self-surrender and so on are best expressed either in music or not expressed at all.

R. Srinivasan says:

> "Music has its own language, the language of emotions; and as human emotions is universal emotions such as joy, fear, depression, despair is universal and so the appeal of music which used such emotions as its language must be universal."[24]

Music is an emotional energy, music is an emotional tool, and the essence of music is emotion. The quest of love is an emotional quest, hence calls for an emotional agent to accomplish its fulfillment-and that agent is music. The *Oxford Wordfinder* defines music as 'the art of combining vocal or instrumental sounds (or both) to produce beauty of form, harmony, and expression of emotion'. Music distinguishes itself from mere sound through its spiritual essence, the core substance of music, which the *Oxford Wordfinder* attempts to describe as 'beauty of form', 'harmony' and 'emotion'. Music aims at a higher quality than bare sound by transforming it into a construction that generates 'beauty of form, harmony and emotional expression'.

Philosophy of Music in Relation with Hindu Religion

Society in India uses music in relation to religion as music and religion converge at so many points that investigation into music invariably means a hard look at religion. India has at least four traditions of art musics, more than seventeen reasonably identified folk musics, primitive music chiefly associated with 25 million tribals, popular music with cinematic music as its chief component and devotional music in almost each region. The magnificent edifice of music in India is thus created by these five categories, all of which have been highly productive. It is therefore easy to see that music and religion are well matched in matter of chronological durability, geographical distribution and in their general coverage of life-areas. They are coextensive as well as co-orbital. 'The worship of God, which was earlier done by the priest alone, lost importance and became the concern of the individual. He looked upon God as the remover of all his worldly distress, failures and sufferings. He craved for His mercy and kindness with a feeling of human inadequacy. All this man expressed in words and tune, and submitted them as offerings in temples – chanting and singing of hymns in form of the deities, which became a part of the temple ritual. This gave rise to the *Bhakti* (devotional) movement where the priest was not so dominant a figure. The hymns used to be chanted in *Sanskrit*, which were beyond the comprehension of an uneducated ordinary human being.

In the medieval age (16th century), a galaxy of saint poets were born, both in the North and the South, who composed verses in regional and colloquial languages, making the metaphysical truth easily communicable. They covered the whole gamut of human emotions directing them to God. The subject matter of such spiritual poems or devotional hymns covered ethics, moral values, praises of God and His deeds of his incarnate forms as mentioned in mythology. A large number of them are prayers to forgive the weaknesses of human beings and to uplift them. These songs became extremely popular for their universal appeal as the common man could comprehend the moral and spiritual thought through the vehicle of the common languages.' [25]

Ashok D. Ranade says,

> "We recognize religiosity to be a basic drive. It is not an instinct and displays a social content. The drive is responsible for a very special psychological experience often described as religious. Hence, religion is to be defined as an institution brought into being to increase the probability and scope, and enhance the quality, of this experience. On the other side of the posited musico-

religious psychological experience is musicality- and equally fundamental human inclination. Musicality is also social and culture-based in content as well as in spread. Specific acoustic experiences, emerging out of this basic musicality need to be nurtured to ensure greater probability, predictability, scope and quality. A totality of this structure is raised in societies and it is subsequently identified as music."[26]

"Musics, like religions, are most meaningfully defined in their own terms. Along with aspects of musical sounds and their structural relationships, religious definitions frequently take into considerations such factors as cosmological and mathematical laws, divine origin or inspiration, psychological and emotional effects, social and ethical implications, relations or contrasts between religious and secular musics, and a wide range of other elements."[27]

In India, because of the importance of religion, the place to look, if one is to grasp any aspect of Hindu culture, is at the concepts, beliefs, and actions connected with that religion. The general area is the essence of those deepest values that bind together every stratum of Hindu society. The philosophical concepts exhibited in words and actions by any individual or group hold many of the keys to understanding their music. Musical analysis made without aesthetic knowledge is not necessarily without value, but must by necessity, is at least somewhat unsure. One cannot comprehend even remotely, the significance of certain of the musical or textual phenomena without having some grasp of the underlying aesthetics. Seeing a man prostrate himself in humility and adoration before another has little meaning until one begins to understand some of the concepts connected with saintliness, reverence for preceptors, an elder man's attitude toward God, and what signifies greatness in person and its implications. The drone in Indian music is not just a device which, when added to melody and rhythm provides mere pleasant sounds disassociated from religio-philosophical values. The drone, called *śruti* (that which is heard), is a musical expression of basic philosophical tenets traceable back to the earliest *Vedas*.[28] When music and religion are discussed, the meaning of this discussion is 'music and *bhakti*'. *Bhakti* is the essence of religion and music is born out of *bhakti*. Music and bhakti are so closely related to each other that the absence of the one destroys the vitality of the other.

"Music is nothing but an expression of bhakti; it is bhakti from which music is produced, and it is in music that bhakti manifests itself in sound form. The beauty of music, therefore, is not told on the grounds of the performer's skills, but it arises from their innate devotional sentiment of the music, which makes the music suitable for offering to the lord."[29]

> It is stated in the *Bhāgavatha Purāṇa*, the fundamental treatise of *Vaiṣṇavism. Kācit samam mukundena svara-jātir amiśritah, unninye pujitatena priyatā sādhu iti*... (A certain *gopi* sang together with *Kṛṣṇa* (in a way that) the notes of the scale did not harmonize. She was honoured by him, as she had pleased him, (with the words) 'splendid'! 'Excellent'![30]

"*Hindus* have wrestled all through the long centuries with the complexities of metaphysical problems. Reality and *māyā*, the great illusion of the outer husk of life, are in constant antagonism. Illusion - *māyā* - is something from which *Hindus* must eventually escape to *Mokṣa* or *Mukti* - liberation. This has had its own effect on artistic concepts and principles and undoubtedly has influenced that tremendous pull inwards that is as often felt as one listens hour after hour to the music floating gently upon the heavy air of an Indian night. As one lives through it, one longs for its final climactic liberation."[31]

Religiosity in itself has some inner connection with the very nature of music. Indian musicians frequently display pronounced religious leanings as revealed in diverse details: "Musicians repeatedly allude to close connections between *Parabrahma* (the Supreme Being) and *Nāda Brahman* (Supreme Being) realized through the medium of sound; the general repertoire of art musicians, on examination, it reveals a considerable number of compositions in praise of deities; there have been numerous instances of *sādhus, faqirs* who were musicians as also of musicians who became near-sadhus. From *Swāmi Haridas* to *Pt. Viṣṇu Digambar* and from *Amir Khusro* to *Sidhi Khan* there is a long line of musicians exemplifying musician-religion bound. The ratio of musicians taking to renunciation proves specifically instructive because instances of dancers, actors exercising similar options are almost unknown." [32]

Symbolism of the Acts of Worship

An aid to understanding the music of another culture can be found in the acts of worship, especially those connected with music. It would follow that religious precepts can be demonstrated by both verbalization of sacred texts and ritual acts. These reflect cultural values in what would seem to be a dramatic way. The interpretation of the symbolism of their acts may not only provide insights into a single culture's values, but also help to place a culture, or some aspect of it, in a more universal light. If the symbols, associated with various acts of worship, are interpreted, insights will be revealed in the entire order. These acts are especially important because they represent physically, dramatically, the acting out of values that go to the ore of the culture.

> "Music has been composed for every act of the Hindu *bhajana* ritual; certain compositions, especially, demonstrate a clear connection between philosophical tenets and musical compositions."[33]

"Traditionally, music in South India has emerged out of religion, centred in and around the temple, and with worship. An efficacious means for achieving religious goals is through song (*kīrthana*); all music in South India is, or is derived from vocal music, and all vocal music springs from religion. The traditional stories about gods and goddesses told in the Hindu scriptures are carried mainly in song."[34] "The dominant awareness in every traditional *Hindu's* consciousness is the omnipresence of God. Devotees are seldom far from their beloved icons. Each home has several icons. In a person's place of work, be it a factory or store, icons are to be found, which are worshipped by employers, and employees, and customers. It is important to understand that the traditional Hindu, in his feelings of the closeness of an omnipresent deity, also feels close to nature. He does not attempt to alter nature, but rather goes along with it; he is aware that he is a part of it. His daily acts, outgrowths of his closeness to nature and God, are ritualistic. His devotions, ablutions, preparation of vegetarian meals and eating of those meals, indeed, every act of his daily life is bound up in observances of traditional rituals closely harmonized with nature. There is consciousness, and deep awareness of all that he perceives. Everything the Hindu does, from the sensual act of cutting vegetables in preparation of a meal, to the classical musician singing an improvised rāga alapana, is done as a ritualistic act in the presence of and dedicated to the Supreme Godhead."[35]

Music, like all other traditional cultural components, is part of an integrated society in which philosophy, science, politics, commerce, and all social phenomena are liable to be viewed in a spiritual perspective.

Today, in villages and cities, children grow up hearing their parents, relatives and neighbours daily sing songs and relate marvelous tales that touch every nuance of *Hindu* life through the deeds of gods and demons, sages and saints. In addition to the song and stories heard in the homes, there are professional singing-story tellers who carry the tradition from village to village. Their performances consist of didactic and devotional songs and stories drawn from the scriptures, i.e. the great epics, *Rāmāyaṇa, Mahābhārata*, and the 'old' religious texts, the *Purāṇas*. Classical and folk theatre and dance, too, carry the religion through themes drawn from the scriptures.

Music in Indian Mythology

Many legends are extant about the origin of music. The *Vedas, the Upaniṣads,* epics like the *Rāmāyaṇa* and the *Mahābhārata, the Srimad Bhāgavata*, other *Purāṇic* works and the *Pañcatantra* contain valuable references to this subject It is also learnt from the Hindu mythology that each god or goddess is inevitably associated with some kind of musical instrument or legend. The beginning of Indian music is lost in the beautiful and fanciful legends of gods and goddesses, who were supposed to be its authors and patrons. Goddess *Sarasvati* is always represented as the goddess of art and learning, and she is usually pictured as seated on a white lotus with a *Veeṇā*, lute in one hand, playing it with another, a book in the third hand and a necklace of pearls in the fourth. The technical word for music throughout India is the word *Sangīta*, which originally included dancing and the drama as well as vocal and instrumental music. *Lord Śiva* is supposed to have been the creator of this threefold art and His mystic dance symbolizes the rhythmic motion of the universe.

In Hindu mythology the various departments of life and learning are usually associated with different *Ṛṣis* and so to one of these is traced the first instruction that men received in the art of music. *Bharata Ṛṣi* said to have brought the art to the heavenly dancers – the *Apsaras* – who afterwards performed before *Lord Śiva*. The *Ṛṣi Nārada*, who wanders about in earth and heaven, singing and playing on his Vīṇā, taught music to men. Among the inhabitants of Indra's heaven we find bands of musicians. The *Gandharvas* are the singers; the *Apsaras* are the dancers and the *Kinnaras* are performers of musical instruments. From the name *Gandharva, the* title *Gāndharva Veda* has come for the art of music. [36]

In great epic *Rāmāyaṇa*, it is mentioned, Kumbhakarṇa, the younger brother of king *Rāvaṇa,* was a great singer. Once the ten-headed *Rāvaṇa* was caught under mount *Kailāśa* and it became impossible for him to get himself free, then he tried to sing some beautiful notes to be able to come out. He needed some instrument to give him support for the recital of his music. (For such purposes, a musical instrument like an *Ektāra* of today was generally used even in those days.) So *Rāvaṇa* chopped off one of his ten heads, cut out a nerve from his huge body and tuned it to the pitch of his voice by tying the other end to his head. *Rāmāyaṇa* was recited by *Lava* and *Kuṣa* (*Rāma's* twin sons) in the most melodious style with jatis, etc. in the, court of *Rāma*, as it is recited today. *Hanumān* sang the glories of Rāma in the form of *Kīrtanas.*"[37]

Lord Kṛṣṇa, the Divine cowherd, in His *Leelās* always attracted the *Gopis* and His cowherds with the sweet, melodious music of His flute. The *Pāndavas*, during their banishment or "*Ajñāta Vāsa*", happened to stay at the palace of king *Virāta*. At the court of king *Virāta, Arjuna*, the third brother, used to give music and dance lessons to Princess *Uttara. Arjuna* had assumed the name of *Brihannala* (a female name) as a music-cum-dance teacher.

Devotional Aspects of South Indian Music

In order to understand the role of music in South Indian culture, it is necessary to observe some of the qualities of the music and how they relate to the entire socio-religious system. Traditionally, music in South India has been devotional or derived from it, and, in large part has emanated from the temple. The temple has been the centre of traditional culture in this part of India since the construction of the first temples in the fifth and sixth centuries A.D. This coincides the rise of *Bhakti*, of which the classical musical traditions are so much a part. We find today that some of the larger temples still feature music for children where the great monuments of South Indian poetry and music are taught.

Musical traditions carried on in and around the temples reaches into every part of the traditional centers. Even music that is not immediately connected to the temples, e.g., folk music, is essentially devotional or reflects the religious permeation in every aspect of daily life. "The words *bhakti* and *bhajana* are associated with an approach to God in which the relationship of the worshipper to the deity is based upon varying attitudes of love. The beginnings of this loving, adorational, mystical approach to God can be found at the dawn *Hinduism* as early as the *Ṛgveda*. We find the *Bhāgavatha Purāṇa* the doctrine of *bhakti* crystallized into a set of loving attitudes and acts, the performance of which would aid the worshipper in the attainment of God. God is conceived of as being personalized. He (and she) is in human form, worshipped in representation of stone, bronze, paint, and photographs. Indeed, the supplicant's attitudes regarding the human, living aspects of the deities during worship, dictate the unique qualities of *Hindu* religious rituals. *Bhajana* as a word and as a phenomenon touches every Indian in every part of the country."[38] Traditionally, South India's greatest classical composers have composed solely devotional music in one form or another. One of the more important classical music forms, the *kriti,* is essentially devotional; texts invariably are about, or addressed to God. The *Śaiva Nāyanārs* or *Nāyanmars and Vaiṣṇava Ālvārs* were singers and God-intoxicated people who transmitted their infatuation to millions of their contemporaries.

"The musical inheritance of the *Trinity, Saint Tyāgarāja, Muthu Swāmi Dīkṣitār* and *Śyāma Sāstri* must have been very rich and they were heir to the composition of *Puandaradāsa, Kṣētrayya, Vīrabhadrayya, Pacmiriyam Adiyappiah* and *Sonti Venkatmanayya.* An analysis of the music of *Dīkṣitār* reveals that it was but an interpretation of the music on his past. It is obvious that *Tyāgarāja* not only has embodied the fine elements of the tradition, but also brings home the glorious possibilities of melodic music in his songs."[39]

Saint *Tyāgarāja* (1767-1847) is considered South India's greatest classical composer, composed hundreds of *kritis*, each expressing in words and music, some aspect of Bhakti. He also composed important sections of the *bhakti* rituals. The Sanskrit term which characterizes an outstanding musician is *Nāda-Yogin*: one who has achieved greatness in his art, who understands the celestial sound which pervades the universe. Many compositions that are performed in public concerts of classical music are sung in *Bhakti* rituals. Although the emphasis is on the musical performance rather than words in a classical concert (as opposed to the meaning of the texts in religious rituals), the quintessential element is the devotional character of the piece. Even in improvising the textless *rāga ālāpana*, many traditional artists enunciate fragments of devotional words and phrases as vehicles for their improvisations. Among traditional Hindus, the performing of or listening to devotional music, remains, a dominant force in their lives in South India. It is the mode through which they give outward expression to their deepest values; it is that endeavour which provides the greatest joy.[40]

There are innumerable important poet-composers who have lived and carried on their dedicated devotional activities in South India. The popular movement in which God is glorified in song is still being carried on in every part of the country. They sing in their loving adoration of Universal *Brahman*. That core of Hindu worship, which emanated from the *Vedas*, still burns brightly; different emphasis and focuses have been placed on varying aspects of the *bhakti* tradition at different times and places and by different *bhaktas*; all sang and spoke in fervent devotion of the one Supreme Godhead whose manifestations are endless.

REFERENCES

1. Philip P. Wiener., *Dictionary of the History of Ideas, Studies of Selected Pivotal Ideas*, p.261.
2. Swāmi Prajñānanda. *A Historical Study of Indian Music*, p. 328.
3. Mircea Eliade, *The Encyclopedia of Religion*, Vol-10, pp.163-164.
4. Suresh Chandra Dey, *The Quest For Music Divine*, p. 1.
5. Baby Nanak Prasad, *Indian Music-Scientific and Practical*, p. 10.
6. Babu Nanak Prasad, *Indian Music– Scientific and Practical*, pp. 10-11.
7. Mircea Eliade, *Encyclopedia of Religion*, Vol- 10, pp. 163-164.
8. Dr. William Pole, *The Philosophy of Music*, p. 12.
9. Swāmi Prajñānanda, *Historical Development of Indian Music*, p. 39.
10. Joad. C.E.M, *Philosophy for our Times*, p. 25.
11. Swāmi Prajñānanda, *Historical Development of Indian Music* , p. 327.
12. Swāmi Prajñānanda, *Historical Development of Indian Music*, p. 328.
13. Arnold Bake, *Oxford History of Music*.
14. Philip P. Wiener, *Dictionary of the History of Ideas, Studies of Selected Pivotal Ideas*, pp.267-68.
15. Selina Thielemann, *The Spirituality of Music*, p. 14.
16. David L. Sills, *International Encyclopedia of the Social Sciences*, Vol-9, p. 566.
17. Rabindranath Tagore, *Gitānjali, LXXXIX*
18. Selina Thielemann, *The Spirituality of Music*, p. 8.
20. Selina Thielemann, *The Spirituality of Music*, pp. 1-2.
21. Prof. Josef Kuckertz, *Essays on Indian Music*, 1999, pp. 24-25.

22. Plato, *The Republic.*
23. *Ibid*, 25.
24. Srinivasan R. *Facets of Indian Culture*, Bombay, 1980, p. 72.
25. Shobhana Nair, "Music of The Soul", *Gentleman*, Mg.Vol-20, No-7, p.48.
26. Ashok. D. Ranade, *Essays in Indian Ethnomusicology*, p. 79.
27. Mircea Eliade, *The Encyclopedia of Religion*, Vol- 10, p. 165.
28. Robert Leopold Simon, *Spiritual Aspects of Indian Music* , p. 1.
29. Selina Thielemann, *Divine Service and the Performing Arts in India*, p.27.
30. Ganesh Vasudeo Tazgore, *Bhāgavatha Purāṇa*, Trans. Ann, 10.33.10, Tr. Ann. Delhi, 1979.
31. Peggy Holrojyde, *The Music of India* , p. 42.
32. Ashok. D. Ranade, *Essays in Indian Ethnomusicology*, p. 80.
33. Robert Leopold Simon, *Spiritual Aspects of Indian Music*, p. 2.
34. *Ibid.*, p. 2.
35. Dr. Annapoorna, L, *Music and Temples: A Ritualistic Approach*, p. 2.
36. Popley. H.A, *The Music of India, Y.M.C.A*, p. 7.
37. Robert Leopold Simon, *Spiritual Aspects of Indian Music*, p. 10.
38. Dr. Annapoorna, L., *Music and Temples: A Ritualistic Approach*, p. 3.
39. *Ibid.*, p. 143.
40. Robert Leopold Simon, *Spiritual Aspects of Indian Music*, Delhi, 1984, pp. 5-6.

3

Nāda-Brahman

The whole universe is a manifested energy according to *Vedic* sages as well as the modern physicists and scientists. The most ancient and primitive human societies across the world have recognized the power of sound vibrations as they affect the human minds and the body. The entire body and the creation is nothing but solidification of sound waves. This is technically called and adored as the *Nāda-Brahman* (Sound Cosmos). In India had ushered in the concept of *Nāda* being worshipped as *Brahman*. There was only one sound in the beginning of the creation and that primordial Causal Sound was the sacred *Om* and later on through its sound vibrations this universe came into existence.

> "The common premise of the religious music of India is that sound either invokes or symbolically represents the power of the universe. Sound as a represent of power, is nowhere more evident than in the din and commotion of a contemporary Hindu temple during the puja or worship ceremonies. Drums, bells, gongs, beaten brass plates, and conch shells all played simultaneously create an overwhelming sonic atmosphere intended to awaken the deity. Sound is power."[1]

Dr. P.C. Chakraborty says:

> "Sound (*Śabda*) is not lifeless mechanism, invented by man. It is more than a mere sound or symbol. It is consciousness that splits up into the two-fold category of *Śabda* (sound) and *artha* (meaning) and what we call *vāk* as the vehicle of communication, is nothing but and expression of *caitanya* (spirit) lying within."[2]

According *to Tantra, Śiva* and *Śakti* create the universe. The *Nāda* or the primordial sound is the outcome of *Śiva Śakti* combination. Thus originated *Nāda* is used to compose *mantras* based on impregnated letters called '*Beejākṣara*'. Music served as the purpose of a vehicle to recite these *mantras* and propitiate the deities concerned while performing *Tantric* rituals. According to *tantra*, sound is all pervading and the most powerful element in the universe. Its proper use may create miracles or cause degeneration to the very existence of the universe.[3]

Śabda or sound is of two kinds -- namely, *dhvani* and *Varṇa*. The unlettered form of *Śabda*, which is not expressed by any alphabetical mark is called *Dhvani*, lettered sound is called *Varṇa*, which means *Akṣaras* expressed from '*A* to *Kṣa*'. Fundamentally, *Dhvani* is the real substance, of which *Śabda* is only a manifestation. This *dhvani* is the subtle aspect of the vital force of *Dhvani* that the *Śakti* appears in and disappears from the body of *Jīva*. Every *mantra*, be it *Vedic* or *Tāntric* is an appearance (*Rūpa*) of *Brahman*. *Veda* or *Tantra* consisting of *mantras*, is only manifestation of *Brahman*, i.e. *Brahman* appears in the form of *mantra*. Just as *Viṣṇu* is the *mūlasvarūpa* (root-being) of those incarnations of His which are called *Rāma*, *Kṛṣṇa* and so forth, so the luminous *mantra mūrti* is the *mūlsvarūpa* of *Śāstra*, which is *Śabda Brahman*.

At the beginning of the creation of the universe the luminous bud of *mantras* blossomed and created the fourteen words, which are the petals of its flower. It is the fragrance of its pollen, which is existence (*sat*), consciousness (*cit*), and bliss (*ānanda*), which fills the three worlds with delight. After the great dissolution (*Mahāpralaya*)

Brahma—the lotus - born (*Brahma* was born on the louts which sprang from *Viṣṇu's* navel) appeared in the center of the thousand petalled lotus, which crowned the stem issuing from the navel of *Bhagvān Nārāyaṇ* lying in the causal sea. Later he meditated for the creation of a universe suited to the age and became immersed in *Samādhi*. At this, *Veda*, which is *Śabda Brahman* appeared by itself in the firmament of *Sri Nārāyaṇa's* heart. It issued out with his breath and then assumed four visible forms corresponding to the *Ṛk*, *Sāma*, *Yajur* and *Atharva* and stood before him."[4]

Sound as Energy

"Sound or the Word has three aspects: *Śabda* - (sound), *artha* (meaning) and *pratyaya* (cognition). There are numerous kinds of sound and each sound has a meaning, vibration and frequency. Sound is Energy and the Energy is both static and dynamic. There are numerous brain centers, which produce different kinds of amplitudes and frequencies. From these combinations particular patterns of energy are produced, which when condensed, take the form of gross matter. Thus the whole *'Mantra-Śāstra'* is based on this Sound principle."[5]

Swāmi Haripremānanda Sarasvati says:

> "Those who are familiar with Einstein's formula, $E=mc^2$ will understand this more clearly. The Law of Conservation of Energy states that Energy can neither be created nor destroyed. Albert Einstein pointed out that energy cannot only change from one form to another but mass and energy too are interconvertible. Energy equivalent E of mass m is given by his famous equation $E=mc^2$ where c is the velocity of light. '*Aum*' composed of three sounds *a*, *u*, and *m* is extensively believed to have supernatural power, quintessentially linked to the Divine. If sound is analyzed, somewhat like light, it is seen to consist of vibrations, which are frequencies of energy radiated or transmitted plus resonance effect. Vibrations can play a crucial role in all biosystems."[6]

Suresh Chandra Dey aptly points:

> "A sustained high 'C' note on a violin can smash a glass; music has growth effects on plants and therapeutic effects on man. Mantric sound cannot be dismissed lightly or with an attitude of skepticism."[7]

In India, music is considered as a subtle divine thread, capable of linking the *Jīvātman* (individual soul) with the *Parmātman* (Supreme Soul). This concept originated in the *Tāntric* idea of *Śabda - Brahman*, the primeval source of creation. It is believed that the Supreme Being is of the nature of *Śabda - Brahman* or *Nāda Brahman.* This Ultimate Sound Principle gets manifested as its vibrations. Through the *Samyoga* and *Viyoga* i.e. the union and separation of these vibrations, *Śabda - Brahman* creates the world of 'forms', from the sub-atomic to the biggest and the mightiest. The entire cosmos is the manifestation of *Śabda - Brahman.* As the *Nāda* evolves, differentiates and expands from the subtle to the gross, it gives rise to articulate sounds - '*Varṇas*', '*sṛitis*' and '*Svaras*' - and moves on to create '*Rāgās*', capturing the '*Bhāvas*' (moods) of the mind. From *Varṇas* arise by permutations and combinations, the world of 'forms'. "Today scientific substantiation of these concepts has been forthcoming through the experimental demonstration that manipulating sound can produce different geometrical figures. "Swāmi Śivānanda of the Divine Life Society, Rishikesh while discussing about sound and image in his famous book '*Japa Yoga*', has said that each sound produces a form in the invisible world and combinations of sound create many complicated figures and shapes."[8]

That means it is possible to reduce all 'physical forms' to 'sound forms' and vice-versa. In other words, form is sound made manifest.

According to the *Tantras* there are 50 basic sounds out of which the world of forms has come into being. P.B. Mukherjee elaborates on the whole story of creation of the Universe by Sound. As the sound (*Nāda*) concentrates and condenses it creates geometric figures. This explains the origin of dimensions, curves, figures, shapes and sizes, but also the fact that as the process of condensation goes on, Sound produces solid, liquid and gas.[9]

Origin of Nāda or Om

The *Om* or the Cosmic Sound vibrated all throughout and everywhere in the Universe. The Indian thinkers expressed this inexplicable in various ways. For this they used *Śabda* - as a tool. When they opened their lips, the first sound, they found was the sound of a vowel, '*a*'. When they started meditating on this first letter, they found the second vowel '*u*' and they found the consonant '*m*' when they closed their lips. Thus, originated the idea of '*Nāda*' in the Indian Thought.

"The '*a*' and '*u*' by *sandhi* become '*O*' and with '*m*' form the '*Praṇava*' or *mantra* '*OM*'- constituted of *A-U-M*. To correctly pronounce *AUM*, the sacred word, one should utter it in such a manner that he dwells upon the final '*m*' making it hum or vibrate in the throat like the hum of a bee, prolonging the sound as long as he is able to do so on the one inhalation."[10]

The three letters of the sacred word *AUM* signify the principles of the creation: *A* – preservation; *U* – destruction; *M* – regeneration, - or, in oriental phraseology, *Braham, Viṣṇu, Śiva* the three gods, - that is the symbolism. In the same way the three syllables represent the three fold elements throughout nature, from the great unseen forces upon which the greatest scientists can only theorize, to the simple nature with which the simplest nature is acquainted. The word *AUM* in its entire sense is simply a symbol to express the divinity, the Supreme Being. *AUM* also stands for the three substances, *Objective, Subjective and Eternal.* The letter '*A*' and its virabtions symbolize the objective substance, or matter. The subjective substance, or mind, is the unseen link connecting matter with the eternal. The vibrations of middle letter 'U' and the eternal substance, or God, represented by the final '*M*', represent it. The word stands for the three realms of life in its manifestation throughout the infinite. Thus we have the natural world, which we can see, the objective, - the subjective world, or that sphere which our senses cannot perceive until they are opened to the impressions of divine things, - and finally the eternal world, - that is, the life of all.[11]

When the seers were able to see the word in their minds they took it as manifested *Nāda*, and called the unmanifested sound stratum, *Nāda Brahman*, the ultimate reality that can be reached through 'Word'. The first sound thus evolved as designated as the mother of all other sounds, and "*a-u-m*" was symbolized as the universe or primordial energy from which came all the words. Meditation on *upāsana* of this *a-u-m* or "*Om*" became the subject of study of the Indian sages. Later they called it *Praṇava.*

"Omkāramcha parābrahma yavadonkāra sambhāvaha

Akāro kāramakāra yethe Sangītā sambhāvaha."
"Akāro Viṣṇurūpancha Ukaaro Brahmarūpakam
Makāro Bhargarūpancha sarvamonkāra rūpakam."[12]
a + u + m = Om.
Akāram - Viṣṇu, Ukāram - Brahma, Makāram - Śiva.

According to *Yoga* School, the origin of *Nāda* is *Omkāram.* This *Om* is nothing but a composition of *a + u + m.* In as much as the sages alone could understand the mystery by which *Akāra* and *Ukāra* became *Makāra*, which was given to others in the form of *Manthram. Prāṇava Nāda*, the *Omkāra* is born of the fusion of air and fire. It is a well-known fact that the *Prāṇava* letter '*Om*' indicates *Parama Śiva* and becomes God himself. It is the prime *mantra* and used it in their daily devotions, as they were sure that any work connected with it ensured success. The hidden state of the *Śakti* or consciousness is *dhavani*, and its outward manifestation is sound. This *dhvani* is the vital force of *jiva*. This universe of movable and immovable things is linked together and pervaded by *Śakti*, which is *dhvani*. This *Śakti* is called by such names as *Nāda* (sound), *Prāṇa* (the vital force manifesting in breath), *Jiva Ghoṣa*, etc.

The *yogis* know this great *Śakti* as *Kulakundalini* moving in the heart. It is she, who makes an indistent and sweet murmuring sound like the humming of a black bee at the aperture in the *mûlādhāra. Kulakuṇdalini* has two aspects namely *Sthûla* or gross form with attributes (*Saguṇa*). In this, like the humming of a moving swarm of black bees, she indistinctly utters the fifty letters. *Sûkṣma*, the other aspects, or subtle form, is attributeless (*Niruguṇa*). It is existence, consciousness and bliss (*sat-cit-ānanda*).

Whereas the *Sūksma* for is that *Dēvata* towards whom the worship of all *sādhakas* is directed. *Brahma* commonly acknowledged, as the author of the *Vedas* is really only the author of the appearance of the *Vedas*. The effect of the *Dhvani* of *Kulakuṇdalini* in the body of *Īśvara* is *Veda*. And the effect *dhvani* of *Kulakuṇdalini* in the body of *Jiva* is *Śabda*. In the *Śabda* is every form of *mantra*, which is that which gives vitality of *Jīva*. [13]

The *yogis* used this *mantra* while practicing their breathing and obtained not only long life but also felt the presence of God in them. *Om* also symbolized God the omnipotent and the omnipresent. Thus they started their preaching (*Pravachana*) or chanting of *Veda mantras* by invoking the blessings of *Om* (*Bhagavan*). [14]

> "As a world principle of creation sound is symbolized in post-*Vedic* times in the syllable *Om*. It dwells in the divinity (*Śiva*) as well as in the human heart. One can be guided by music to the divine principles of the cosmos."[15]

Lewis Rowell says:

> "*Nāda* is an extremely important term for musical sound with a wide range of meaning and association. The word *Nāda* is correctly identified as a derivative from the verbal root *Näd* (to stand, thunder, roar, or bellow), in the sense of a loud sound, a spreading sound, with powerful reverberations. The semantic development of the term is of considerable intrinsic interest, in that it demonstrates, how phonetic similarities reveal the persistence of common root meaning in words that have become specialized."[16]

In *the Kaṭopaniṣad*, "*Om* has been given the highest position: That Word is the supreme symbol, that word is the supreme support."

It is stated in *the Kaṭopaniṣad:*

> "*Nacikētā* asked: "What lies beyond right and wrong, beyond cause and effect, beyond past and future?

> *Dharmarāj* said: "The word that the Vedas extol, austerities proclaim, sanctities approach - that word is *Om*.
> "That word is eternal Spirit, eternal distance; who knows it attains to his desire.
> "That word is the ultimate foundation, who finds it is adored among the saints.

"The self-knows all, is not born, does not die, is not the effect of any cause; is eternal, self-existent, imperishable, ancient."[17]

Yama tells *Nacikētā:*

> "*Nacikētā,* I will tell you of the power of the word that has been praised in the *Vedas* and repeated in live by devotees. The word is the essence of the *Vedas*. It is the speech of devotees and the experience of the learned. It is '*Om*' and '*Om*' only."
>
> "The mind must concentrate on '*Om*'. '*Om* is fearless liberation. Those who concentrate on it shall never be afraid anywhere."[18]
>
> "*Chhāndogya Upaniṣad* interprets Om as the basis of foundation of speech (*Vāk*): All speech is held together by *Om.* Verily *Om* is the world-all."[19]

"In the *Bhagavad Gītā,* Sri Kṛṣṇa has said:

> "*Aum ity ekāksaram brahma vyāharan mām anusmaran/*
> *Yah prayāti tyajan deham sa yāti paramām gatim*" [20]

"All the gates of the body closed, the mind confined within the heart, having fixed his life-energy in the head, engaged in firm *yoga*; uttering the one-syllable '*Om*', Brahman, thinking of Me, he who departs leaving the body, attains the Supreme Goal."

Abbe J.A. Dubois says:

> "The most powerful *mantram* is the mysterious monosyllable '*Om*' or '*Aum*'. The Hindu conception of the word *Aum* is thus explained by one authority: As long

> as there has been a *Hindu* faith, the power of sound has been recognized in the sacred word. In that word lie all potencies, for the sacred word expresses the one and latent Being, every power of generation, of preservation, and of destruction." [21]

Nāda - Śabda – Sphoṭa

"*Sphoṭa* is another literary term with an extremely specialized meaning: deriving from a verbal root meaning 'to burst', *Sphoṭa* signifies the eternal and imperceptible aspect of sound as the vehicle of meaning, flooding the mind with a burst of pure meaning in response to the uttered sounds. It is an instantaneous and indivisible perceptions, fusing in a single stoke the separate phonetic elements of a word or the words in a sentence. The idea behind *Sphoṭa* adds some valuable background to this linguistic survey, but the word has seldom been applied to music."[22]

"According to the philosophers like *Pāṇini, Patañjali, Bhatṛhari, Nāgeśa, Punyarāja, Helarāja* and others, The Causal Sound (*Nāda, Śabda* - or *Sphoṭa*) is the substratum and fountainhead of the Cosmic World-Process. These philosophers, musicologists and *Tantriks* regard *Nāda* as the material cause of the Universe and identify it with the *Brahman* of *Upaniṣads. Patañjali* has said in the *Mahābhāṣya* that the latent force of psychic energy remains in the form of primordial causal sound, known as '*Sphoṭa*'. According to him, words are divided into two, *nitya* and *kārya,* - eternal and created. The *nitya-Śabda* - is the supreme reality, which transcends the limitations of time and space. It is the *parāvāk* as well as the *parā-Brahman.* The conception of *vāk* as *Vag Dēvi* has glorified the idea of *Akśara* or *udgīta*. The *Sphoṭa* as such is free from all kinds of determinancy and gross body of speech (*Dhvani*). So the *Sphoṭa* is both immanent and transcendent, - determinate and indeterminate in its nature." [23]

Dr. S.K. De says;

> The *Sphoṭa,* which has been likened to the Neo-Platonic '*logos'*, is often translated by the terms 'expression',

'concept', or 'idea'; but none of these terms brings out its essential nature. The *Sphoṭa* is explained as the sound of a word as a whole, and as conveying a meaning apart from its component letters (*varṇas*). The *Sphoṭa* does not contain exactly the sounds of the order peculiar to the letters, but the sounds of something corresponding to them are blended indistinguishably into uniform whole. When a word is pronounced, individual sounds become reflected in some degree in the order of the *Sphoṭa* in which the particular sounds are comprised; and as soon as the last sound dies away, the *Sphoṭa*, in which the idea corresponding to all these sounds is comprised, becomes manifest and raises to our consciousness the idea thus associated. The sounds of a word as a whole, therefore, and a part from those of the constituent letters, reveals the *Sphoṭa*." [24]

The *Sphoṭa* can be compared with the divine mystic word, *Om* or *Praṇava* wherefrom all the forms of speech or *vāk* are supposed emanate.

According to Dr. P. C. Chakraborty,

"The assumption of a spiritual phenomenon like *Sphoṭa*, to which all sounds are reducible and from which all meanings follow furnishes a clue to the origin of sound. *Sphoṭa* is indivisible (*akhanda*), and represents *Caitanya* in its purest form. Its sacred and lofty nature was much exaggerated by the grammarian so that it was finally identified with *Brahman*."[25]

Ākāśa: The Medium of Sound

Nāda is said to be the primordial sound generated from *Ākāśa* which cannot be translated as sky. Space though a little better term than the sky, but it does not come very close to the real meaning of '*Ākāśa*'. *Ākāśa* is one of the five elements (*Ākāśa, Prithvi, Jala, Agni* and *Vāyu),* and it is the first and foremost of them.

Lewis Rowell says:

> "The concept of *Ākāśa* is not a simple concept but rather an entire semantic field that includes such things as breath, soul energy, motion, space, wind, and most important of all, ether. The word *Ākāśa* is a derivative of the verbal root *'kāś'* "to become visible, shine, be brilliant". The idea of *Ākāśa* developed in later *Vedic* times and is especially prominent in the cosmological speculations of the *Upaniṣads.* One passage from the *Taittirīya Upaniṣad* refers to *Ākāśa* as the first, evolutes from the universal sound (*Ātman*). "From this Soul, verily, space (*Ākāśa*) arose; from space, wind; from wind, fire; from fire water; from water, the earth, from the earth, herbs; from herbs, food; from food, semen; from semen, the person." [26]

"In another grand cosmic vision, the *Bṛhadāraṇyakā Upaniṣad* describes the *Ākāśa* as part of a multidimensional world tapestry: past, present and future are "woven, warp and woof" across the *Ākāśa*, while the *Ākāśa* is itself "woven, warp and woof" across the Imperishable (*Ākāśara*), the 'unseen Seer, the unheard Hearer, the unthought Thinker, the ununderstood Understander, that is *Brahman.* If sound, then, is identified as the primary quality or attribute of the substance that pervades the cosmic tapestry, it is clearly understood the cultural priority assigned to speech, hearing, and the inherent power of sound."[27]

The supernal *Ākāśa* is the imperishable source and perpetual basis of sonorous rhythms that issue from the heights to form the planes and build the world and also to function by casting harmonic spells for their sustenance.

Classification of Sound or *Śabda*

Four kinds of *vāk* in the *Ṛgveda*

> "*Catvāri vāk-parimitā padāni tāni vidur-brahmaṇā ye maniṣhinah/*
>
> *Guhā triṇi nihitā nengayaniti turiyam vāce manuṣya vādanti//* [28]

Speech is of four kinds, *vaikharī* the spoken, *madhyamā* the conscious but unspoken language, *paśyanti* the consciousness that sees and creates the language construction, and *parā* that sees everything in its total unity before breaking into any classification. "Patañjali, Bhatṛhari, Nāgeśa, Gaudapada and *Sāyaṇa* have also divided the speech into four parts, *parā, Paśyantī, madhyamā* and *Vaikharī.*

The four kinds of speech 'correspond to four different stages, through which *Nāda* passes till it becomes perfectly audible. Thus, we may start with *bindu* or the final point as the crude germ of sound proceeds from the *mulādhāra* to the *visuddha*, in order to see how *Śabda - Brahman* or *parāvāk,* transforms itself into popular speech. From *bindu,* arises *Nāda*, which is called *Śabda-Brahman*; it is featureless, intellectual in essence, and possesses the characteristics, which are favourable to the cosmic creation. It is the essence of the world that is often signified by such words as *rava* and *parā.*

The nature of the *parāvāk* convinces us that it is aluminiferous consciousness residing in the *mulādhāra,* creative but indestructible. It is what is known as the *Śabda-Brahman* or the essence of the *Logos.* When *Nāda* or *Parāvāk* gets manifested a little and the internal air that serves to reveal it comes up to the navel region from the *mûlādhāras*. We have *Paśyanti* form of the *vāk,* which is revealed by the same air, when it passes to the region of the heart. It has intelligence as its only ingredient. The *Vaikharī* form of speech is what men speak. It is generated when the internal air passes through the throat and reaches the mouth."[29]

The '*Śabda -*' itself is classified into *Parā, Paśyantī, Madhyamā* and *Vaikharī.* The grossest of these four is *Vaikharī*, the dense audible sound, sound in its maximum differentiation. *Madhyamā* is the stage where thought takes the form of sound or word. It is an inner subtle, more ethereal state at which it is inaudible to physical ear. *Paśyanti* is still higher, inner, more, ethereal state. It is the preceding stage where 'thought' assumes a 'form' where sound vibration becomes 'visible' in the mind. At that stage, there is no impress of language on the form. That is, here the barrier of language has no meaning. Beyond it lies the subtlest, highest and most transcendental stage of *Parā* where neither thought, nor names nor forms find a place, as there are neither waves nor wavelengths there. It is the ultimate unifying substratum - the undifferentiated, yet potential sound of *Śabda - Brahman*. This is the stage of Godhead, the goal of deep meditation.

P.B. Mukherjee says:

> "*Parā*, which represents *Īśvara-Śakti* is the potential (*kāraṇa*) state of the Sound which is *Avyakta* or undifferentiated. The *Parā* sound is not like the *Vaikharī*, different in different languages. It is the unchanging primal substratum of them all, the source of universe Once if we look beyond the common etymological significance of the four divisions of *Parā, Paśyantī, Madhyamā* and *Vaikharī* and concentrate on their higher dimensions, we find the concept of *Vāk* or *Parā Vāk* (Eternal Causal Sound which is *Nāda Brahman*) revealing its fundamental and total significance as Creative Cosmic Life, as Revealing Supernal Light and as basic Original joy *(Ānandam)* which is the '*causa sui*,' 'the Magnum Matrix' of whatever is and becomes, of the entire process and *Līla* of Being and Becoming."[30]

Swāmi Prajñānanda asserted that:

> "*Vāk* or speech is the cause or fountain-head of music, the science and the theory of vāk should be studied with care in connection with music. The work *vāk* comes from the root, '*Vāc*' that means 'to speak'. The word *Vāk* therefore connotes the idea of voice or sound, and this sound manifests itself in three main aspects, parā (supreme) or *kāraṇa* (causal), sûkṣma (subtle) and *sthûla* (gross). The *parāvāk* is the cosmic ideation (*sṛṣṭikalpana*) of the Lord, the Creator (*īśvara*). *Vāk* has the same sense as '*Śabda*. *Artha* is meaning or object. *Pratyāya* is mental apprehension. All things have a threefold sense, supreme (*para*), subtle (*sûkṣma*) and gross (*sthûla*). *Parāvāk* is

the causal stress, which, in terms of *pratyāya,* is the cosmic ideation (*sṛṣṭikalpana*) of *Īśvara.*" [31]

"Sound or *Nāda* is the basic substance out of which the entire edifice of music is created by man's creative faculty or *Pratibha* and his urge for delight through creation. The original unmanifested sound i.e., *Mahā- Nāda* rests in a stare of involution against the background of the fundamental illimited silence i.e. *Mahā - Mauna.* From this primordial, transcendental state, starting with *Mûla Spanda* or original vibration it descends to the subtle, less subtle and gross or *Sthûla* level and becomes physically perceptible phenomenon. This sound, holds within itself the potential for becoming an expressive utterance, *Nāda* is synonymised with *Vāk.*

In Indian philosophical parlance *Vāk* as the vital force of the ultimate is the primordial source of the entire universe of expressive sound and the ideas and objects represented. At this highest-level *Vāk* is *Parā* i.e. transcendental. *Nāda* is the *Śakti* of *Brahman,* synonymous with *Parā Vāk.* By worshipping the *Śakti* of *Brahman,* which is closely related to *Brahman,* one can attain *Brahman* itself, just as a man moved by the luster of gem can move in its direction and attain gem itself. This *Nāda -Brahman-Vāda* of music is comparable with *rasa-Brahma-Vāda* of poetics signifying the aesthetic experience at its highest level–akin to *Brahmānānanda.*" [32]

Dr. Gauri Nath Sastri states that *Parāvāk* assumes the state of *Paśyanti* when, through its innate autonomous spontaneity, it externalized itself. As the order of the denoter and its denotation does not arise in that state, we find no differentiation. It is the light of consciousness, alone which shines with all its luster, and, consequently, it is described as the cognizer or the seer.

In *Madhyamā,* which is purely intellectual, the differentiation between the denoter and its denotation becomes slightly manifested. It is described as the intermediate stage between indistinct and distinct manifestation. And the name *madhyamā* owes its origin to this fact. The stage of distinct manifestation of the difference between the denoter and denotation is called *Vaikharī,* which exhibits the sequence of letters and syllables. Each of the three stages, *Paśyanti, madhyamā* and *Vaikharī*, is further divided into three stages, gross, subtle and super-subtle. Thus the gross form of *Paśyanti* is represented by the prelude to a song as denoted by the technical term, *ālāpa*, in which there is no differentiation of letters and which is singularly captivating. The gross state of *madhyamā* is represented by the sound, which arises when the fingers play upon musical instrument, say, a drum (*mridanga*). The gross stage *Vaikharī* is represented by what produces the various letters. The subtle conditions of each of these manifestations are respectively represented by the desire to sing, the desire to play upon a musical instrument and the desire to speak. And the super-subtle conditions are represented by the pure knowledge which lies as the source of the aforesaid desires." [33]

According to J.N. Sinha, the causal sound or *Nāda* is produced in the basic *cakra* by the action of volition of the self on the vital air. It is called the *parāvāk*. When it ascends to the *svadhisthāna cakra*, it unfolds itself and becomes *paśyanti*, and when it ascends to the *Anâhata Cakra*, it is united with intellect or *Buddhi* and becomes *madhyamā*. Gradually it ascends upward and reaches the *visuddha-cakra* in the throat, and becomes *vaikharī*. From there it rises towards the head, spreads over the palate, the tongue, lips, teeth, the root of the tongue, etc. and roduces articulate sound."[34]

According to Swāmi Prajñānanda, the Divine psyche or *Ātman* is the foundation (*adhisthāna*) of music. The Divine psyche sings eternally the immortal song of the Absolute Music, which is formless and colourless in essence and yet it manifests as phenomenal music with gross raw materials of tone, tune rhythm, grace etc. The philosophy of music states that Absolute Music is subjective, whereas its objective form is visual, audible and phenomenal music. Swāmi Prajñānanda has very nicely harped on the integrational approach of Sārañgadēva. In the *Sangītā-Ratnākāra*, Sārañgadēva has synthesized all the doctrines of *Patañjala-Mahābhāṣya, the Yoga darśana, Tantra and Vedânta* in his enunciation of the philosophical foundations of music. He adores reverentially *Nāda Brahman*, who assumes the body of sound: *Nāda tanu*." [35]

"Indian *Yoga* and *Tantra* have expounded the aspect of *Nāda*, marvelously. They describe four stages from the gross physical to the mental, then supramental and transcendental states. The gross physical is *vaikharī*, the second stage is *madhyamā*. The third is *paśyanti* and the fourth is *parāvāk*. In Hinduism the word '*Aum*' has been referred to as the beginning of creation. The state of nascent creation i.e., the state of *parāvāk*, the word is no other than the content and referent. This has significant implication that the entire creation of the universe is the result of Divine Imagination or thought. In this state, thought, word and the thing are one.

Parā means highest; *vāk* means thought-vibration. *Paśyanti* is a state where a vision of the configuration of *Nāda* starts. *Madhyamā* is that state where thought feeling prevails without verbal expression. *Vaikharī* is the state of the sense where experience is had through the direct employment of the five senses of hearing, seeing, touching, smelling and tasting and verbalization starts. *Brahma* means *mantra* or word. *Bhrāmaṇa* is the text that explains the *Vedas*. The Āraṇyakā pertains to the knowledge developed through meditation in the forest i.e., the text in which truths mentioned in the Vedas are given as experienced by man. *Upaniṣad* deals with fundamental metaphysics and the path of spiritualization as expounded in the *Vedas*."[36]

Nāda Yoga

There are various forms of *Yoga*. This philosophy is extremely systematic in its development, and begins with the doctrine of the body and proceeds through the active powers of the mind up to the higher principles of spirit. *Hatha Yoga* deals with the body land its training through specific methods of training, etc., and later by means of the systems of *Āsana*, *prāṇayāma* and *Mantra Yoga*. *Rāja Yoga* deals with the training of the mind and the psychic power and this includes *Prathyāhāra*, *Dharaṇa*, *Dhyāna* and *Samādhi*. *Karma Yoga* deals with the freedom of soul by means of work, largely work for others. *Bhakti Yoga* is a system of *Yoga* aiming at perfection through devotion. It is a doctrine of love. *Jñāna Yoga* we have a system, which endeavours to obtain union with God, or the universal consciousness by means of wisdom."[37]

Nāda Yoga, the most ancient practice in India, is an approach to sounds with reverence not just as objects for self-aggrandizement or sensual entertainment but as integral part of ones own unity with his inner and outer cosmos. The fundamental principle of *Nāda* is that our world is based on one primordial *Nāda*, that the entire Universe is a system of Sound-principles. It refers to the study of the powerful influence that *Nāda* exerts on ones mind or consciousness. The *Nāda Yogis* are of the view that all the constituents and ingredients of this phenomenal world, which have assumed gross forms, are based on the causal vibrations of the Sound-principle.

"Music is the language of the soul, the inner voice, the voice of pure reason and the Ultimate Reality. The practice of *Nāda Yoga* makes our mind subtler and subtler so that it becomes completely purified of all objective notions. Once the psychic being rises above the world of subject-object relationship it will have direct access to *Nāda Brahman*."[38]

Suresh Chandra Dey says:

> "The *Yoga* of Music, of which *Nāda Yoga* is an essential part, can be developed and embellished to the point of perfect absorption with *Nāda Brahman*, by resorting to an integral surrender of all actions, feelings, expectations, ambitions, etc, at the lotus feet of the Supreme Lord." [39]

In the *Bhagavad Gitā*, Lord Kṛṣṇa gave the following advice and exhorted Arjuna to become a yogi:

> *"Tapasvijbhyodhiko Yogi Jñānibhyohpi mathohdhika:*
> *Karmibhyaschādhiko Yogi Tasmad Yogi bhavārjuna."* [40]
>
> The *Yogi* is deemed superior to ascetics, superior to men of knowledge even; he is also superior to ritualists. Therefore be you a *Yogi, O Arjuna*.

The path of *yoga* is certainly the royal way, the most rapidly effective and revolutionary means of spiritual realisation. This wonderful exhortation of God calling upon the human beings to resort

Yoga- sādhana, which has been held by Him to be the highest and noblest path cannot be taken amiss.

> "*Japāt koti guṇam dhyānam; dyānāt koti guṇam layah;*
> *Layāt koti guṇam gānam Ganāt paratarant nahi.*" [41]

> *Of all the paths, the yogic path of gāna, which means Sangīta (music) in the wider sense, is prescribed to be the best and it has been further emphasized that there is nothing beyond music.*

God's natural preference is for music, which is full of '*prēmabhakti*' (loving devotion) arising out of his countless gregarious (singing) devotees, who are especially fond of partaking the '*nāmamamṛtam*' (the nectar of the Lord's name) and dance in ecstasy.

"Even many scientists have believed that the human body is not the ultimate stage of existence. It is only a gross (*Stûla*) layer, which is called the '*Annamaya Koṣa*'. There is a subtler (*Sûkṣma*) body than the gross one and it is called the *Prāṇic* or vital body, which refers to the *Prāṇamaya Koṣa. Praṇa* is the life-principle and vital force, which has five functional divisions such as *Praṇa, apāna,* etc. There are still five subtler sub-divisions, which are responsible for producing reflex actions of the same vital energy, the *Prāṇa.* Beyond this layer of body there exists a mental body through which we are able to think rationalize and understand. This constitutes the mental layer of our consciousness and is called, The *Manomaya Koṣa*. Still subtler than this is the layer of intelligence of the astral body, which is called *Vijñjanāmaya Koṣa.* Some people experience this in dreams and visions. The fifth layer, which is the subtlest, is the layer Absolute Consciousness and it is known as *Ānandamaya Koṣa.*

In *Yogic* parlance, beyond these layers of sheaths of existence, i.e., *Annamaya Koṣa* (gross physical), *Prāṇamaya Koṣa* (Vital), *Manomaya Koṣa* (mental), *Vijñjanāmaya Koṣa* (subtle physical or intelligence of the astral body) and the *Ānandamaya Koṣa* (layer of the Absolute Consciousness), there is a secret circumconscient or environmental consciousness in which are determined our unseen connections with the world outside us.

By environmental consciousness means something that each man carries around him, outside his body, even when he is not aware of it, by which he is in touch with others and with the universal forces. It is through this that the thoughts, feelings, etc. of others pass to enter into one- it is through this also that waves of the universal force—desire, sex, etc. come in and take possession of the mind, vital or body. Therefore, all believers of *yoga* philosophy accept that the physical body is not everything. It happens to be just a 'starting point'.[42]

Similarly, the external world of sound, which is received by our auditory organ, is not the be-all and end-all of the principles of Sound. In our body also, there are infinite sound vibrations on the different layers of consciousness, the permutations and combinations of which go to form the human bodies (and bodies of other creatures also), the vital energy, the mental faculties and the physic being.[43]

According to the *Nāda Yogis*, there was only one Sound in the beginning of the Creation and that primordial Causal Sound was the sacred *Om* and later on through its sound vibrations this universe came into existence. The word of the Bible means the Supreme Word or the Supreme Causal word and the Supreme Causal Sound. (Holy Bible, John: 1-1). The *Om* or the Cosmic Sound vibrated all throughout and everywhere in the Universe. Thus, according to the tenets of *Nāda Yoga*, the entire body and the entire creation is nothing but solidification of sound waves. This is technically called and adored as the *Nāda Brahman*.[44]

In the science of Music, every sound has a form of its own and it is not just one vibration. By proper concentration the notes of music can be solidified. Sound can be converted into energy and again reconverted into a material object and then the object can be disintegrated into atomic particles. The *Nāda Yogis* are of the view that all the constituents and ingredients of this phenomenal world, which have assumed gross forms, are based on the causal vibrations of the Sound- principle. Music is the language of the soul, the inner voice, the voice of pure reason and the Ultimate Reality. The practice of *Nāda Yoga* makes our mind subtler and subtler so that it becomes completely purified of all objective notions. Once the psychic being rises above the world of subject-object relationship it will have direct access to *Nāda Brahman*.[45]

Nāda Yoga sādhana

While there are different approaches to the practice of *Nāda Yoga*, the practice of *Svara Sādhana* is also adopted for the four gradual stages, which have been recommended. Those who are singers and are accustomed to do *svara sādhana* with the Indian musical instrument called *Tānpura* or *Tambûra* may sit down in any of the five *yogi* postures (suggested *āsanas*), for the meditation with the *tambûra* rested on the ground horizontally across the body (in front) of the singer.

According to Indian strings the *tambûra* strings, four in number, are set to tune in the following order; the first string (furthermost to the right) is set to the *Pañcama* note of the *mandra saptaka* (lower octave); the second and third strings set to the tonic note, *Ṣaḍja* or the *Madhya saptaka* (middle octave) and the fourth string set to the *Ṣaḍja* of *mandra saptaka* (lower octave). Alternatively sometimes the first string is set to the *madhyama svara* (*ma*) instead of the *Pañcama svara* (*pa*), of the *mandra saptaka* (lower octave) without any other change. While trying his process, the *sādhaka* of *Nāda yoga* need not belong to high order of vocal musicians. Any one who has musical sense with fundamental knowledge and acquaintance with the tones of the octave (*svara-saptaka*) can take recourse to this beautiful and charming method, without worrying about the technicalities of the musical system. With a very calm composed mind, *Om* may be uttered softly and hummed out in elongated fashion, basing on the tonic, *Ṣaḍja* (*sa*) of the middle octave (*Madhya saptaka*).

The same technique as in case of *Bhramāri Prāṇayāma* may be employed. The ear holes can be plugged with cotton pads in the beginning stages and these should be taken out in the fourth stage. There should be a perfect blending of the soft human voice with the base *nāda* (*mûlanāda*) i.e., '*Sa*' or the *Ṣaḍja* note of the middle octave while uttering and humming '*Om*' in an elongated fashion; the heart and mind should be totally stopped at the fourth stage. When the strings of the *Tambura* are arranged in the first combination of '*pa*' (*Pañcama*) and '*sa*' (*Ṣadja*), all the notes of the octave, except *madhyama* (*ma*) are produced by way of rich resonance of the four strings. When the strings are arranged as per the second combination of '*ma*' (*madhyama*) and '*sa*' (*Ṣadja*), all notes of the octave, except '*niṣāda*' are *sahāyaka nādas*. It is perhaps the desire of the Goddess of Music, and it is Her gift of Grace to mankind that with the *tambûra* strings set (or tuned) to only two base notes (*mûla nāda*), six auxiliary notes (*sahāyaka nādas*) are produced, i.e., the ratio is three times that of *mûla nāda.* [46]

Sri Swami Sivananda says:

> "By knowing the nature of inspiration and expiration, by having a comprehensive understanding and practice of the *Svara Sadhana* (science of breath), comes into being the knowledge of the past, present and future. This science, the hidden of the hidden, the secret of the secret, the revealer of *Satya or Brahman.* the bestower of bliss and supreme knowledge, is a pearl, a precious gem on the head of the wise. This knowledge is easily understood if faith, interest and attention are sincerely bestowed on the part of aspirants. It excites wonder in the unbelievers In the *Svara* are the Vedas and *Śāstras*. The *Svara* is the reflection of *Para Brahma*. Wrong *Svara* is the cause of a host of ailments. Observance of right *Svara* confers health and longevity. This will doubtless bestow on you wonderful benefits." [47]

Nāda Yoga employs *Nāda* or 'resonance' for alleviating all those problems connected to mind, psyche or consciousness, but also for raising one's level of consciousness through the various subtle. Psychic centers in the body, called *Chakras*. The sound vibrations consisting of two forms are *Âhata* (Struck Sound) and *Anâhata.* (Unstruck Sound). All the systems of philosophy whether *Vedic, Âgamic* or *Tantric* have broadly speaking, accepted the concept of *Nāda* as struck *(âhata)* and unstruck *(anâhata)*, and have held that while *anâhata* is for liberation and is not pleasing, the *âhata* is pleasing and leads to *anâhata*. "Unmanifest sound is causeless that emanates by itself without application of any outer force, friction, shock, etc. It is named as '*Anâhata*', which means, the sound that is produced without any type of striking. It is eternal, causeless and unmanifest.

According to *Tantras*, this '*Anâhata Nāda*' manifests itself in the '*Śunya*' (void), which is named as '*bindu*'. In the materialistic language, it may be said that *Anâhata Nāda* is manifested, when *Śiva* and *Śakti* meet together, it is spontaneous. *Anâhata Nāda* can be heard by meditating with concentration on the special plexuses called *Anâhata. Cakra,* poised in the region of heart. This *charka* contains twelve petals, each with the twelve first letters of the *Dēvanagari* alphabet. This *chakra* is considered to the place where the Lord Śiva should be worshipped in the form of '*Praṇava*' or '*Om*'." [48]

Hereward, C. says:

> "The *Anâhata Cakra* is situated in the heart. It is blood red, has twelve petals and is the seat of the *Prāṇa*. The *Hindus* have a saying that 'He who has awakened this *chakra* can walk in the air'- that is, he experiences levitation. The mystics are supposed to have aroused this center, hence their ability to 'levitate'. It is in the *Anâhāta chakra* that the 'Sound' is heard – the Pulse of Life. In this center is the 'tree which grants all desires' and beneath it the 'jewelled altar'. This *chakra* is the critical point in *Yoga* development." [49]

Swami Sivananda says that *Anâhata* sounds or the melody, are the mystic sounds heard by the *Yogi* at the beginning stage of his meditation. This subject is termed *Nada-Anusandhāna*, an enquiry into the mystic sounds. This is a sign of purification of the *Nādis* due to the practice of *Prāṇayama*. The sounds can also be heard after the uttering of the *Ajapa Gāyatri Mantra*, "*Hamsah Soham*", a lakh of times. The sounds are heard through the right ear with or without closing the ears. The sounds are distinct when heard through closed ears. The ears can be closed by introducing the two thumbs into the ears through the process of *yoni-Mudra*. One should sit in *Padma* or *Siddha āsana,* closing the ears with right and left thumb to hear the sounds very attentively. Occasionally it can be heard through left ear also. Practice must be to hear from the right ear only. It is because of the influence of the solar *Nādi, Pingala.* The *Anâhata* sound is also called *Omkara Dhvani.* It is due to the vibration of *Prāṇa* in the heart."[50]

The Inner and Outer Music

Nāda Yoga divides music into two categories: The inner music or *Anâhata,* and the outer music or *Âhata.* While the outer music is heard through the sense organs viz., ears, where the mechanical energy is converted to electro chemical energy to be perceived by the brain, the inner music owes its reception to the subtle heart *chakra,* also known as *Anâhata. cakra,* which is not a sensory organ. As its name implies, *Anâhata,* refers to one's own sound vibrations, which is so close to one's own self that any one else cannot simply share it. *Anâhata* is totally personal and private exclusive to its "possessor" alone. The system of *Nāda Yoga* not only assures to the practitioner of inner music the resultant harmony, relaxation, but also promises self-realization, which is often, the singular goal for those who undertake meditation.

The Inner Music (Anâhata Nāda)

The term "*Anâhata*" refers to the sound that is produced not by striking or hitting any object against any other object. It is also referred to as "Unstruck" or "non-material" sound. This term is also interpreted variously. It refers to the cosmic sound, *Om,* which represents a primal vibration that has evolved in to all manifestations in the universe. It is *brahmari,* the sound of a black bee, a sound, unbroken or unending and familiar to the practitioners of *prāṇayāma.* it is the thud, thud and thud of our heartbeats. *Nāda* itself is *Anâhata.* It is a sound, which is not produced through any striking. It has to be spontaneous and automatic, infinite, a sound without barriers or boundaries.

The Outer Music (Âhata Nāda)

Unlike inner music, the outer music is not esoteric or hidden. Unless one's hearing is impaired, anybody can listen to or appreciate the outer music. The outer music is manifold, unlike the inner music, which is unique and absolute. The outer music, as generally understand with its infinite varieties, affects our moods and minds in various ways. It draws our attention, affects our temperaments and behaviors too! While agitating us or relaxing, it affects us in myriads of ways. When one feels down and out, it is the music that could inject hopes or sunshine.[51]

Suresh Chandra Dey says:

> "The various treatises on music have described that when the current of the vital air or *Prāṇa Vāyu* comes in contact with the will-power or *iccha-Śakti*, there originates a vibration (*spandana*), resulting in a subtle audible sound, which is called '*Anâhata Nāda*'. Then gradually it becomes grosser and grosser, and manifests at least through the vocal cord (or the instruments) and is known as *Âhata Nāda* or musical sound. Obviously *Âhata Nāda* refers to the *Vaikharī* state of *Vāk*. As regards *Anâhata Nāda,* it can be said that it relates to the *Mādhyamiki Vāk*, which, according to Pratyagātmānanda Sarasvati, is the '*Axis Spanda*' upon which all kinds of 'causal *spanda*' must revolve, whether it be for the process of evolution or involution and also the two other higher stages of *Vāk*, viz., *Paśyanti* and *Parā*."[52]

The *Om* or the Cosmic Sound vibrated all throughout and everywhere in the Universe. Thus according to the tenets of *Nāda Yoga*, the entire body and the entire creation is nothing but solidification of sound waves. This is technically called and adored as the *Nāda Brahman* (Sound Cosmos). "*Matañga*, (5th-6th century A.D.), the author of the *Bṛhaddeśī,* identifies the causal music (*Nāda*) with the presiding deities of creation, preservation and destruction (*Brahma, Viṣṇu, Maheśvara*). He has said:

Nāda rūpah smrito brahma Nāda rūpo Janardanah/
Nāda rūpa parā-śakti Nāda rūpo Maheśvarah."

That is, the divine idea, that was in a seed from before creation i.e., projection (*Sṛiśti),* manifested with its richness and beauty."[53]

Matañga said that without *Nāda* it is impossible to attain knowledge and without the same it is impossible to arrange the welfare of the creatures. This is because the transcendental Luminous Self is *Nādarūpam* and *Brahman* or *Hari* Itself *Nādarūpi:*

"No Nādena bina jnanam
No Nādena bina Śivam
Nāda rūpam param jyotih
Nāda rūpi svayam Harih"

He mentioned that the fine arts of vocal music, instrumental music and dancing would have been impossible without *Nāda*. The entire Universe, is, according to him, *Nādātmakam* or inseparably identified with *Nāda*. The Holy Trinity, *Brahma* (the Creator), *Viṣṇu* (the Preserver), and *Maheśvara* (the Destroyer), representing the various gunas (*Sattva, rajas, and tamas*) and different aspects of the Creation and even *Parā Śakti (Mahā Māyā)* are personified in the form (or principal) of *Nāda*."[54]

Matañga begins his word '*Bṛhaddeśī*' with '*Dhvani*', *Bindu, Varṇa, Nāda* - Its importance and five types of *Nāda* based on the origin; various parts of the physical body in human beings. *Matañga* does not mention about these two types of *Nāda, Anâhata* and *Âhata*. He begins with *Dhvani* and *Nāda*, and his work indicates his inclination towards the *Tantra* and *Âgamas*. He elucidates the creation of *Dhvani* and *Varṇa*, according to the *Tantra* tradition. Matañga has enumerated five grades of evolution of the musical sound and there are: subtle (*Sûkṣma*), subtlest (*atisûkṣma),* manifested (*pûrṇa*), unmanifested (*apûrṇa*), and mechanical (*slaksma*). He has laid great stress upon its source or the basic psychic content; the *Nāda*, and he says in his *Bṛhaddeśī* that there can be no music or musical creativity at all without *Nāda* as the base of the primal energy:

"Na Nādena viṇa Gītām
Na Nādena viṇa svarah
Na Nādena viṇa nritam
Tasmon Nāda tmakam jagat." [55]

Swāmi Prajñānanda says, "The *Nāda* is the determinate (*Saguṇā)* form of the absolute *Brahman*, and its real indeterminate (*Nirguṇā*) aspects is the *Ātman,* which is the pure and Absolute Consciousness. He further says, the world of appearance is the projection of the *Nāda*, the *Śabda-Brahman* and the absolute happiness is *Brahman* itself. He has stated that music being the highest art, confers upon man absolute bliss and happiness. According to him, Sound is produced by the friction of heat-energy (*Agni*) and vital air (*Prāṇa Vāyu*). It produces tones and tunes or it can be said that the vibrations of the sweet and soothing sound units produce music. Swāmi Prajñānanda admits the *Parā Vāk* is essentially identical with the Ultimate Reality, the *Brahman*."[56]

"Matañga's description of the generation of musical sound, with its many symbolic associations with the gods, elemental substances, and the structure of the universe, has become one of the most powerful cultural models for the idea of musical sound. Few later authors have deviated from his line of thinking, which reinforces so many of the traditional continuities of Indian thought. As a consequence, the theory of sound as emerging vital substance became established as one of the pillars of Indian musical teachings."[57]

In *Sangītā Makaranda,* Nārada, after naming the two types of *Nāda: Āhata* and *Anâhata*, describes and defines the *Anâhata Nāda* in short. He explains that it is named as *Anāhata Nāda*, because it originates from the space by itself, and then elaborates the use of unmanifest sound. This '*Anāhata' Nāḍa* resides in the heart of *Anāhata Chakra*. He says that *Yogis,* sages and great souls attain the salvation through great mental concentration upon this *Nāda*."[58]

"Ākaṣa sambhavo Nādo Ya !"
Soṣanahasamjñitha! [59]

"The most significant account of Indian music theory, the *Sangīta Ratnākara* was written by Sārañgadēva, between 1227 and 1247 in *Deogiri* in Central India. The *Sangīta Ratnākara* may be seen as an important reflection of contemporary music practice, and it points at the changes that had occurred since the *Nātya Śāstra.*"

> " *Hṛdaye anahathah chakramh Śivasya Prānavākṛuthe*
> *Pujasthānam thadischanthi Dalovdradeṣabhiyuthamu*"

'Sārangadēva in his *Sangīta Ratnākara* comes nearer to *Sangīta Makaranda* of Nārada. He describes the *Anâhata Nāda* in the same way as Nārada, with more elaborations. In the second section, '*Pindotpatti Prakāram*' the importance of *Nāda* is discussed which is similar to that of ' *Bṛhaddeśī*' of Matañga, followed by manifest and unmanifest forms of *Nāda*. As *Nāda* is generated by the soul (*Ātma*) residing in the physical body of human beings, the formation of the body from the very beginning is described at length:

> "*Āhathe anāhathashchethe thredha nādo nigādhathe*
> *Soṣayam prākāśate pinde thasmathu pindoṣithiyathe*"

Sārañgadēva refers to the two types of *Nāda* as *Suguṇā* - concrete and *Nirguṇā* - abstract which are the means of the worldly enjoyment and salvation respectively. The same attributes are allotted to the unmanifest or *Anâhata* sound as by *Nārada* in his *Sangīta Makaranda*. The single-minded dedication with deep concentration upon the '*Anâhata*.' sound would result in salvation.

According to Sārañgadēva, this concentration is not possible for everybody. '*Nirguṇā*' sound has neither pleasing nor unpleasing proper ties to the human ears and mind. It is very difficult to concentrate on something, which has no form, foundation, cause or any property to meditate upon. *Anâhata Nāda* is a subtle, abstract sound residing within the body, which can be heard by directing one's mind inward with full concentration. A condition practically met with highly spiritual people. '*Âhata Nāda* with its concept of *Suguṇā* - the natural friction of things accessible to everyone produces concrete sound. This *Âhata* or *Suguṇā* sound is based on *sṛutis* and *Svaras*. Our ancestors, i.e., sages and seers have systematized the *Āhata Nāda* and regulated it accordingly to be practiced and enjoyed by all the people. This music provides entertainment as well as spiritual enlistment and breaks the cycle of birth and death. Either *Anāhata* or *Āhata Nāda* serves the purpose of spiritual enlistment and attainment of salvation. The result lies in the mental and spiritual standard of the candidate who practices it. Āhata *Nāda* is easier to practice as it is this on which the concept of music is based. According to Nārada, (*Sangīta Makaranda*), *Nāda* is to be focused upon by Yogis, munis, etc. It is not concerned with music, but gods reside or take refuge in it. *Nārada* as such does not have any specific definition or description of the *Âhata Nāda* as the *Nāda* in general indicates *Âhata Nāda* only.'

Sangītā Ratnākara by Sārańgadēva expresses *Nāda* as follows:

"*Chaitanyam sarvabhoolānām vivrutam*
Jagatatmāna Nādabrahma TadĀnandam Adviteeya Mupāsmahe" [60]

The alphabets are pronounced with the help of *Nāda*. These alphabets make words, sentences and languages.

Nakāram Prāṇanāmānam
Dakāramanalam Vidhuhu
Jatah Prāṇāgni Sāmyogā thena
Nādobhidēyate'

Nā stands for *Prāṇa* and *Da* for fire. The combination is *Nāda* sound. As a vehicle of expression it has developed world culture and helped in its dissemination. Its range, vitality and endurance have been proved by modern scientific inventions. It is from prānava the primordial sacred syllable; the *Vedas*, *Āgamas* and *Śāstras* emerged. [61]

The *Sāñkhya* sages called the manifest word as *Om Prakṛti* and its substratum as *Nāda Puruṣa*. According to *Sāñkhya* School the sound that is spread all over the creation of God is called, *Brahmānanda*. *Brahmānandam* is the medium of all human behavior.

According to *Bhakti* School, the letter *Om* itself is God. Hence it is not only a symbol for something else but also the 'thing in itself'.

As a result the Śaivaites tried to interpret the letter '*Om*' as the very incarnation of *Śiva* in Cosmic Dance. For the Vaiṣṇavites also '*Om*' is the *Prāṇa* of the *mantra. Bhaktās* or devotees as much worship the letter "*Om*' as they worship their favorite God in the idol form. This understanding led them to the idea of revelation and meditation.

"*Vedic* Philosophy refers to the concept of *Nāda Brahma* ('Sound god') as the source of all vibrations, audible or inaudible, in the cosmos. This concept is represented iconographically in sculpture of a later period by the figure of *Śiva Tāṇḍava* (dancing *Śiva*), who drums the cosmos into existence. The sacred syllable *Om* is the oral representation of this sound genesis and in its written form has at least a thousand-year history as a wholly graffito. Repetition of a magic mantra or syllable such as *Om* or verse consisting of such syllables with or without lexical meaning is an ancient meditation practice based on a belief in the efficacy of controlling vibration within the body."[62]

Selina Thielemann says:

> "In the *Vedic* tradition, sound is identified with the supreme reality, *Śabda-brahman*, the prime object of worship and meditation. Being given concrete shape in the chanted syllable, sound acts as the principal vehicle of communication between man and the forces of the universe."[63]

The *Vedas, Vāk (Vāg Dēvi)* or the Divine Mother sang the creation into being. God's eternal life force, *Parāśakti*, entered or rather assumed the perennial Casual Sound (*Nāda*) through the monosyllabic seed-sound, *Om (Prāṇava)*, and thereby the phenomenal world with its multiple forms evolved. This process of physical, vital, mental and soul-contact or Holy Communion with the omnipotent, omniscient and omnipresent God, who is the ultimate principle of Harmony and beauty forever, is a spiritual art and scien_e of Integral *Yoga*. It aims at a complete union, perfect integration and absolute identification of God, in all His manifested as well as unmanifest *Līla* (Divine sport) at the individual, cosmic as well as supra-cosmic levels of existence.

Nāda is Brahman

The term *Brahman* has been from the ancient *Vedic* times to the modern age the most important unified concept of Hindu religion and Indian philosophy. The musicologists, especially in India, who have identified the casual music (*Nāda*) with the presiding Deities of creation, preservation and destruction have emphasized that *Nāda,* being the source of all forms of *Vāk* is called *Śabda-Brahman* or *Nāda Brahman.* In this process *Śabda* - or *Nāda-tattva (*principle) has been completely identified with *Brahman-tattva*, by the philosophers and musicologists.

Devoted musicians have regarded *Nāda* as *Parama Vidyā* (Ultimate knowledge) and they have offered their prayers to The Divine Mother through the famous songs. Matañga describes about the causal sound or *Nāda*, from which music, with all its manifestations evolved. He says that the *Nāda* as the determinate (*suguṇa*), *Brahman,* shines as *Brahma*, the creator, *Viṣṇu*, the preserver, *Maheśvara*, the destroyer. According to Achārya Bhatṛhari, the study of the science of sound leads mankind to the realization of all-pervading God and he supported the doctrine of *'Śabda - Brahman* or *Nāda Brahman*. In his magnum opus, the *'Vākypādīyam*,' he has fully expounded *Śabda-Brahmanvada.* He has dealt with the theory of emotional *Dhvani*, based on the *Sphoṭavāda*. In his *Vākypadīya* and in the *Brahmakānda* of the *Vākypadīya;* he has established the doctrine of *Śabda - Brahman*. He was a staunch advocate of the doctrine of sound (*Sphoṭavāda.)* and advocates that the *Śabda-tattva* and the *Brahma-tattva* are interchangeable.[64]

> "*Anādinidhanam Brahma Śabdatattvam yadakṣaram*
> *vivarterthabhāvena prakriyā jagato yatah!*"

"Bhatṛhari's concept of *Śabda-Brahman*, the ultimate reality, has been interpreted as an evolutionary principle. His assertion goes on the lines as enshrined in the ancient Hindu Scriptures. In his philosophical system, Consciousness and Word are interchangeable terms. "The Ultimate Reality is the Absolute Consciousness and Consciousness and Word being identical, it is the Absolute Word." Bhatṛhari's concept of Absolute *Brahman* has been characterized as a dynamic principle. It produces the Universe and appears to be the material and efficient cause of all that exists. Consequently this *Śabda-* - *tattva* (or *Nāda tattva*) of *Bhatṛhari* and his followers is universally acceptable because of its cogency sensible approach and its close affinity with the Indian metaphysics of Sound."[65]

"Bhatṛhari maintained the theory of eternality of sound (*Sphoṭa)* in a different way. He said in the *Brahmakānda* of the '*Vākypadīya* that *Brahman*, without beginning and end, is the indestructible essence of speech or sound. It is manifested in the form of things, and from it springs also the creation of the world appearance."[66]

Śankara has also supported the evolution of the world from the causal sound on the logical basis of perception and inference.

> "*eta iti vai rajapatirdēvanasrjatasrgramiti*
> *Śastramabhisoubhagetyanyah prajah.*"[67]

Dr. Gouri Nath Shastri says:

> "*Nāda Brahman* is the purest of all lights that dispels the gloom of nescience. It is Being (or existence) in essence in that it exists for all time and beyond time as well. It has neither birth nor death. *Nāda Brahman* has two-fold aspect as 'transcendent' beyond time in which it is above all predication in thought and language and as 'immanent' in time in which it is the subject and predicate of all judgments."[68]

Suresh Chandra Dey says that the Supreme Reality in the philosophy of Sanskrit grammar has been called the Eternal Verbum (*Śabda-Brahman*) or the Supreme Word, which is a highly subtle and met empirical principle which transcends all that comes within the ken of human experience and all that possesses a pragmatic significance; even moral and religious values are not predicable of it. 'The eternal Verbum lies beyond time and space; it is non-relational and featureless, and eludes all descriptions by means of positive and negative predicates.'[69]

According to him, 'Indian philosophy has very beautifully synthesized all the doctrines of *Pātañjala-Mahābhāśya*, the *Yoga-darṣana, Tantra, Vedānta*, post-Vedantic thoughts and in the enunciation of the philosophic foundations of music. Consequently, it regards *Nāda* as the highest knowledge and an inseparable ingredient of the *Satyam, Śivam, Sundaram* and *Ānandam* aspects of *Parā Brahman* or the Absolute Divinity."[70]

In *Shrīmad Bhagavad Gītā*, Lord Kṛṣṇa has told Arjuna that the Imperishable and Immutable is the Supreme Brahman:

> "*Akṣaram Brahman param swabhavo' dhyatmamucyate!*
> *Bhutabhavodbhavakaro visargah karmasamjnitah*"// [71]
>
> The imperishable is *Brahman,* the Supreme. Its dwelling in the individual body is called *Ādhyātma*. The offering which causes the origin of beings is called *karma*."

In *Akśara Brahman Yogah,* Lord Sri Kṛṣṇa describes Brahman as the omniscient, the Ancient, the Over ruler, minuter than atom, the sustainer of all, of form inconceivable, self-luminous like the Sun and beyond the darkness of *Māyā* (illusion), The Supreme Resplendent *Puruṣa*."

According to Sri Aurobindo the *Brahman* state is that of a Supreme existence, supremely aware of itself, *Svayamprakāśa*; It is *Saccidānanda* (*Sat, Cit, Ānanda*), Existence-Consciousness-Bliss. Even when it is described as beyond That, *Parāt Parām*, it does not mean that it is a state of Non-Existence or Non-Consciousness, but beyond even the highest spiritual substratum of cosmic existence and Consciousness.

Sri Aurobindo says,

> "The Divine has projected the universe out of His own being with a purpose. That purpose is to manifest Himself, His nature of existence, consciousness and Bliss, *Saccidānanda*. It is the aim of *Yoga* to work out this Supreme will by the liberation of human life from the holds

> of ignorance, limitation and death and its transformation in the divine nature of knowledge, infinity and immortality."[72]

Throughout the ages, the saints, seers, yogis and poets have tried to describe the *Brahman* in their respect ways and yet almost everybody feels that the *Brahman* has always eluded our grasp and it has remained above all descriptions. ...Beyond all words in the Holy Scriptures.

The *Taittirīya Upaniṣad* has attempted to define *Brahman* when it says that it is the all-pervading principle, the self of all beings, the reality that is one only without a second and besides whom there really exists nothing else.[73]

In the *Yajurveda*, it is said that every thing in this whole round of the Universe is God-made, God-protected and God-pervaded or enveloped by Him.[74]

The *Sāmaveda* sings in praise of the Supreme *Brahman* saying that it has no equal. [75]

The *Ṛgveda* offers its hymn to the Almighty Lord as follows:

> "*To the thoughtful men who Truth discern*
> *And deeply things Divine explore,*
> *That God reveals His hidden lore*
> *But fools His secrets may not learn.*"[76]

The *Upaniṣads* describe the phenomenon of happiness as the Bliss of *Brahman*, manifested in *antahkārana* (the internal organ, the mind) due to contacts with objects mundane, whereas the unsurpassable or Absolute Happiness is *Brahman* itself. According to Swāmi Prajñānanda, the philosophy of Music is absolutely concerned with the theory and value of Causal Sound, which is *Nāda* in Sanskrit. *Nāda Brahman* stands for the Ultimate Principle of Casual Sound, which is the causative, creative and dynamic Energy of the Supreme Being or the *parama Puruṣa*. Philosophers, Musicologists and *Tantriks* regard *Nāda* as the material cause of the universe and identify it with the *Brahman* of the *Upaniṣad*.[77]

Nāda, Śabda, Sphoṭa, Dhvani and Vāk

We may examine the deep significance and connotations of different terms often used by the grammarians, such as Śabda -, *Nāda-Sphoṭa, Dhvani* and *Vāk* etc., in our effort to understand the concept of *Nāda* Brahman properly. Basically, there is no difference between *Nāda Brahman* and *Śabda - Brahman*, which are quite often identified with *Parā Vāk* and *Parā Brahman.* Such distinctions do not affect the immutable integrity of the Real Fact or the Ultimate Principle, but these arise only in our habitual reviews and mental reports thereof, and our pragmatic reactions thereto.

In the ultimate analysis every object has in it a system of constituting forces, which are in ceaseless movement and produce some significant sound. But this Sound is of the supersonic order, not audible to the normal ear of common man; particularly audible to the *Yogic* ear of the *Yogi* or *Sādhaka*; within in the twinkling of an eye the Absolute ear of *Brahman.* Needless to say, *Nāda Brahman* is the Absolute Ear, the Absolute Vision and the Absolute Emanation of The Eternal Sound-Energy of Integral *Brahman (Pûrṇa Brahman).*

Om, which is the primordial *Ekākśara Bija-Mantram*, is the Omnipresent, Omnipotent and Omniscient *Mantra Śakti* and the indwelling *Nāda Brahman* in each object and subject of the phenomenal world. When Lord Sri Kṛṣṇa says in the *Bhagavad Gītā* that among the various *Yajnas*, He stands for or represents *Japa-yajña* and further declares to Arjuna that He is the *Omkāra (Prānava) Mantra* in all *Vedas*, Sound in *Ākāśa* and manhood in men.

> *"raso ' ham apsu kaunteya prabhā ' smi śaśisûryayoh !*
> *Pranavah sarvavedsu śabdah khe paurusam nrsu" //*[78]

Suresh Chandra Dey says that it is proved beyond doubt that God is eternally and absolutely identified with *Om* — the Casual *Mantra* of the Universe, which is inseparable and indivisible from *Nāda Brahman. Nāda Brahman* is the purest word-consciousness, the highest goal of Nature's music and the mightiest Sound-Energy pervading each and every level of creation and at the same time it is the Transcendental Reality (*Paratparā Satta*) far above and beyond the *triguṇatmaka (Sattva, rajas* and *tamas)* Universe. It is *Parā Vāk, Parā Śabda* -, the Eternal *Sphoṭa*, the Fundamental Stress or *Prāṇa Spanda. Vāk*, which is also called *parā Śabda,* or *parā Vāk* does not mean just word or sound - vibration, as we understand in the ordinary sense. It actually means the fundamental Causal Stress and what Swami Pratyagātmānanda Sarasvati calls, 'the magnum matrix of all cosmic vibrations, the concept of *Nāda Brahman'* in Indian Music."[79]

REFERENCES

1. Mircea Eliade, *The Encyclopedia of Religion*, Vol.– 10, p.185.
2. Dr. Chakraborthy. P.C., *The Cultural Heritage of India,* p. 674.
3. Dr. Vijaya Lakshmi. M., *A Critical Study of Sangita Makaranda*, p.76.
4. Sir John Woodroffe, *Principles of Tantra*, Part-II, pp.175-177.
5. Suresh Chandra Dey, *The Quest for Music Divine*, p.32.
6. Swāmi Haripremānanda Sarasvati, *Yogataravali, Adi Śankarāchārya,* (commentary), Yoga Magazine of the Bihar School of Yoga, Monghyr, August, 1977.
7. Suresh Chandra Dey, *The Quest for Music Divine,* p.33.
8. *Ibid.* p.1.
9. Mukherjee, *The Metaphysics of Sound: An Appendix to Japasutram*, pp.71-71.
10. Hereward, C., *Higher Psychical Development*, p. 68.
11. *Ibid.*, p. 70.
12. Telang. M..R., *Sangīta Makāranda of Nārada,* Ed.
13. Sir John Woodroffe, *Principles of Tantra*, Part- II, pp. 179-18.
14. Dr. M. Vijaya Lakshmi, *A Critical Study of Sangita Makaranda*, p. 77.
15. Philip. P. Wiener, *Dictionary of the History of Ideas, Studies of Selected Pivotal Ideas,* Vol-III, p. 268.
16. Lewis Rowell, *Music And Musical Thought in Early India,* pp. 43-44.
17. *Kaṭopaniṣad,* 2, 12, 16, 17.
18. *Kaṭopaniṣad,* 12, 15.
19. *Chhāndogya Upaniṣad,* 1:27.

20. Swami Chidambarananda., *The Bhagavad Gītā*, 8:13, p. 466.
21. Abbe J.A. Dubois, *Hindu Manners and Ceremonies*, p. 141.
22. Lewis Rowell, *Music and Musical Thought in Early India*, p. 42.
23. Swāmi Prajñānanda, *A Historical Study of Indian Music*, pp. 330-332.
24. Dr. De, S.K., *History of Sanskrit Poetics, Bengali Literature in the 19th Century*, pp. 143-144.
25. Dr. Chakraborty. P.C, *The Philosophy of Sanskrit Grammar*, p. 674.
26. Lewis Rowell, *Musical and Musical Thought*, p. 48.
27. *Ibid.*, p. 48.
28. *Ṛgveda* I-164-45.
29. Dr. Chakraborthy. P. C., *The Linguistic Speculations of the Hindus*, pp. 49-50.
30. Mukherjee. P.B., *The Metaphysics of Sound: An Appendix to Japasutram*, pp. 71-73.
31. Swāmi Prajñānanda, *A Historical Study of Indian Music*, p. 340.
32. Dr. Sumati Mutatkar, *Bharathiya Samskriti*, p.117.
33. Dr. Gouri Nath Sastri, *The Philosophy of Word and Meaning*, pp.74-75.
34. Sinha. J.N., *Indian Psychology, II, Emotion and Will*, p.11.
35. Swāmi Prajñānanda, *A Historical Study of Indian Music*, pp.342-343.
36. Gautam.M.R., *Evolution of Raga and Tala, In Indian Music*, p. 13.
37. Hereward. C., *Higher Physical Development*, p. 4.
38. Suresh Chandra Dey, *The Quest for Music Divine*, p. 76.
39. *Ibid.*, p. 74.
40. Swami Chidbhavananda, *The Bhagavad Gita*, Ch: VI, 46. p.409.
41. Tinkodi Bandopadhyaya, *Sangita Shatadala*, Vol-1.
42. Suresh Chandra Dey, *The Quest for Music Divine*, p.75.
43. *Ibid.*, p.76.
44. *Ibid.*, p. 75.
45. *Ibid.*, p. 77.
46. Suresh Chandra Dey, *The Quest for Music Divine*, p. 81.
47. Sri Swami Sivananda, *Practice of Yoga*, p. 315.

48. Vijay Lakshmi M., *A Critical Study of Sangītā Makāranda of Narada*, p. 77.
49. Hereward. C, *Higher Psychical Development*, p. 148.
50. Sri Swami Sivananda, *Practice of Yoga*, p. 375.
51. Vijay Lakshmi M., *A Critical Study of Sangītā Makāranda of Narada*, p. 79.
52. Suresh Chandra Dey, *The Quest for Music Divine*, p.76.
53. Swāmi Prajñānanda, *A Historical Study of Indian Music*, p. 342.
54. Suresh Chandra Dey, *The Quest for Music Divine*, p.23.
55. Swāmi Prajñānanda, *A Historical Study of Indian Music*, p.343.
56 Swāmi Prajñānanda, *A Historical Study of Indian Music*, p.408.
57. Lewis Rowell, *Music And Musical Thought In Early India*, p.47.
58. Vijay Lakshmi M., *A Critical Study of Sangītā Makāranda of Nārada*, p. 79.
59. Telang. M.R., *Sangītā Makāranda of Narada*, (Ed), p.21.
60. Ranganathan. N., *Musical Forms in Sangitaratnākara*, p. 416-417.
61. *Ibid.*, p.417.
62. Mircea Eliade, *The Encyclopedia of Religion*, Ed, p.186.
63. Selina Thielemann, *Singing The Praises Divine, Music in Hindu Tradition*, p.2.
64. *Vākypadīya*, I: I.
65. Suresh Chandra Dey, *The Quest For Music Divine*, p.16.
66. Swāmi Prajñānānanda, *A Historical Study of Indian Music*, p.333.
67. *The Vedānta sūtra*, 1.3.28.
68. Dr. Gouri Nath Shastri, *The Philosophy of Word and Meaning*, pp.74-75.
69. Suresh Chandra Dey, *The Quest for Music Divine*, p.17.
70. Suresh Chandra Dey, *The Quest for Music Divine*, p. 272.
71. Swami Chidbhavananda, *Shrīmad Bhagavad Gītā*, Ch. V111: 2, p.452.
72. Pandit. M.A, *Sādhana in Sri Aurobindo's Yoga*, pp.12-13.
73. *Taittirīya Upaniṣad*, 2:1
74. *The Yajurveda*, 40: 72.

75. *The Sāmaveda*, 1: 85
76. *The Ṛgveda*, 7: 135.
77. Swāmi Prajñānanda, *A Historical Study of Indian Music*, p. 330.
78. Swami Chidbhavananda, *Srimad Bhagavad Gītā*, Ch. VII: 8, p. 422.
79. Suresh Chandra Dey, *op. cit.*, New Delhi. p. 20.

4

Vedic Music

The Vedas were considered as revealed literature and sacred collection of verses conceived by the Sages and seers (*Ṛṣis*) through divine vision and hence their unique authority and influence was undeniable. In order to ensure the purity of the *Vedas*, the slightest change was forbidden, and there has been virtually no change in these texts for about 3,000 years. The *Vedic* cult was brought into ancient India with the *Āryans*, around 1400 to 1000 B.C. The four Vedas formed the basis of their culture. The oldest of these texts is the *Ṛgveda*, which came into existence around 1200 to 100 B.C. and which contains verses that are to be rendered at sacrifices. The remaining three *Vedas* are of later date, approximately 100 to 800 B.C; these include the *Yajurveda*, as collection of sacrificial formulae, chronologically followed by the *Sāmaveda*, the compilation of the sung melodies, and by the *Atharvaveda*, which deals with magic formulae.

> "The *Vedas* are succeeded by a number of commentaries and explanations embodied in the *Brāhmaṇas*, *Āraṇyakās* and *Upaniṣads*, philosophical texts of the 8th to 6th centuries B.C. The oldest of these texts, the *Brāhmaṇas*, contain prescriptions for the Vedic ritual. The *Āraṇyakas* (*āraṇyaka*, pertaining to 'forest'), of later date than the *Brāhmaṇas*, are strictly secret texts, hence the name *āraṇyaka*, which refers to these books being either

> composed or studied in the seclusiveness of the forest. The *Upaniṣads,* composed towards the end of the *Vedic* period and containing the chief tenets of Indian philosophy, form the category of texts known as *Vedānta*, the 'end of the *Veda*'.[1]

The name '*Veda*' (knowledge) stands for the *Mantras* and the *Brāhmaṇas*. *Mantra* means a hymn addressed to some god or goddess. The collection of *Mantras* is called '*Samhitā*'. There are four *Samhitās* – *Ṛk*, *Sāma*, *Yajuh* and *Atharva*. These are said to be compiled for the smooth performance of the *Vedic* sacrifices."[2]

According to Swāmi Prajñānanda:

> "There were only *Trai* or three Vedas, *Ṛk, Sāma* and *Yaju*, and so in the *Vedas* and *Brāhmaṇa* literature we often find the word, *Tray*, i.e. three *Vedas* only, and the *Atharva Veda* evolved afterwards and was added in the list of the *Chaturvedah*."[3]

Dr. Chandradhar Sharma elaborates:

> "Some times the Vedas are referred to only as '*Trayi*', omitting the *Atharva*. *Ṛk* means a verse, *Sāma* means a song, and *Yajuh* means a prose passage. Thus we see that the *Samhitā-bhāga* or the *Mantra*-portion of the *Veda* is the *Hymnology* addressed to the various gods and goddesses."[44]

The *Ṛṣis*, to whom the hymns of the *Vedas* appeared as revelations, are the authors of those hymns. The seven *Ṛṣis* (*saptarśis*) are referred to in the *Shatapātha Brāhmaṇa* as *Goutama, Bharadwāja, Viśwāmitra, Jamadāgni, Vaśistha, Kaśyapā* and *Atri*. The seven *Ṛṣis* are represented in the sky by the seven stars of the Great Bear. The *richas* or the hymns were often composed on the spur of the moment. There were some social, political and religious organizations among the *Āryans* in the *Ṛgvedic* period (3000-2500 B.C). Their vast literature proves that the *Āryans* were highly cultured and civilized. From ancient times the *Vedas* have been reputed to constitute an extensive literary corpus held in reverence as the source of all knowledge. Thus *Śankarāchārya* describes it as 'the mine of all knowledge' (*Sarvajñānākarasya),* 'lighting up all Truths like a lamp' (*Pradipāvatsarvārthavadyotinah*). *Patañjali* has earlier indicated its traditional extent:

> *'Ekaśatam adhvaryuśākhāh sahasravartmā sāmavedha ekavimaśatidhā bāhvrcyam navadhātharvano vedah.!'*

That is to say the *Ṛgveda* had twenty-one branches or recensions, the *Yajurveda* had one hundred and one, the *Sāmaveda* as thousand, the *Atharvaveda* nine. Most of these have now disappeared. Of the *Ṛgveda*, only one complete recension, that of *Sākala,* survives; possibly thirty-six hymns of the *Bāskala śākha* are available and of the *Vālakhilya* only eleven. Of the *Yajurveda* only six recensions survive. Of these *Kathaka, Maitrāyani, Taittiriya*, and fragments of *Kapiṣthala-katha* recensions belong to *Kṛṣṇa -Yajurveda*. The *Śukla-Yajurveda* or *Vajasaneyisamhitā* survives in the *Kanva* and *Mādhyandina* versions. Of the *Sāmaveda*, three recensions survive, viz., the *Ranayaniya*, the *Kauthuma* and the *Jaiminiya*. Of the *Atharvaveda, Saunaka-Samhitā* is current, while the *Paippalāda-samhitā* is known."[5]

In its several thousand years of history, Indian music has been transmitted primarily as a sounding reality. Notation systems exist since the *Vedic* period. The *Ṛgvedic* notations, that are accessible to us only since a few centuries, belong to the oldest notation systems in the world, if one presumes that they have been passed on as a secret science since the time of the *Ṛgveda*. For the melodies of the *Sāma-veda*, a specific system of notation was devised and has been maintained over approximately 3000 years.[6]

> "The *Vedic* texts originally kept secret and orally transmitted by male *Brāhman* singer-priests. The *Ṛgveda* (stanzas of praise), *Sāmaveda* (chant based on *Ṛgveda* texts, *Yajurveda* (sacrificial prayers), and *Atharvaveda* (magic formulas) were passed down through *Śākhas* (lineages) that supported schools for training *brahmans* of particular *gotras (*sub-castes). The recitation of this

> massive corpus of material required a prodigious and well-ordered memory and knowledge of the codified rules of musical adaptation."[7]

Swāmi Prajñānanda says:

> "By *Vedic* Music is meant the music of the *Sāma-Veda* or *sāmagāna* that evolved out of the *ṛcs* or stanzas or verses of the *Ṛgveda*, set to tunes."[8]

On the whole, the hymns are sophisticated sacerdotal compositions valued for their wisdom and use in worship, especially sacrificial ritual in which certain mantras out of them were employed for the invocation of the gods, for making offerings to them etc. But they are not simply liturgical formulae, not mere folk poetry, nor any; historical or legendary record of primitive tribal conflicts. Their value as a cultural document is incidental. Their primary value lies in their being their expression of wisdom, which is also the literal, meaning of the word '*Veda*'. There is no other document in the history of civilization which is so ancient and yet in many ways so alive.

The Performance of the Vedic Sacrifice

"A *Vedic* sacrifice needs four main priests, *Hotā*, who addresses hymns in praise of the gods to invoke their presence and participation in the sacrifice; *Udgāta*, who sings the hymns in sweet musical tones to entertain and please the gods; *Adhvaryu*, who performs the sacrifice according to the strict ritualistic code and gives offerings to the gods; and *Brahma*, who is the general supervisor well-versed in all the *Vedas*. The four *Samhitās* are said to be compiled to fulfill the needs of these four main priests; *Ṛk* for the *Hotā*, *Sāma* for the *Udgāta*, *Yajuh* for the *Adhvaryu* and *Atharva* for the *Brahma*."[9]

"There were also additional priests for each of the main *Brāhmiṇs*, and they were known as: a) *Maitravaruṇa, Acchāvāk* and *Grāvastuta* (of the *Hotā*), b) *Prastotā, Pratiharta* and *Subārhmanya* (of the *Udgātā*) c). *Prati-Prastotā, Neṣtā* and *Uneetā* (of the *Adhvaryu*) d). *Brāhmapacchmsi, Agnidhra* and *Hotā* (of the *Brahma*). The *Udgātā* and his assistants generally sung the *sāmans* before the sacrificial altars. Regarding the officiating priests of the *Somayāga*, the officiating *Brahmans* were divided into six classes. There, first, the *Hotā*, who used to chant the hymns of the *Ṛgveda*, second, the *Udgātā*, who used to sing the verses of the *Sāman*, third, the *Pota*, who used to prepare the materials for oblation, fourth, the *Neṣtā* or *Karta*, who used to pour the *Soma*, clarified butter etc. into the sacred fire, fifth, the *Brahma* or *Upadraṣta*, who used to superintend and direct all the ceremonies and, sixth, the *Ṛksa*, who with a *vajra* or club of *Palāṣa*-wood and whose head was studded with spikes, used to stand at the door to ward off improper visitants. These, with the *Yajamāna* or initiator of the sacrifice, formed the seven classes of priests, necessary at the *Somayāga*."[10]

The *sāmans* were sung both within the precinct of the sacrificial building and outside. *Sāmans* used for invoking the *Devas*, were called *Sthotriya* or panegyric or *sthutiniṣpādaka* i.e. performer of laudation. The song contained one or the combination of more than one '*Ṛk*'. The *sthotria-gāna* contained one '*Ṛk* ' as word. The *sthotria* was the style of singing with the inclusion of three *ṛcs*. Both rhythm and tempo were in use and their tune section was similar to *Sāma* or the principal beat and *viṣāma* or the first beat. Anything offered or sacrificed to the *Devas*, is called *dravya*.

The *Devas* and the *dravya* and *Tyāga* or sacrifices are the indispensable parts of a *yajña* or ritual. By *Dravya* is meant *havya* or *ājya* (articles for oblation). They comprise of animal flesh, juice of *Soma* creeper, clarified butter, sacrificial frumenty, milk, curd and bread or cake. An act of sacrifice is known as *āhuti* or burnt offerings. Some sort of desire or expectation, in return, lay behind every act of ritual or sacrifice: be that for the attainment of piety or for the welfare of one's country and its people or for one's own welfare. The *Yajamāna* (a sacrificer or worshipper through priests) was one for whose benefit any sacrifice or ritual was performed. Three classes of *Yājakas* or *Ritvikas* (officiating priests) were engaged in important sacrifices. They followed the *Vedas, Ṛk, Sāma* or *Yaju.*

The *Ṛgvedic* priests used to chant *Ṛk-mantras* in distinct and loud voice, the *Yajurvedic* priests in a subdued and mellow voice, and *Sāma-Vedic* priests used to sing the *sāmans*."[11]

Lewis Rowell says:

> "Only the members of the three highest classes in traditional *Hindu* society, the *dvija* (twice born), may learn and recite the *Vedas*, and their teachings is reserved for members of the priestly class (*Brāhmans*)."[12]

According to Wayne Howard,

> "Every *Brāhman* belongs by birth to one *Veda*, one *Sakha* (school) of this *Veda*, one *Gotra* (ancestral family), and one *Sûtra* (manual of aphoristic rules)."[13]

> "The auspiciousness of the *Vedic* ritual depends on the elaborate correctness of the performance, with all its secret convolutions, thereby obliging the deities to deliver boons to the supplicants. Tales of a single mispronounced syllable bringing ruin to kingdoms and madness to the singer-priest are legend."[14]

Guru-Śiṣya Paramparā

Śikṣa is the first branch of *Vedic* learning. It deals with the science of correct pronunciation of vowels, consonants and syllables. Basically six aspects are dealt with: *Varna* (syllable), *Svara* (notes), *Mātra* (duration), *Bāla* (articulation), *Sāma* (a kind of balance in the total utterance) and *Santāna* (the spacing of the words). Some of the well-known *Śikṣa* are *Pāṇiniya*, *Yagñyvālkya Vashisthi*, *Kātyāyani*, *Manduki* and *Nāradiya*, the last being associated with the sage, *Nārada*.

Music in India has been passed on in a tradition best described as Guru-Śiṣya Paramparā (preceptor-disciple tradition). This method has occupied an important place in Indian culture. A guru is regarded as the metaphysical father of his disciple and is ranked higher than biological parents.

> "The sounding constructions as such are transmitted orally. The teacher handing over the musical material in every detail to his disciple does this. The organization of music

> is based on teacher-pupil successions which have enabled a smooth progression and a high degree of preservation of the musical heritage over long periods of history."[15]

The *Gurukul* system dates back to the *Vedic* period. In the *Gurukul* system of education, a pupil or *Śiṣya*, after his initiation (sacred thread ceremony), lived in the house of his *guru*, or teacher, and studied the *Vedas* and other subjects under his guidance, for a period of 12 years. *Gurus* were expected to teach everything they knew to the disciple. The institution was accessible only to the upper classes. The *Gurukuls* were well supported by kings who considered it their duty to make them financially viable.

According to Selina Thielemann:

> "The important term in the transmission of Indian Music is '*Paramparā*' (tradition or succession) which denotes the performing tradition as such. The *guru-śiṣya paramparā* (teacher-pupil-succession) functions as the fundamental of transmission not only of musical traditions, but also of any intellectual tradition in the Indian cultural nexus. In Indian musics, the function of the teacher is not limited to the teaching of the practical aspects of music, but in an ideal case, the disciple will learn both the theory and the practice from his guru. The teacher-pupil relationship begins with a formal initiation ceremony and is thereafter maintained not just for a limited period of instruction, but for a lifetime."[16]

There were four kinds of *gurus: Achārya, Pravakta, Shrotriya* and *Adhyāpak.* It is from the *samhitā* period that we have names of *Achāryas* such as *Angiras, Gārga, Atri, Bṛhaspati* and *Vaśishtha.* There were two types of *Śiṣyas*: one, who paid fees to the *Guru,* was known as *āchārya-bhāga*; the other, who earnt by performing domestic chores in the *guru's* house, was described as *dharma-Śiṣya. Vedic* age was divided into three parts, ancient, middle, and later.

Dr. Dutt says:

> "This division was also known to the *Vedic* people, as it is

> evident from the V, 21.5 *mantra* of the *Ṛgveda* where *ṛṣi Bharadvāja* had a talk with *Indra*."[17]

The *Ṛgvedic* age is divided into four layers (strata) according to the age of compilations. The first layer is composed of second and seventh *maṇḍala*, the oldest parts of the *Vedas*. Then comes the second layer composed of first and eighth *maṇḍalas*. Then comes the ninth *maṇḍala*. The fourth and the last layer is the tenth *maṇḍala*.[18]

The Ṛgveda

The *Vedic* hymns which were practiced orally from generations to generation, were collected together and were known as the *Ṛgveda*. The *Ṛgvedic* age was so called because the hymns of the *Ṛgveda* were in practice. The *Ṛgvedic* age was not composed of single period, but it took several centuries to build itself. The *Ṛgveda* is the main book of collection and all the three *Vedas, Sāma, Yaju,* and *Atharva* were designed after the *mantras* of the *Ṛgveda* differing in their aspects and applications. The *sāmans* were made out of the *ṛcs* or stanzas of the *Ṛgveda*. So the *Ṛgveda* attains a very high position in the domain of *Vedic* literature.

Dr. Arnold says:

> "It is believed that the poetry or collection of *Ṛgveda* is historically homogeneous, being the work either of one poet or the poets connected in time and in family."[19]

According to him, The *Ṛgveda* comprises mainly with the texts of the *Ṛgveda*, the meters, the arrangements of the *Ṛgveda* in homogeneous parts and the historical development of the art of verification.

Lakshman Swarup writes:

> "The *Ṛgveda* is the most sacred scripture of the Hindus. It is the earliest literary monument of the *Āryan* race. All its hymns could not have been composed simultaneously. They must have covered a long period. Early and late strata can be distinguished in the stanzas themselves. It is not merely a book. It is literature itself."[20]

Ṛcās

M.R. Gautam writes:

> "The first music consisting of one *svara* was '*ārcikā*' from the *Sanskrit* root *Richa* which means a *Ṛgvedic* hymn. *Ārcikā* denotes a musical chant chanted by *Ṛgvedic* reciters. It is repetition of one *svara* or chanting on one *svara* e.g., *aum, aum, aum*, on '*sa*' or any other *svara*. There is a great profundity in the content of significance of the word."[21]

In *Sangīta Ratnākara* Śāraṅgadēva mentions:

> *"Arcko gāyikshch ch sāmiko cha svarānthar:*
> *Yeka svarādithananana chthunamibhitha yima:*"[22]

The *Richas* compiled in the *Ṛgveda* are the prayer to the *Āryan* gods, composed by the *Āryans*. The *Ṛgveda* is the prayer book of the *Āryans*. They have composed the prayers of their gods *Indra, Agni, Marut, Ashvinau, Viṣṇu* and others. In these prayers, the *Āryan* composers have described the exploits of their forefathers with the *Indus* people as favours of gods conferred on them.

Swāmi Prajñānanda says:

> "The *Richas* of the *Ṛgveda* show that the prayers though composed in praise of a particular god, they yet contain the description of the favours of the god conferred on a particular *Āryan* hero in a particular historical event of his fight with *Dasa* and *Dasyu*, who were proved to be identical with the Indus people. The *Richas* of the *Ṛgveda* show a complete picture of a composite Vedic culture. From the *Richa* we find that the *Āryans* who composed the *Richas*, assimilated many elements including gods as well as many other connected things from the Indus civilization."[23]

Yāska, the great commentator, has interpreted the *Richas* of the *Ṛgveda* in naturalistic way, where as *Sāyana* is another great commentator, who has explored the layers of mystery that were hidden in the Richas. *Yāska* has written his *Nirukta* before the famous grammarian *Pāṇni* (500 B.C.) and *Patañjali* (400 B.C.). *Yāska* has written *Nighantu* and *Nirukta* in 700 B.C. and they form one book and his name was mentioned in the *Mahabharata* in the *Śānti-parva. Yāska* believes that the *Richas* of the *Ṛgveda* were the *mantras* in praise of the supernatural gods. So he has treated the *Ṛgveda* as purely the religious literature, dealing with the gods who represented the Nature, and so his interpretations of the *Richas* and also of the gods were purely in the naturalistic way. *Yāska* has believed that the struggles in the Indus cities happened between the gods and the demons. So it is found that most of the words of the *Richas* are interpreted in a traditional way. *Sāyana* is a notable fourteenth-century commentator on the *Ṛgveda (Sāmavidhana Brāhmaṇa)* and author of numerous works. *Sāyana* explained the texts of the *Ṛgveda* in a naturalistic manner. *Sāyana* has quoted the rules of *Yāska,* when necessary, because, as a *Vedic* grammar or science of etymology, the *Nirukta* of *Yāska* is the only faithful reference book and there were no other grammar or science.[24]

The Vedic Meter

The *Richas* compiled in the *Ṛgveda* show perfection in the matter of language, poetry and meters (*Chandas).* There are as many as fifty-two meters of the in the *Ṛgveda.* A hymn may contain any number of stanzas, but usually it consists of not less than three or more than fifteen stanzas, generally uniform in character, except in the case of strophic and mixed lyric hymns. It is also not uncommon for the last stanza of a hymn to contain one or even two additional verse. The most typical forms of the stanza are:

a). *Anuṣtubh,* which consists of four diameter verses.

b). *Tristubh*, which consists of three diameter verses.

c). *Jagati,* which consists of trimeter verses, each of twelve syllables.

d). *Gāyatri,* which consists of three dimeter verses, *pankti* of five.

e). *Mahāpankti*, of six.

f). *Vijra* of three triştubh verses.

g). *Dvipāda-virāj* of two decasyllabic verses."[25]

In all meters, the rhythm of the later part of the verse is much more rigidly defined than that of the earlier part. In the early part of the verse, there is a general preference for long syllable, in the latter part of the verse for short syllables. The dimeter verses falls naturally into two parts of members, each consisting of four syllables. The second and fourth syllables are preferable long. In the cadence, the fifth and seventh syllables are almost always short.

The trimeter verses may be analyzed into two parts, which regularly follows either the fourth or the fifth syllable, or into three members. a) the opening, which consists of the first four syllables; b). the break, consisting of the fifth, sixth and seventh syllables, and c). the cadence, which includes the remaining syllable, beginning with the eighth. In the case of *triştubh* verse, the two parts consist either of four and seven syllables, or of five and six syllables each. In the case of *Jagati* verse, the second part is in each case longer by one syllable. The cadence of trimeter verses shows the same general rhythm as that of dimeter verse. It is only in a small part of the *Ṛgveda* that a short tenth syllable is at all common; while the short eighth syllable is chiefly found in the shape of a syllable containing a short final vowel.

A *Vedic* meter is said to be a measurement by number of syllables.

Dr. Macdonell says:

> "The metrical unit in the Vedas is the first *(pāda)* or quarter in the sense of the verse or line which is a constituent of the stanza. The verse is further more or less regulated by a quantitative rhythm (unaffected by the musical accent) in which short and long syllables alternative. In every meter the rhythm of the latter part of the verse (the last four or five syllables) called the cadence, is more rigidly regulated than that of the earlier part."[26]

The name 'Ṛk' or the unit of the Vedic hymn knows the stanzas. A stanza may consist of a combination of metrically identical or of metrically different verses and either two or three stanzas may further be combined to form a strophe.

"Theoretically, the meter of the chants was determined by the selection, number, and arrangement of *mātras* (syllable lengths) that were to be chanted in a single measure of breathe. These units of meter are known as *parvan* (division), of which there are approximately three hundred examples varied by *mātra* patterning. Discussion of *vṛtti* (tempo) in the Sanskrit musicological texts employed the same terms used in contemporary Indian classical music: *vilambita* (slow), *madhyama* (medium), and *druta* (fast)."[27]

"The meters really play the role of the rhythm of the *Vedic* music. The main *Vedic* meters are seven in number, and they are:

1) *Gāyatri* is of 24 letters, consists of three octo-syllabic verses = 8+8+8 = 24.

2) *Usnika* is of 28 letters, consists of two octo-syllabic verses, together with a verse of twelve syllables = 8+8+12 = 28.

3) *Anuṣṭupa* is of 32 letters, consists of four octo-syllabic verses, divided into two himisticle = 8+8+8+8 = 32.

4) *Vrihati* is of 36 letters, consists of three octo-syllabic verses, together with a verse of twelve syllables = 8+8+8+12= 36.

5) *Pankti* is of 40 letters, consists of five octosyllabic verses, divided into two hemisticles of two and of three verses respectively = 8+8+8+8+8 = 40.

6) *Tristupa* is of 44 letters, consists of four verses of eleven syllables divided into two hemisticles = 11+11+11+11+ = 44.

7) *Jagati* is of 48 letters, consists of four verses of twelve syllables divided into two hemisticles = 12+12+12+12+ = 48

Among these meters, *Gāyatri* triples are commonest, and the other are rare in use in the *Vedic* hymns. Besides these seven main meters, there are seven types of '*atichandas*' or subordinate meters, and they are:

1. *Atijagati* consists of 52 letters.
2. *Sarcari* consists of 56 letters.
3. *Atisarcari* consists of 60 letters.
4. *Asti* consists of 64 letters.
5. *Tyasti* consists of 68 letters.
6. *Dhriti* consists of 72 letters.
7. *Atidhriti* consists of 76 letters.

Besides, there are again seven types of '*vichandas*', and they are:

1). *Kriti* consists of 80 letters.

2). *Prakriti* consists of 84 letters.

3). *Akrti* consists of 88 letters.

4). *Vikrti* consists of 92 letters.

5). *Sankrti* consists of 96 letters.

6). *Utkriti* consists of 104 letters.

7). *Atikrti* consists of 108 letters.

These meters really determine the norms of different hymns of the Vedic compositions."[28]

Macdonell says:

> "One extremely significant model for the clusters of three source verses (*trcas)* may be the celebrated *Gāyatri meter*, which is employed for nearly one-fourth of the *Rg-Veda*. The standard *Gāyatri* stanza consists of three identical lines of eight syllables, each (if normal) unregulated at the

> beginning of the line but concluding with two iambs. Of all the texts composed in this popular *meter*, the most famous is the *mantra* that is also known as the *Gāyatri*, a short prayer addressed to the sun god *Savitri* as the 'stimulater'."[29]

"The initial verses of chapter 7 of the *Maitri Upaniṣad* classify the *meters* in group together with gods, planets, seasons various forms of breath as well as different types of hymn and chant and each group is assigned a specific direction.

Maitri Upaniṣad 7:1 identifies the Gāyatri *meter* with *Agni* (the god of fire), with the *trivrt* hymn *rathantara* chant, with the spring season, with upward breath, with the stars and with the *Vāsu* gods; these entire rise in the east. *Maitri Upaniṣad* 7:2 identifies the *tristubh meter* with *Indra* (the king of the gods), with the *pancadāsa* hymn, with *bṛhat* chant, with the summer season, with *vāyna* breath, with the *Soma* juice and with the *Rudra* gods; all these rise in the south. *Maitri Upaniṣad 7:3* identifies the Jagati meter with the *Māruta* gods, with the *saptadāsa* hymn, with *vairupa* chant, with the rainy season, with *apana* breath, with the planet Venus and with the *Āditya* gods; all these rise in the west. *Maitri Upaniṣad 7:4* identifies the *Anuṣtubh* meter with the *Viśva* gods, with the *ekavimsa hymn,* with *vaiārja* chant, with the autumn season, with *sāmana* breath, with the god *Varuṇa* and the *Sādhya* gods; all these rise in the north. *Mairi Upaniṣad 7:5* identifies the *pankti* meter with the gods *Mitra* and *Varuṇa,* with the *trinavga* and *trayastrimsa* hymns, with the *sakvara* and *raivata* chants, with the two cold seasons, with *udāna* breath, with the *Angiras* (descendants of the *sage Angiras* to whom many hymns of the *Ṛgvedic* are ascribed) and with the moon; all these rise from above.

Maitri Upaniṣad 7:6 refers to those elements that rise from below i.e. from the underworld; this verse does not contain any identification of meter hymn or chant.

The different modes of chant mentioned here are explained in the *Chhāndogya Upaniṣad* (2:11-2:20): *Gāyatri* Chant (2:11), *Rathantara* chant (2:12), *Vāmadevya* chant (2:13), *Bṛhat* chant (2:14), *Vairupya* chant (2:15). *Vairāja* chant (2:16), *Sakvari* chant (2:17), *Revati* chant (2:18), *Vajnāyujniya* chant (2:19), and *rajana* chant (2:20). Each type describes the chant in terms of specific cosmic principles such as vital breath (*Gāyatri* chant), fire (*Rathantara* chant), the sun (*Brhat* chant), rains (*Vairupya* chant), seasons (*Vairaja* chant) etc.[30]

Vedic Chant and Intonation

"There were some peculiarities among the followers of the *Ṛg-Veda* that they also used the second and third tones of the *Sāmagana*. In the *ārcikā* age, only one tone was in use. The *svaras* used were *Gāndhara Riṣabha* and *Ṣaḍja*. The scale was descending one beginning with *Gāndhara*. Similarly the *Āhvārakas* not only used one tone in singing songs and chanting *Stotras* but also used first and third as well as the seventh or *kruṣta* as the highest tone in the *sāman* scale. From this it can be inferred that they belonged to the *svarāntara* age, when it was customary to sing the *sāmagāna* with four tones only. The *svaras* in this new scale was, *ga, ri, sa, ni*. The followers of the *Taittirīya* recension used four tones in their songs. By the term '*dvitiyādi*' attributed to their songs, is meant the combination of second, third, fourth and fifth (*mandra*) tones. Consequently their songs too, were within the *svarāntara* class. The *Tandibhallas* used to present the *sāmagānas* with half of three *Vedic* tones like *parathama, dvitīya,* and *tritīya* and from this it is evident that they used to follow the mode of singing prevalent in the *gathika* period. The singing of the *sāmans* assumed different forms in different *Vedas* and their recensions and the *Brāhmaṇas,* and their unfolding took place in different ages. Hundreds of years elapsed on the path of their variegated manifestation. Apart from this, evolution of the tones took place by stages, in accordance with the development of man's taste and aesthetic sense."[31]

M.R. Goutam writes:

> "As regards *svarāntara,* it seems that *sāma-scale* reached its second stage of evolution. Till then the music was confined to only three notes. But when an extra note was

> added, it was naturally *svarāntara*. That is today a *tāna* is created with each note in successive and cumulative order i.e., a *tāna* with one note, then with two notes, then three notes, then four, five, six and finally seven notes."[32]
>
> "The way of chanting *Ṛgvedic* hymns has definite musical importance, as the three accents employed, the *udātta, anudatta* and *svarita*, a distinct difference in pitch."[33]

Macdonell says:

> "The *Vedic* like the ancient Greek accent was a musical one, depending mainly on pitch, as is indicated both by its not affecting the rhythm of meter and by the name of the chief tone, '*udātta*, raised'.[34]

"The verses of the *Ṛgveda* were recited on three pitches: *Udātta*, the regular (literally 'raised) pitch, *Anudatta*, a lower (literally 'not raised) pitch, and *Svarita*, a 'sonant' pitch, which is either raised above the ordinary pitch or connects the regular and the lower pitches. The 'regular' and 'lower' pitches, i.e. *udātta* and *anudatta*, are determined by the prose accents of the text syllables, and the distance between them is in most cases that of a major second. The *Ṛgvedic* notation system is accessible to us only since approximately 200 years, though it may have existed as a secret science for insiders since several centuries, uses only two symbols: a short vertical stroke below the syllable for *anudatta*, and a short vertical stroke above the syllable for the *svarita*; the *udātta* is not marked. This way of notation confirms the widespread assumption that the *svarita* (sonant) is actually higher than the main recitation pitch (*udātta*). In most *Ṛgvedic* traditions, the *svarita* on short syllables is recited on a higher pitch than the *udatta*. A *svarita* on a long syllable is recited on two successively higher pitches."[35]

"In order to protect the magical power of the sacred words, mathematical formulas were applied to the text, further expanding the already voluminous quantity of material to be memorized by the priests.

These *Vikrti* (alterations) involved reordering, adding, and repeating syllables, words, phrases, and even verses in order to obscure the secret text while invoking the power of the gods. One such *Vikṛti*, named *Ghana* ('dense'), places words in the order, 1-2, 2-1, 1-2-3, 3-2-1, 1-2-3; 2-3, 3-2, 2-3-4, 4-3-2, 2-3-4, and so forth, transforming a phrase such as "*Agni* with a poet's power" into *Agni* with, with *Agni*, *Agni* with poet's, poet's with *Agni*, *Agni* with poet's, with poet's, poet's with, with poet's power, power poet's with, with poet's power." This fascination with verbal mathematics can also be heard in the *Stotra* chant form used in the performance of *Vedic* sacrifice, in which the priests chant verse phrases in ordered sequences. Internal variation and signaling words in the first phrase of each verse, as well as the use of small sticks placed on a cloth in front of the chanters, help the chanters to keep their place."[36]

Selina Thielemann elaborates the *Vedic* chant in detail:

> The correct intonation of the *Vedic* hymns was of essential significance for the success of the sacrifice. For the recitation of the *Ṛgveda*, two ways became relevant, determined by different interpretations of the text. The principal and unmodified way of recitation, *samhitāpatha*, maintains the oṚginal text version in which the words, determined by the phonetic rules of the Sanskrit Language, occur in their composite rather than isolated form. The second way, *pāda-patha*, singles out the words and separates them from their phonetic compounds or *sandhis* to which they are tied in the text.

Exemplified on the basis of the beginning of the opening hymn of the *Ṛgveda*, the two ways of recitation would appear as follows:

Samhitā-Patha

agnim ile purohitam yajñasya devam ṛtvijam hotāram ratnadhatanam (1)

agnih purvebhir ṛṣibhir idio nutanair uta sa devam eha vaksati (2)

Pāda-Patha

Agnim / ile / purohitam / yajñaṣya / devam / ṛtvijam / Hotāram / ratnadhatanam (1)

Agnih / purvebhih / ṛṣibhih / idiah / nutanaih / uta / sa / devam / eha / vāksati (2).

("I invoke *Agni* as the domestic priest, god of the sacrifice, ministrant, invoker, best bestower of treasure. *Agni* to be invoked by past and present seers, may he conduct the gods here.").

Based on the *pāda-patha* i.e. on the version in which the words are isolated from each other, a number of modifications or *vikṛtis* (literally 'variation', 'modification') were developed. These *vikṛtis* are methods of recitation in which the textual rendering is determined by the emphasis given to the syllables and by the division of the words. Separated from the text, the sacred words are joined together in different ways so that the reciter could memorize them more easily and employ them more effectively. The principal *vikṛtis* are known as *krama, jata* and *Ghana;* these are complemented by a number of rare *vikṛtis* named *mala, sikha, rekha, dhvaja, danda* and *ratha.* The *vikṛtis* distinguish themselves on the basis of their characteristic word combinations that influence the melodic line of the recitation. The principles of word permutation employed by the respective vikṛtis can be illustrated as follows; each letter of the alphabet stands for one word of the verse beginning with 'a' and ending with 'z':

"The following example taken from the LP "The *four Veda*" (AHM 4126), demonstrates the *samhitā -patha,* the *pada-patha* and a number of *vikrtis,* all of which are transcribed below:

"Devim vacam ajanayanta devas tam visvarupah pasavo vadanti sa no mandresam urjam dudhana dhenur vag asman upa sustutaitu // [37]

"The gods gave birth to the goddess of speech, of whom manifold animals are talking. This cow, pleasant to us, (giving), strengthening libation with (her) milk, may (she) come near to us (in the form of) aptly (spoken) speech."

Samhitā-patha: The words are joined together: *abcde...xyz....* Devim vacam ajanayanta devas tam visvarupah pasavo vadanti / sa no mandresam urjam dudhana dhenur vag asman upa sustutaitu //

Pāda-path: The words are separated: *a / b / c / d / .../ x / y / z / ... Devim / vacam / ajanayanata / devah / tam / visvarupah / Pasavah / vadanti // sa / nah / mandra / isam / urjam / dudhana / dhenuh / Vaj / asnab / upa / sustuta / a / etu //*

Krama: Each word is recited twice, the first time preceded by the previous word, the second time followed by the subsequent word: *ab / bc / cd / de / .../ wx / xy / yz / ...*

Jata: Each word is recited once, followed by the subsequent word recited twice, is then again repeated twice, followed by the subsequent word: *abbaab / bccbbc / cddccd / ... / xyyxxy / yzzyyz ...*

Ghana: The word combinations are based on three successive words joined together as follows: *abbaabccbaabc / bccbbcddcbbcd / / wxxwwxyyxwwxy / xyyxxyzzyxxyz.*

Māla: Each pair of words is recited first in straight, then in Reverse order: *ab / ba / ab / bc / cb / bc / .../ xy / yx / xy / yz / zy / yz /...*

Sikha: Similar to jata, but here, the respective third word is included in each combination: *abbaabc / bccbbccd / xyyxxyz..*

Rekha: The word combinations are progressively increased by one Word and recited in straight and reverse orders: *ab / ba /bcd / dcb / bc / cdef /fedc / cd / defgh / hgfed / de /efghij / jihgfe / ef / fghijkl / lkjihgf / fg /...*

Dhvaja: The first and second words counted from the beginning are followed by the second and first words counted from the end; the second and third words from the beginning are followed by the third and second words from the end etc. *ab / yz / bc / xy / cd / wx / .../ xy / bc / yz / ab //*

Danda: Similar to rekha, the word combinations are progressively. Increased by one word, but under repetition of the full sequence of preceding words: *ab / ba / ab / bc / cba / ab / bc / cd / dcba / ab / bc / cd / de / edcba /...*

Radha: This mode of recitation includes repetitions in straight and reverse orders, omission of intermediate words as well as progressive increase of the number of words joined together: *ab / ef / ba / fe / ab / ef / bc / fg / cba / gfe / ab / ef /bc /fg /cd /gh /dcba /hgfe /* [38]

The syllabic or numerical notation in the songbooks did not prescribe specific melodic movement of discrete tones but simply represented entire melodic phrases or tonal aggregates learned orally. It is also possible that *Vedic* chanting utilized microtones not specified in the notation in much the same way that contemporary Indian notation omits subtle tonal shadings in its orthography. More specifically prescriptive of melodic shifts, however, are the series of three accents utilized in the notation of the *Ṛgveda: anudatta* (central tone). *Svarita* (passing tone), and *udātta* (raised tone).

> "The expert singers and chanters of the *Vedic* age knew fully well the specific laws and method of application of the three registers: bass, medium and high i.e., *mandra, madhya* and *tāra*. The three ancient register notes or *sthānasvaras*, raised, not raised and balancing circumflex i.e., *udatta*, *anudatta* and *svarita* came to be used as three

> kinds of pitches of speaking as well as singing voices. The rhythm and tempo were used in accordance with different types of feet of the Vedic meters, *Gāyatri, Jagati, Anuṣṭupa,* etc."[39]

Duration and Tempo

The temporal aspects of the chant were regulated, as one would expect by the syllabic quantities of the text- as measured in *mātras* (a unit equal to one short syllable) and their multiples. Three basic durations were recognized: short, long and protracted (*pluta*), in an invariant ration of 1:2:3 *mātras*. *Pluta* is in many respects the most interesting of the three and played a special role in the delineation of musical rhythms, but its role is minuscule in Vedic recitation. *Pluta* occurs three times in the *Ṛgveda* and it is in all cases related to the special type of speech function. Certain combinations or distortions of syllable have the effect of prolonging or reducing these *mātra* values by halves or quarters, resulting in a complex but precise representation of the durations of the orginal text.

> The *Pāṇiniyasksa*, the oldest and most authoritative of the phonetic manuals, prescribes the following values: "One *mātra* is equivalent to the cry of the blue jay, two *mātras* to that of the crow, three *mātras* to that of the peacock, and one-half *mātra* to that of the mongoose." The three tempos were taught and found more by tradition and instinct than by any precise calculations.[40]

Wayne Howard says: "the *mātralakṣanam* (a treatise of uncertain date) provides a specific ratio for the three 3:4:5, in which each of the *matras* is divided into three, four, or five *kālas* (apparently in the sense of absolute time units). In this treaties the moderate and slow speeds are referred to as 'augmented' *(vrddha)* and each of the three is associated with a color and a deity: fast with red, for the red horses of the wind god *Vāyu*; moderate with dark blue, for the blue back of *Bṛhaspati*, the 'Lord of Prayer'; and slow with white, for the white horses of *Surya*, the sun god."[41]

The Role of Memory

Mukhopadhyay says; "For many centuries the *Vedas* were transmitted orally, with many controls to insure precise rendering of the text. As a consequence, the texts have survived with greater accuracy than the musical system with which they were performed. Young trainees were put through memory-building routines that boggle the mind: recitation of the text both with and without consciousness of its meaning, recitation both forward and backward, recitation both with phonetic junctures (*sandhi*) between words and with separations between words, metrical recitation and recitation in a continuous flow and recitation of pairs of syllables in distorted (*vikrti*) sequences and complex designs, with and without *sandhi*, accents, and pauses."[42]

The aim was to instill an automatic and total command of the text that would rule out even the slightest possibility of error. A chanter was expected to respond immediately with the correct opening letter when his teacher cited the chapter and verses.

According to Lewis Rowell,

> "These routines proved to be powerful techniques for learning a text and preserving its accuracy by periodic refreshment, but the ancient *Vedins* were not content to stop here. Convinced that memory was too important a thing to be left to the mind, they built in redundancy by developing additional reinforcing techniques. Perhaps the most valuable of these were the *mudras*, the finger positions and motions which were used to represent the more musical aspects of the chant and which are as essential in performance as they are in learning and remembering."[43]

Gonda says:

> "The *mudras* were designed to convey a wealth of musical information with just a few ample and convenient motions of the hand. The individual *svaras* are marked off on the right hand by touching the finger joints with the tip of

> thumb. The same hand is also used to indicate certain melodic sequences, tonal prolongations, and tones that are to be shaken -- by gliding the thumb across several finger joints or rubbing the side of one of the fingers. The special function of the Right hand was, and is, the 'good' hand in Indian tradition."[44]

Division of the verses of the *Ṛgveda*

"The *Ṛgveda* is divided into ten books or *maṇḍalas*. The first seven are quite homogeneous in respect of their character and internal arrangement. The first book or *maṇḍala* is considerably the longest, containing a hundred and ninety-one hymns, hymns which are, with single scattered exceptions, ascribed to fifteen different authors or *Ṛṣis*. The *ṛṣie* stand together in a body and with the exception of those of *Agastya*, the last in the book, are so arranged that those addresses to *Agni* come first, those to *Indra* succeed them, and then follow promiscuously those to other divinites. Of the next six books, each is ascribed entirely to a single poet, or poetic family; the second, containing forty-three hymns, to *Kurma Garstsmada;* The third, sixty-two to *Viśvāmitra*; the fourth, fifty-eight to *Vādadeva*; the fifth, eighty-seven to *Ātri* and poets of his kindred; the sixth seventy-five to *Bharadvāja;* the seventh, one hundred and four to *Vasiṣtha*. In all of them, the hymns are arranged in strict accordance with the method above stated as observed in the subdivisions of the first book. The eighth contains ninety-two hymns, assigned to a great number of deferent authors. This book has special name. It is entitled the *Pragathas* (the word etymologically signifies a kind of song from the root '*ga*' to sing).

The hymns of the ninth book are one hundred and fourteen in number, addressed to the *Soma*, being intended to be sung while that drink was expressed from the plant that afforded it and was clarified, are *pavamanāyas*, or 'purificational'. The word '*soma*' means simply extract. The eighth and ninth books stand in a peculiar connection, with the *Sāmaveda*; nearly half the verses of the *pavamanāyas* occur again in that collection, and of the *Pragathas*, more than a fifth or nearly two-thirds as many verses as from all the other books of the *Ṛgveda* (excepting the ninth) taken together. The tenth book again stands apart from the rest, wearing the appearance of being a later appendage to the collection. It is a very long one, comprising like the first, a hundred and ninety-one hymns. Of these, the first half is arranged upon no apparent system; the second commences with the longer hymns and diminishes their length regularly to the close."[45]

Dr. Arnold says:

> "The hymns of the *Ṛgveda* are arranged in three principal groups, of which the largest extends from i.51 to the 2nd of vii, and consists of fourteen collections of hymns arranged in the ascending order of the number of hymns contained in each; the hymns to *Agni* coming first, then those to *Indra*, in each collection."[46]

Periods of the Ṛgveda

Dr. Arnold has divided the most striking features of the collection of the *Ṛgveda* into three main categories:

1. The use of the family name of the authors in the separate hymn.
2. The use of a special refrain verse.
3. The use of meters or rhythms peculiar to the collection.

Some or all of those indications confine to confirm ascription of the hymns of the *mañdala* vii to *Vaśiṣtha* and that of the hymns of *mañdala* vi to *Bharadvāja*. In the same way we find reason to ascribe the collections I 36-43, 44-50, viii 1-5, 6-11, 32-34 and 49-59 to *Kanva,* I 165-191 to *Mana,* I 58-64 and 74-93 to *Gotama*, viii 19-22 to *Sobhari,* 23-26 to *Vyāsva,* 35-38 to *Syāvasva*, and x 20-26 are not only different from those which prevail in later literature, but also almost peculiar to each family.

He has divided the period of compositions or collections of the *Ṛgvedic* hymns into three, and they are *bardic*, normal and *gretic*.

Among them:

- a) the *bardic* period suggests the period of originally and rivalry between the *bardic* families.
- b) the normal period suggests that all the hymns reached to perfection rather than originality in this time.
- c) the *gretic* period suggests that though the groups of the hymns formed a comparatively small part of the *Ṛg-Veda* at this time, yet they seemed to have a character of their own and belonged to a period of transition. To enunciate these three assumed periods it can be said:

1. To the *bardic* period, the metrical grounds were assigned to collections i. 127-139, which were connected with the name of *Divadāsa;* and the hymns ix 98-111, each of which corresponded to some one of the collections in the class. The collections i. 140-164, ii, and V each contained a nucleus of hymns of similar metrical distinctiveness, which might be ascribed to *Dirghatamas*, *Gṛtsāmada*, and *Atri* respectively. It is supposed that the composition of the hymns of this group were extended over a long period of time and in each family over several generations.
2. To the normal period, it is found that two metres were almost exclusively employed, namely Tristubh and *Gāyatri,* and in these, there were great regularity both of external and internal form. Such collections were i. 1-11, 12-23, 24-30; iii, iv and ix, 1-97. The refrain verses and authors names were very rare in these collections, the name of *Kauşika* was most prominent and in the meter there was little to differentiate one collection from another;
3. To gretic period, the following groups of hymns i. 31-35, 94-115, and those which extended from X. 33 to X 84 employed almost exclusively *tristubha* and *Jagati meters*, and included a large proportion of hymns in which gretic rhythm was favoured. The authors' names were again wanting though the refrain verses sometimes occurred.

According to Arnold:

> "the three supposed periods, the *bardic* and the *gretic* were inventive, as the bards were occupied in constructing fresh

metrical schemes, as well as in producing verses following established schools. They show confidence that a 'new' song would be more pleasing to the gods than one which is old fashioned. The faculty of inventing and appreciating new and delicate variations of rhythm seemed to be a special gift of the *Ṛgvedic* peoples of both the *bardic* and *gretic* period."[47]

The Deities of the Ṛgvedic Hymns

Among three parts of the hymns, one part is composed of hymns to *Agni*, the second of hymns to *Indra*, and the third of hymns to other deities.

According to Dr. Arnold:

> "Brihaṣpati, *Vastopati*, *Kṣetrapati* and *Sadasaspatiand Dadhikra* appear to be most prominent in the normal period; the *Apati*, as well as the *Apriya* hymns and most of these which have a ritual character, are found chiefly in the *gretic* period and the popular *Ṛgveda*."[48]

"There are various groups of hymns, small and large, and they are known as the *Kaṇva* groups, *Soma Pavamana* groups, etc. These groups are again known as groups like *ārchaic*, strophic, normal, gretic and popular. Different *Vedic* gods were conceived in these different groups of hymns. In the *ārchaic* groups, there is the clear conception of a company of deities living in the sky (*svarga*), and these gods were invited to the sacred ceremonies by the fire-messenger to descend.

The *Soma* or drink-ceremony is associated with the hero, *Indra*. In the earlier parts of the *Ṛgveda*, we find two other groups of deities those have secured a very high position; and these gods are *Aṣvina* and *Marutah*. *Aśvina* has been depicted as some phenomenon of the sky, whereas *Marutah* as representing the storm clouds. *Uṣas*, the Dawn, and *Puṣan* have taken a subordinate position."[49]

Dr. E.V. Arnold says:

> "To the primary conception of *Indra* as the warrior-god, several others are attached, which may have been originally independent of him and much earlier in date and they are *Vritraghna*, the slayer of dragon, the down maker, the storm-god and conguneror of some misery foe, such as the *Panāyah* or *Vala*. In the *ārchaic* hymns *Vāyu* or Wind appears as the charioteer of *Indra*. In the latter parts of the *Ṛgveda*, *Brihaspati* takes the place of *Vāyu* or Wing-god. The group *Mitra-Varuna-Āryamān* is very commonly met with in the *ārchaic* period. In the latter times a group of seven gods appear as the sons of *Āditi*."[50]

According to Swāmi Prajñānanda,

> "In the *Ṛgveda*, (1.142.9), the names of the four deities, *Ida*, *Bhārati*, *Mahi* and *Sarasvati* were found. In the Rig-Veda 1.13.1, the name of *Bhārati* was again dropped. Gradually *Ida*, *Bhārati* and *Sarasvati* were conceived as one and the same, and *Sarasvati* became predominant with all the qualities of the other two. So *Sarasvati* is worshipped from the early *Vedic* period."[51]

The Sāmaveda

The *Sāmaveda* is interesting chiefly, because it is the '*Veda* of music'. The *Sāmaveda* is devoted a good deal to the worship of *Indra*, who has to befuddle himself with *soma*, in order to get the necessary courage to slay demons.

"The melodies of the *Sāmaveda* are generally believed to predate the textual material and may have been derived from *Aryan* folk tunes or aboriginal chants which, as popular melodies, may have originated in circles which attributed a decidedly magical power to them. Most of the melodies in the *Sāmaveda* are identified by name indicating either an ancient *ṛṣi* (sage) composer who may have originally set the *Vedic* text to the folk melody, or simply a name indicating the folk melody to be used. One such melody was named rathamtara, considered a particularly powerful melody essential for certain sacrifices."[52]

"The *Chhāndogya Upaniṣad* belongs to the *Sāmaveda* and discusses primarily the role and function of chant as part of the *Vedic* sacrifice. The hymns of the *Sāmaveda*, the *Veda* of songs, are largely based on the text of the *Ṛgveda*. The word *Sāman* denotes any kind of 'song' or 'tune' and is possibly derived from the Verbal root *'sa'*, 'destroying sin'. The melodies of the *Sāma-Veda*, which belong to the oldest preserved melodies in the world, are no more based on three pitches, as was the *Ṛgveda* recitation, but take a pentatonic scale for their fundament. The five notes of the *Sāma-Vedic* melodies were known as *prathama* ('the.first', the tonic), *dvitiya* (the 'second', *tritiya* (the 'third'). *Caturtha* (the 'fourth') and *mandra* (pleasantly sounding or low, the 'fifth'), Following the deve!opment of these basic pitches, two complementary notes were added: *atisvarya* (strongly resounding, the lower 'sixth), and *krusta* (clamorous, the upper 'seventh'). These seven notes, referred to as *prakrti*, or 'natural' notes came to form a Heptatonic scale (*saptaka*, containing 'seven'). Along with the principal pitches, a number of '*vikrti*' (modified) notes were employed, such as *jatya* (pleasing), *abhinihita* (touched slightly), *ksipra* (quick) and *prasilista* (coalescent). For the chanting of the *Sāma-Vedic* hymns, seven *vacah sthananis*, or degrees of pronunciation, were prescribed: *Upansu* (whispered), *Dhvani* (murmured), *nimada* (distinct but slow), *upamidamat* (fastened), *mandra* (soft), *madhya* (medium), and *tāra* (loud).[53]

"Since the hymns of the *Sāmaveda* are chanted on the basis of fully developed melodies, the original *Ṛgveda* text had to be modified in order to meet the requirements of the melody. Six types of modification are evident in the rendition of the *Sāmaveda:*

1. *Vikara*	The simple distortion of the word, e.g., *agne* could be changed *to agnāi.*
2. *Visleṣaṇa*	The splitting of the syllables of a word and singing individual syllables – e.g., *vitaye* could be split up as *voyi toya toyi.*

3	*Vikarṣaṇa*	Changes the quantity of *mātrās*, e.g., *ya* to *yi* for *ye.*
4	*Abhyāsa*	A sudden break in the *pada* and repetition, as for example, in *toyāvi toyāyi.* The purpose for breaking being perhaps that the word was sung to a different tune.
5	*Virāma*	A brief pause. It generally occurred in the middle of a word and was meant for convenience of breathing. .
6.	*Stobha*	The addition of new but quite meaningless syllables, e.g., *hā-u, auhovā*, etc.."[54]

For the *Sāma-Vedic* melodies, a notation system was used which employs both numeral and syllables to indicate the pitches. The numerals denote the pitches in a descending sequence, e.g. '2, 3, 4' refers to three successively lower pitches. In many cases, the *Sāma-veda* offers a number of different melodies are given for verse 6.16.10 of the *Ṛgveda*, which functions as the opening hymn of the first hymn book (*grāmageyagāna)* of the *Sāmaveda* In each version; the word alterations are carried out in a different way:

Agna a yhai vittaye gṛnano havyadataye /
Ni hotā satsi barhisi //[55]

("O *Agni,* proceed to the feast, having been invoked, proceed to the offering of oblations. Sit down, priest, on the sacrificial grass.").

Sāma-Veda, Grāmageyagāna; 1. 1.

Om // o gna // om //o gna i a ya hi vo i to ya i to ya i grnano ha vya da to ya i to ya i / na i ho ta sa tsa i ba au ho va hi si //

Sāma-Veda, Grāmageyagāna: 1.2.

a gna a ya hi vi ta ya i grnano ha vya da ta ya i /
ni ho ta sa tsi ba rha i si ba rha i sa au ho va ba rhi si //

Sāma-Veda, Grāmageyagāna: 1.3.

a gna a ya hi va i ta ya i grnano ha vya da ta ye /
ni ho ta sa tsa i ba ha iso ha i //

(The insertion of the *stobha* '*auhova*' in between the syllables of the word '*barhisi*' in melodies 1.1. and 1.2 can be noted).[56]

"The verses are grouped in strophes which, when accompanied by their music, are known as *Sāmani,* i.e. 'melodies'. The *sāman* - stanzas are preserved in three forms. First, in the *Ṛgveda*, ordinary poetry accented in the usual way, and not accompanied by melodies. They are contained mostly in the first fifty hymns of the first book, and in books viii and ix. Most of these stanzas are composed in the meter *Gāyatri*, or in strophes known as *pragatha,* which are compounded of *Gāyatri* and *Jagati* verse lines. Both the words *Gāyatri* and *pragatha* are derived from the verb *ga*, 'to sing' and show that the stanzas and strophes, composed in these meters, were from the start intended to be sung. Secondly, they occur in the *Sāma-Veda* itself in a form called *ārcika*, that is 'collection of stanzas'. This is a kind of libretto, or textbook containing the stanzas, which are to be memorized for 'making upon them', as the *Sāman*-melodies. Here also there is a system of accents, peculiar in its notation, but apparently still with reference to the unsung *sāmans*. In the third in *sāman*-version, the *gānas* or songbooks, we find the real *sāmans* as they are to be sung. Here not only the text but also the musical notes are given. Still this is not a complete *sāman* yet. In the middle of the sung stanzas, certain exclamatory syllables are introduce, the so called stobhas, such as *om, hau, hai, hoyi, or him;* and at the end of the stanzas certain concluding exclamation, the so called *nidhānas*, such as *atha, a, im,* and *sat*."[57]

Nature and Division of the *Sāmaveda*

The *Sāmaveda* can be regarded as the ritual *Samhitā*. In the *Ṛgveda, suktas* are arranged according to the families of the singers (*sāmagas)*. In the *Sāmaveda* they are arranged according to the stanza units. The *Sāmaveda* is the music edition of a part of *Ṛgveda*, which is to be employed in a sacrifice. The relation between *Ṛgveda* and *Sāmaveda* can be ascertained that the former supplies the text-part (*pādapatha*) in the original form with accents and the latter indicates a stage of language music (*hāsa or mantragīti*).

The accents of the *Ṛgveda* are in the *Sāma-Veda*, and they have been indicated by numbers, 1,2,3 etc. This use of accents by numbers can be explained by saying that the relation of the *Ṛgveda* was afterwards transformed into artistic song of the *Sāma*, the basic material being the same. Or it can be said that *Ṛgveda* gives the text in historical arrangement, *Sāma-Veda*, apart from the selection with accents and new arrangements, gives the same text as in the *Ṛgveda* with the same orthography, which are signs of notes only in the *gāna*-texts and songs are given in the form, in which they are used in practice.

Wayne Howard says:

> "The *Samhitā* of the *Sāmaveda* is arranged in two different formats: One according to meter and the particular deity addressed, and the other according to the requirements of the various rituals."[58]

According to Swāmi Prajñānanda

> "The first and smaller, the *ārtika*, is composed of hundred and eighty-five verses, whereof five hundred and thirty-nine are found likewise in the *Ṛgveda*. The first twelve decades are addressed solely to *Agni*; the thirty-six next following to *Indra;* single invocations of *Agni* and other divinities are scattered here and there among them and a part of one of the last is addressed to *Soma*. Thus the verses are taken indifferently from all the books of the *Rik* excepting the ninth: the extracts from the eighth are greatly preponderant in number. The remaining eleven decades are from the *Soma*-hymns of the ninth book. The second portion, called the *staubhika* (from the root '*stobh*'—'to praise') contains twelve hundred and twenty-three verses, eleven hundred and ninety-four of them occurring also in the *Ṛgveda*."[59]

Groupings of the *Gānas* in The *Sāmaveda*

"The *sāmans* used to be enchanted notes (*Vedic*) on the verses.

It can rightly be said the *sāman* used to be enchanted on different verses or different *sāmans* could be chanted on the verse. The verses on which a *sāman* was chanted, was called a *yoni* or womb, the source of the melodies. The *Sāmaveda* proper was the *arcika*, which was a collection of five hundred eighty five *yonis*. The *purvarchika*, together with the *Āraṇyakā- Samhitā* and *uttrarcika*, represents the text-part (*pādapatha*) of the *Sāmaveda*. The *Grāmageya*, the *Āraṇyageya*, the *Uha* and the *Uhya gānas* together constitute the song-part (*ganapatha*) of the *Sāmaveda*. There was difference in meaning and significance between the *gānas*, *Grāmageya* and *Āraṇyageya*. The *Grāmageya - gāna* was unsophisticated simple *Vedic* song, meant for all classes of people, whereas the *Āraṇyageya- gāna* was sophisticated and artistic meant for the experts only. The *Uha* and *Uhya- gāna* were purely mystical (*rahasya*) type of *Vedic* songs, meant for the spiritual purpose. The word *grāma* connotes the idea of common locality or village, and the word *āraṇya* connotes the idea of selected or desired and definite place, and so the two types of *ganas* or songs were characterized by their specific places or spots and meanings or significances."[60]

The Somayāga

The *Somayāga* or *Soma*-sacrifice with the help of the *Soma*-plant or creeper was very ancient The *Soma*-sacrifice is very elaborate in nature. Not only its processes very complicated, but it also needs much paraphernalia and wealth. As many as sixteen priests conduct this sacrifice. Though the sacrifice is so expensive, it was at one time a must for every *Brāhmaṇa* family. They expected to perform it at least once during the course of three generations, failing which other *Brāhmaṇas* looked them down. Soma is the name of a deity (*Dēvata)* who is regarded as a king. So he is also known as *Rāja Soma*. *Soma* has his abode in heaven (*dyuloka*), but is represented on earth by a creeper said to grow on the Mujwan mountain situated towards the North of the Himalayas.

Soma resembles *Agni* in the fact that the anthropomorphism of the god is constantly coming into collision with the actual form of the plant and thus is prevented from attaining any clear development. Hence myths of a concrete character cannot spring up around the name, and the deeds, which are given to *Soma* simply borrowed by him from the other gods, especially *Indra* and *Agni*, with whom he is very nearly associated, since the former is the great *Soma* drinker and the latter for his part is a god of ritual like *Soma*.

The *Soma* is the great object of priestly interests, and the most elaborate imagery seems to have formed round the simple operations of pressing and straining the juice: the monotony of the ninth book is only equaled by its obscurity in detail, and, it must be admitted, much of the obscurity hides no real depth of thought but merely puerile fancies. For the juice pressed from the *Soma* plant the *Ṛgveda* offers various names, such as *andhās*, applied also to the whole plant, *pitu*, and often *madu*, the intoxicating beverage, it is even called food, and very often honey, a term which is applied also to milk and to ghee.

Dr. A.C. Das says:

> "The existence of 'the *Soma* cult' was from time immemorial in the Indo-Āryan community. It furnishes an evidence of the vast antiquity of *Sapta Sindhu* and of the *Āryan* culture. "The *Soma* Cult' is as old as the cult of *Indra*-worship, for the *Soma* sacrifice was mainly performed for propitiating *Indra*, and strengthening him in his daily and annual fight with *Vṛtra*. It was an institution peculiar to the *Āryans* of *Sapta-Sindhu*, and distinguished them from all other branches of the *Āryan* race, who either on account of their disbelief in *Indra*, or from the difficulty in procuring the genuine *Soma*-plant in any country other than *Sapta-Sindhu* or the Himalayas, did not take to the sacrifice, or discontinued it, when they left the country."[61]

"The hymns of the *Sāmaveda* were rendered to accompany the *Soma* sacrifice, the offering of the sacred juice that formed the center of the *Vedic* ritual. The ceremony was conducted by the main priest, the *Udgātār*, and his assistants including the *prastotār* and the *pratihatār* sing the hymns along with the *Udgātār*. The chant was performed in either five or seven parts depending upon the ritual requirements. The version with seven divisions comprises, 1. *Humkāra*, the chanting of the sacred syllable *Aum* by all priests; 2. *Prastāva*, an introductory section with narrow tonal range, sung by the *prastotār*; 3. *Udgitha*, the main section sung by the *Udgātār*, 4. *Pratihāra*, the first responsorium sung by the *pratihātr*, 5. *Upadrava*, the second responsorium which repeats the end of the *pratihāra* with variation of the text syllables, sung by the *Udgātār*, 6. *Nidhāna*, the concluding section sung by the three main priests *Udgātār*, *prastotar* and *pratihatār*, 7. *Pranava*, the concluding chanting of the syllable *Aum*."[62]

The Notation of the the Sāmagāna

"In the process of evolution of both the *Vedic* base notes or accent tones and the *sāman* tones, several strata are discernible. After the evolution of the five *sāman* notes, *prathama, dvitiya, tritiya, caturtha,* and *mandra*, the *saptaka* (octave) was completed with addition of the lower sixth, *atisvarya,* and the upper seventh, *kruṣta.* Besides the principal notes, there were some optional or secondary notes, such as, *jatya* or independent, *abhinihita* or absorbed, *ksaipra* or hastned, *praslista* or constructed. The principal notes were called the *prakṛti* ones, while the optional or secondary notes, the *vikrti* ones."[63]

Sri K. Vasudeva Sastri is of opinion that it appears extremely probable that the notes of the *Sāmaveda* are all *Prakriti svaras* but with the *śrutis* constituting each *svara* or note arranged in a descending order so that the lowest *śruti* of each note become the dominant *śruti* of that note. Considered in this light, it will be found, if we take into account the composition of *Prakriti svaras* that the lowest *śruti* of each *svara* is the highest one or very nearly that, of each of the notes of *Kharaharapriya* of *Carnātic* Music or *Kāfi* of Hindustani Music."[64]

According to Swāmi Prajñānanda:

> "The early songs were monotonous and recitative in nature, but gradually they were developed into music proper with the development and growth of intellect and creative faculty of man in the society. Mainly three transitional phases are

found in the evolution of songs of yore. They are: a) speech, b) speech-music or recitation, and c) song proper. The *Vedic* music was a developed and systematic one, and it possessed some rhythmic process and harmonic relation between the notes."[65]

Tables of Scales and Notes

Samic Notes	*Ancient Indian notes*	*Ancient European Notes*	*Modern Indian notes*	*Modern European Notes*
1.	Ma	F	Sa	C
2.	Ga	E	Ni	B
3.	Ri	D	Dha	A
4.	Sa	C	Pa	G
5.	Ni	B	Ma	F
6.	Dha	A	Ga	E
7	Pa	G (F)	Ri (Sa)	D

The *sāmic* notes have a tendency to descend, which was tradition among all the *Sāman*-singers. The comparative table of Scales and Notes of *Samic*, Ancient India, Ancient Europe, Modern India, and Modern Europe are shown in the above table.

The *Sāmaveda* at first, used only three notes. That is, why a song of three notes was known as *samuka.* Later on other notes were added and a full scale of seven notes was evolved. In the *Sāmavedic* music, songs mostly with five notes (pentatonic) only are found. There are very few songs with six or seven notes. However, the pitch of all the seven notes was recognized. *Svaras* (musical notes) were called *Yamas* in *Sāmavedic* parlance.

The *Sāmavedic* notes started with *madhyama (laukika)*. The names given to the notes starting with *madhyama* were the following: *Krusta (madhyama), Prathama (Gāndhara), Dvitiya (Riṣabha), Tritiya (Ṣaḋja), Chaturtha (niṣāda), Mandra (Dhaivata), Atisvara (Pañcama)*. The notes of the *Sāmavedic* scale resemble those of

Kharaharapriya of Karnataka Music and *Kafi* of Hindustani Music. In course of time, the scale became one of ascending order, but the interval of the notes remained the same. The scale with this interval of notes i.e. with notes resembling those of *Kharaharapriya or Kafi* came to be known as *Suddha*. The *Sāmavedic* notation is numerical. The figures one, two, three, etc., are given on the top of the words of the song to indicate the various notes.

1	2	3	4	5	6	7
Ma	*Ga*	*Ri*	*Sa*	*Ni*	*Dha*	*Pa*

The figure, which is indicated on the top of the first letter of a *Sāmavedic* song, becomes the keynote of that song. For instance, if a *Sāma* starts with the figure 2 on it, then *Gandhara-svara* becomes the keynote for that particular song. If a *Sāma* begins with the figure 3 on it, then *Riṣabha,* which is indicated by the figure 3 in the scheme becomes the key-note for that song."[66]

The *Sāma- gītas* have several parts. There are in all five parts and they are known as *bhakti.* They are:1). *Hiṅkāra or Humkāra 2). Prastāva 3). Udgita 4). Pratihāra 5). Nidhāna.* There was a special manner in singing the *Sāma.* There were in all three singers. They were called *Prastotā, Udgāta* and *Pratihartā.* The main singer was the *Udgāta. Prastotā* amd *Pratihartā* were his assistants.

In the beginning all the three singers sing '*Hum*' together as if to intone their tonic correctly and clearly. The '*Hum*', which they sang, was '*Hiṅkāra*' *bhakti.* Then the second part of the *sāman prastāva* is sung by the *prastotā. Prastāva* means introduction. This introductory part is sung with an *Omkāra*. Then this is followed up by *Udgīta* or the main part of the song. This is sung by *Udgāta.* As the *Udgāta* sings the *Udgīta*, the *pratihārtā* waits for it to end but before it actually ends, he picks up its last word and continues with the *pratihārā* part of the song. In the end all the three join in singing the *nidhāna* or final part of the *sāman* in unison.[67]

Swāmi Prajñānanda, elaborates:

"A historical study of Indian Music is meant to unravel the

mystery of different grades of Indian Music in different periods. It affords a man full scope for visioning the genuine structure, type and temperament of songs and melodies musical instruments and dances, prevailing different times. India has a glorious tradition of history of her achievements in the field of music, bearing the stamp of distinctive trait, quality as well as of spirit."[68]

A well-trained voice, perfect *śruti*, *svara śudhi*, faithfulness to tradition, spotless personal character are emphasized as the most important fundamentals in *Vedic* music which laid a strong foundation to the development and evolution of Indian Classical Music.

REFERENCES

1. Selina Thielemann, *The Music of South Asia*, p.50.
2. Dr. Chandradhar Sharma, *A Critical Survey of Indian Philosophy*, p. 14.
3. Swāmi Prajñānanda, *The Form and Function of Music in Ancient India: A Historical Study*, p. 158.
4. Dr. Chandradhar Sharma, *A Critical Survey of Indian Philosophy*, p.14.
5. G.C. Pande, *The Dawn of Indian Civilization (Up to C. 600 BC)*, p. 550.
6. Selina Thielemann, *The Music of South Asia*, p. 71.
7. Mircea Eliade, *The Encyclopedia of Religion*, Vol-10, p. 186.
8. Swāmi Prajñānanda, *Historical Development of Indian Music*, p. 406.
9. Dr. Chandradhar Sharma, *A Critical Survey of Indian Philosophy*, p. 14.
10. Swāmi Prajñānanda, *The Form and Function of Music In Ancient India, A Historical Study*, pp. 206-207.
11. Swāmi Prajñānanda, *The Form and Function of Music in Ancient India a Historical Study*, pp. 206-207.
12. Lewis Rowell, *Music and Musical Thought in Early India*, p.18.
13. Wayne Howard, *Sāmavedic Chant*, New Haven, p. 2.
14. Mircea Eliade, *The Encyclopedia of Religion*, Vol-10, p. 186.

15. Selina Thielemann, *The Music of South Asia*, p. 71.
16. *Ibid.*
17. Dr. Dutt. B. N., *Dialectics of Hindu Ritualism*, p.14.
18. *Ibid.*
19. Dr. Vernn Arnold, E., *Vedic Meter in its Historical Development*, p. 1.
20. Lakshman Swarup, *The Ṛgveda and Mohenjadaro. Indian Culture*, Vol. IV, 1937, No-2, pp.149-169.
21. M.R. Gautam, *Evolution of Rāga and Tāla in Indian Music*, p.12.
22. Subrahmanya Sastri. S., *Sangīta Ratnākara of Śāraṅgadēv*, with Kalānidhi of Kāllinātha and Sudhākara of Simhabhupāla, Ed. Madras, Vol-I, 1947, verses, 39, p. 120
23. Swāmi Prajñānanda., *The Form and Function of Music in Ancient India, A Historical Study*, p.167.
24. Swāmi Prajñānānanda, *The Form and Function of Music In Ancient India: A Historical Study*, p.186.
25. Dr. Vernn Arnold. E., *Vedic Meter in its Historical Development*, p. 1.
26. Prof. A. A. Macdonell, *The Vedic Grammar*, p. 437.
28. Vernn Arnold. E, *op. cit.*, p. 437.
29. Prof. Macdonell, A.A., *op. cit.*, pp. 3-10.
30. Selina Thielemann, *op. cit.*, p. 59.
31. Swāmi Prajñānānanda, *op. cit.*, p. 213.
32. Goutam. M.R., *Evolution of Rāga and Tāla in Indian Music*, p.15.
33. *The Music of India'* in *The New Oxford History of Music*, p. 200.
34. Macdonell, *A Vedic Grammar for Students*, p. 448.
35. Selina Thielemann, *op.cit.*, p. 51.
36. Mircea Eliade, *The Encyclopedia of Religion*, p. 186.
37. The *Ṛgveda*, verse 8. 100. 11.
38. Selina Thielemann, *op.cit.*, p. 51.
39. Swāmi Prajñānanda, *Historical Development of Indian Music*, p. 64.
40. Lewis Rowell, *Music and Musical Thought in Early India*, p. 67.
41. Wayne Howard, *Matralakṣaṇam*, translation and ed, Indira Gandhi National Centre for the Arts, pp. 11-15.

42. Mukhopadhyay. K.L., *History of Science and Technology in Ancient India: The Beginnings,* pp. 506-13.
43. Lewis Rowell, *Music and Musical Thought in Early India,* p.65.
44. Gonda. J., *Vedic Rituals,* p. 57.
45. Swāmi Prajñānanda, *op.cit.*, p. 170.
46. Dr. Vernn Arnold. E., *The Vedic Meter in its Historical Development,* p. 437.
47. *Ibid.*
48. *Ibid,* p. 263.
49. Swāmi Prajñānanda, *op.cit.*, p. 175.
50. Vernn Arnold. E., *op.cit.*, p. 263.
51. Swāmi Prajñānānanda, *Historical development of Indian Music*, p. 53.
52. Mircea Eliade., *The Encyclopedia of Religion,* p.187.
53. Selina Thielemann, *op.cit.*, p. 59.
54. G.C. Pande, *History of Science, Philosophy and Culture in Indian Civilization*, Vol-1, Part- 2, p. 113.
55. *Ṛgveda,* 6.16.10.
56. Selina Thielemann, *op.cit.*, pp. 60-61.
57. Swāmi Prajñānanda, *op.cit.*, p. 188.
58. Wayne Howard, *Sāmavedic Chant*, New Haven., pp. 8-9 and 14-25.
59. Swāmi Prajñānanda, *op. cit.,* p. 190.
60. *Ibid.*, pp. 190-193.
61. Dr. A.C. Das, *Rig Vedic India,* p. 60.
62. Selina Thielemann, *op. cit.*, p. 61.
63. K. Vasudeva Sastri, *op. cit.*, pp. 71-72.
64. *Ibid.*
66. Swāmi Prajñānanda, *op.cit.*, p. 237-38.
67. Gautam. M.R., *Evolution of Raga and Tala In Indian Music,* p. 25.
68. Swāmi Prajñānanda, *A Historical Study of Indian Music*, p.1.

5

Svaras and Rāgas

Music was practiced by the *Ṛṣis, Gandharvās*, and other inspired mortals and was considered sacred, because it softened and refined the mind and elevated its devotee to the Creator of the Universe. The soul of a nation is enshrined in the temple, in its literature and in its arts. All these are venerated in India and are represented to have emanated from God who is believed to be the fountain-head of all that is True, Good and Beautiful in life - *Satyam, Śivam* and *Sundaram*.

> "Inspired words, *mantric*-sounds, beautiful poetry and holy music are very powerful means or catalytic agents for total spiritual awakening and tuning the present level of human consciousness with the higher realms of celestial *Ānanda* (delight) and the highest regions of Divine consciousness. The Gods and Goddesses are particularly fond of pure and devotional music, which pervades all the layers and stages of creation and every moment of existence. Hence of all the modes of spiritual *Sādhana*, music is considered to be the highest and the best by the seers and sages."[1]

The ancient Aryans assigned a divine origin to music. To a Hindu, God is infinite and the entire sublime idea that is symbolically and beautifully expressed when the sages and *Ṛṣis* of India described

Sangīta and *Sāhitya* as two limbs of the Goddess *Saraswathi*. Music is perhaps the oldest of the Arts and it can be traced back to the *Vedic* period for there is the *Ṛgveda*reference to *Vīeṇā*, the perfect string instrument and *Vana* the hundred stringed instrument and the wonderful music concert of ineffable melody (in Yama's court) of music of *Vana*, *Vīeṇā* and other musical instruments. India venerates music and none of its arts is more perfect, more loved, more widespread more interwoven with its life than its music. India's musical tradition was that *Brahma* first created music from the *Sāmaveda*. Indian classical music is monophonic and based around a single melody line or *rāga* rhythmically organized through *tālas Carnātic* music is largely devotional; most of the songs are addressed to the Hindu deities.

Historical Background of Svaras and Rāgas

The earliest scriptural documentation of Indian music is found in the ancient philosophical texts, beginning with the *Sāmaveda* and continued by the *Brāhmaṇas*, *Upaniṣads* (especially the *Chhāndogya Upaniṣad*, which belongs to the *Sāma Veda* and deals specifically with song) and *Sutrās* and *The Purāṇas*. Chapters on music are contained in the *Vāyu*, *Markandeya* and *Viṣṇudharmottara Purāṇas*, while other texts such as the *Harivamṣa* and *Bhāgavatā Purāṇas* are rich of musical reference without specific chapters. Prior to the *Purāṇas*, dates the *Nātya Śāstra* attributed Bharata, the earliest treatise on India's dramatic art, in which music is explicitly discussed in six chapters towards the end.

SOME IMPORTANT SANSKRIT TEXTS ON INDIAN MUSIC

I. The Nāradiyaśikṣā of Nārada

There are several Nāradas starting from the author of *smṛiti* in various periods, ranging from pre-*Vedic* period to the tenth or more accurately up to fifteenth century A.D. Various persons bearing the 'non-de-plume' of Nārada, or originally named as Nārada came under this category. As it is said about Bharata, that Bharata is a general name for a person related to *'Nātya Veda'*, the name 'Nārada also stands for a person connected with music. Nārada and music are inseparable. Music is named as *Gandharvam* and according to many authorities *Gandharvaveda* was brought to the earth by *Nārada (a Gandharva)*.[2]

According to Swāmi Prajñānanda,

> Nārada is one of the *Gandharvas* among *Tumburu, Vīshwavāsu*, etc., who has expounded *the Gandharva* music. *Gandharva* music is as old as *Vedic* music. *Mārgi* music was a later development. This fact is very well established in '*Nāradiya Śikśa*' of *Nārada* which deals in both *Vedic* and *Loukik* music side by side with their uses of meters, tones and tunes."[3]

According to him too, there are four *Nāradas* each one an author of different work. *Nārada - I* is the compiler of *'Nārada Śikśa'*, which deals with the meters of the *mantra's* texts as well as *Vedic* songs and recitations. *Nārada –II* has authored the *'Sangīta Makaranda.' Nārada – III* is the author of *'Pañcama Sāra Samhitā' and* Nārada – *IV* is the author of *Chatvarimshchatta Rāga Nirupanam'*.

Nārada of *'Nāradiya Śikśa* is accepted to be the first and foremost by all the scholars. *'Nāradiya Śikśa* is given priority over the *'Nātya Shastra'* itself because of its subject (*Vedic* Music). *Nārada* of *'Nāradiya Śikśa '* is the one who is mentioned by the other ancient authors: *Bharata, Dattila* and others, besides several *Purāṇas* also in the context of music (*Gandharva*).[4]

M.R. Gautham says:

> "*Nāradiya Śikśa* deals with the origin of the *sāma* scale, *kruṣta, prathama, dvitīya, triītya, caturthā, mandra* and *atisvārya*. The work also mentions the six *Grāma rāgas* namely *Madhyama Grāma, Ṣaḍja Grāma, Sādhāritha Grāma, Pañcama Grāma, Kaiśika Grāma, Ṣādava Grāma* and *Kaiśika madhyama Grāma*. But the structure and form of the *rāgas* not given, with the result one cannot get an idea of the *svara*-arrangement of the above *rāgas*. But the real significant point is that the term *rāga* has been used, in its technical sense."[5]

The word *'rāga'* occurs four times in the *Nāradiya Śikśa*: thrice in the second section *(Kānda)* and once in the fourth section of the first chapter *prapāthaka*. It may be asked as to what the word *'rāga'* signifies. Nārada says that *grāma-rāgās* fully convey the idea and significance of the '*rāga*', which means that pleases and soothes the mind of all living beings. *Nārada* has described about the *svaramandala*, which is constituted of *tāna, rāga, svara, grāma, Mūrcchanā*, etc.

Nārada says,

Sapta-svarāstrayo grāma mūrcchanāstekavimsatih /
Tāna-ekoanāpancasadityetat-svaramandalam /

Further he says,

Tāna-rāga-svara-grāma-mūrcchanānam tu lakshmanam /
Pavitram pāvanam punyam naradena prakirititam //[6]

According to *Nārada, tāna, rāga, svara, grāma* and *Mūrcchanā*, that constitutes the *svara-mandala*, are sacred and purifying, because they bring permanent solace and tranquility to the minds of men and women."[7]

Prajñānanda says: 'the *grāmas* are named after the initial notes of the ancient *grāmas* like *Ṣadja, Madhyama* and *Gāndhāra*. The practice of the *grāma*-rāgās was also current in the pre-Christian era, and they are found mentioned in the Great Epics like *Rāmāyaṇa, Mahābhārata* and *Harivamṣa*. It is said that the *Gāndhāra-Dēśa* was situated on the Northwest frontier of India, as it is at the present day, and it is believed that it was the ancient site where the civilization and culture of India had its dawn. For this reason it was known as the sacred region of the bright spirits of *Dēvas*. And it is a fact that the *Gandharvas* are fully conversant with the use and application of the *Gāndhāra-grāma* in their system of music, which was known as '*Gandharva*'. Nārada is said to be the promulgator of the *Gandharva* school (*Sāmpradāya*), and so it is believed that he knew that the *Gāndhāra-grāma*, which was suitable for the *Gandharva* type of music for the *Gandharvas*, would not be suitable for the music system of the world, as the tonal arrangement of the *Gāndhāra-grāma*, was some what difficult to improvisation in the practical field."[8]

"*Nāradiya Śikśa* is divided into 2 parts, each containing 8 *Kāndikas* or chapters with 238 *Slokas*. In the first part of *Prapāthak*, the author describes about notes, *Grāmas, Mūrcchanā, tana, Grāma Rāgās, Vedic* and *Loukik* scales and things related to *Gandharva* music. The second part or *Prapāthak* deals with *Vedic* music, its rules and regulations. In the musical field *Nāradiya Śikśa* serves as a connective link between the *Vedic* and post-*Vedic* musical traditions. While the *Vedic* music is meant for the *Vedic* scholars and priests and to be utilized for rituals and spiritual purposes, *Loukik* music is meant for common man, which is termed as *Gandharva* for the spiritual attainment but with a little difference. It might be said that *Gāndharvam* is used in *Tantric* and other rituals and other types of worships."[9]

II. The Nāradiyaśikṣā of Bharata Muni

The *Nātya Śāstra* (literally 'science of drama') represents the oldest and most important source of information on Indian music theory and on the music practice in earlier times, and the *Purāṇic* descriptions are largely based upon the theory laid down in the *Nātya-Śāstra*.

There is no precise date of origin for the *Nātya Śāstra*, but most sources place the text somewhere between the first century B.C. and the first century A.D. The work is ascribed to an author named *Bharata*, a word originally denoting the actor in a drama; hence, a treatise on the activities of a *Bharata* was called *Bharata Śāstra* ('science of the actor').[10]

Of the six chapters referring to music, chapter 28 classifies instrumental music, chapter 29 discusses stringed instruments and chapter 30 hollow musical instruments, chapter 31 deals with musical meter (*tāla*) and tempo (*laya*), chapter 32 describes *dhruva* songs and finally chapter 33 offers a detailed introduction to percussion instruments.

a). *Notes of the scale (28. 21-23)*

The seven notes (*svaras*) of the Heptatonic scale are identified as *Ṣaḍja (sa), Ṛṣabha, (Ri), Gāndhara (Ga), Madhyama (Ma), Pañcama (Pa), Dhaivata (Dha)* and *Niṣāda (Ni)*. Four kinds of notes within the scale are distinguished on the basis of their relation to a specific interval of microtones: sonant (*vādi)*, consonant (*samvādi)*, assonant (*anuvādi),* and dissonant (*vivādi*).

b). *Basic scales (grāma, 28. 23-28) and derived modes (Mūrcchanās, 28. 28-34 and Jāti, 28. 25-151)*

Two basic Heptatonic scales (*grāma*) are distinguished on the basis of their initial notes: *Ṣaḍj-grāma* (beginning from *Sa*) and *Madhyama-grāma* (beginning from *Ma*). Each Heptatonic scale comprises 22 microtones (*Śruti*), whose succession in *Ṣaḍj-grāma* respectively *Madhyama-grāma* occurs as follows:

Ṣaḍj-grāma:

Sa (4) – Ri (3) – Ga (2) – Ma (4) -- Pa (4) – Dha (3) – Ni (2)

Madhyama-grāma:

Ma (4) – Pa (3) – Dha (4) – Ni (2) – Sa (4) – Ri (3) – Ga (2) – Ma

This means that in *madhyama grāma, 'Pa'* is lower by one *śruti* than in *Ṣaḍj-grāma.* Each *grāma* or basic scale has seven *Mūrcchanās* or derived scales each of which starts from a different note. *The Mūrcchanās* further divided into heptatonic, hexatonic, and pentatonic scales. Further note combinations lead to the constitution of the seven 'pure' and eleven 'modified' *jāti* that may be considered as basic melodic models. The *jātis* are characterized by the treatment of the notes within the scale or melodic model, especially by differences in emphasis given to the single notes, hence the *jātis* may have served as the basis for the later evolution of the *rāgās* (melody types). Bharata used 2 *veeṇās* having 7 strings in each."[11]

The science of the microtones was much developed in Bharata's time. He has devised it with the help of two kinds of *Veeṇā, achala*, having fixed frets and *chala*, having shiftable frets. He has also formulated the principles as well as materials of the *Gandharva* on the basis of those, as delineated in *Brahma's* monumental work, '*Brahmabhāratam*'. He has called his drama the '*Nātya Veda*', which is known also as the *Pañcama Veda* or *Gandharvaveda*. Like Nārada, *Bharata* seems to have been a scion of the clan of the *Gandharva*. The Lord *Brahma* has desired to compile a science of dramaturgy (*Nātya Veda*), and thus contemplating upon the four *Vedas*, he has collected the materials thereupon and compiled the *Nātya Śāstra*. He has selected the plots of drama from the *Ṛgveda*, music from the *Sāmaveda*, the art of acting from the *Yajurveda*, and aesthetic qualities from the *Atharvaveda*. It is evident from these lines that the science of drama or dramaturgy, together with music, already existed in the *Vedic* time, and *Brahma* or *Brahmabhāratā* carried on his investigations in the field of drama, dance and music in a novel way, with the help of the materials, as contained in his *Nātya Śāstra*, after following the footsteps of his grand predecessor, *Brahma* or *Brahmabhāratā*.[12]

Bharata has stated:

> *"Samkalpya bhagavanevam sarvān vedānānusmaran /*
> *Nātyavedam tatascakre caturvedānga-sambhavam //*
> *Jagrāha pāthya-mrgvedāt sāmebhyo gītameva ca /*
> *Yajureveād dabhinayān rasānatharvanādapi //* [13]

Bharata has formulated ten specific characters or essentials like *graha, amśa, nyāsa, alpatva, vahutva,* etc. to determine the genuine forms of the *jātis (rāgas)*. He has mentioned about the emotional sentiments and moods of the *jātirāgās* so as to create the corresponding sentiments and moods in the minds of the appreciators. He has also admitted that the *jātis* are the precursors of forerunners of all kinds of *mārga* and *Dēśī rāgās* to be evolved in future.

III. Dattilam of Dattila

Dattilam is a short treatise in Sanskrit written by *Dattilamuni*, who was the son of Bharatamuni, in the early centuries A.D. The work consists of only 244 verses, which are described as *kārikās*.

> "The author expresses clearly his intention of being concise and brief in dealing with the science of music. He classifies

> music under *Gandharva.* According to him *Gandharva* consists of four elements: *Svara, Tāla, Pāda* and *Avadhāna.* In this work, *Dattila* follows the traditional and rational method in treating this subject. He considers music as a temporal art extending over time and conceived in terms of temporal relationship within various elements, while fine arts like sculpture, painting etc., as spatial arts extend over space in various ways."[14]

Dattilam has 12 chapters: *Śruti, Svarā, Grāma, Mūrcchanā, Tāna, Sthāna, Vrithi, Suśka, Sadhārana, Jathi,* and *Alankāra.* While describing *śruti*, he says, '*śrutis* occupied a dominant position and the *svaras* arose from śrutis. *Śrutis* are 22 specific sounds in the octave, which can be distinguished separately, and distinctly by the human ear. Out of the 22 *śrutis* only certain specific *śrutis* were given the status of *svarās*, which made the *svaras* dependent on *śrutis*. Thus he establishes that *śrutis* came first and *svaras* were born out of *śrutis.* He defines *svara* as that which is to be measured by *Mēya.* In describing the *svaras* with its varieties and kinds, *Dattila* seems to have followed *Bharata.*

Each of these *svaras* gives rise to different varieties having the auxiliary *Suddha, Sādhāraṇa, Antara, Chatuśruti, Kaiśiki* and *Kākali.* He also describes the *lakśana* of *svaras* – *Graha, Amsa, Vādi, Anuvādi, Samvādi, Vivādi,* etc., *Vādi* has been defined as the predominant note. It is the natural *svara. Samvādi* depended upon harmonic affinity, but it was defined only in relation to *vādi* and is the second important note in a melody. *Vivādis* are defective *svaras* and indicates dissonance and its presence distorts a melody. He states that *Vīvādi* is the king. *Samvādi* is the Minister, *Anuvādi* is the soldier and *Vivādi* is the enemy.

He defined *grāma* after śruti and *svarā* since he was of the opinion that *svarā* depended upon *Śruti* and *grāma* upon svarā. He says that there exists mainly 2 *grāmas* named after the *svaras, Ṣaďja* and *Madhyama* as Bharata followed.[15]

IV. Bṛhaddeśī of Matañga

Nātya Śāstra of Bharatamuni and *Bṛhaddeśī* of Matañga are two major works available from the ancient period. *Nātya Śāstra* is a work on dramaturgy and *Bṛhaddeśī* by *Matañga* is a work solely dealing with the theory of music. *Matańga* in his work, *Bṛhaddeśī* that refers to *Dēśī-rāgas,* introduces folk material into classical music, in 8th Century A.D. "Matañga has tried to follow Bharata in many aspects. He himself claims to have thrown light on *Rāgas* and allied aspects of music. It was from the time of Matańga that the term rāga took emergence. He has followed *Bharata* in describing *jātis* based on twenty-two śrutis and adopted the same experiment of *dhruva Veeṇā,* and *chala Veeṇā.* He was of the belief that the *svaras* originated from the Gods and he assigned four varieties of *śrutis* to the four castes."[16]

"In the fifth-seventh century A.D, we find the evolution of Philosophical ideas in Indian music, which was connected with evolution of microtones (*śruti)* and tones (*svara*) from the causal sound or *Nāda*. We find this idea clearly in *Matańga's Bṛhadēśī,* when he says,

> *"Idanim sampravaksyami Nāda-lakśana -muttamam /*
> *Na nād ena veeṇā gītam na nād ena veeṇā svarāh"/* [17]

According to Swāmi Prajñānanda:

> "Matañga describes about the causal sound or *Nāda,* from which music, with all its manifestations evolved. He says that the *Nāda* as the determinate *(Saguṇa) Brahman*, shines as *Brahma*, the creator, *Viṣṇu,* the preserver and *Maheśvara,* the destroyer."[18]

Dr. Bhagyalekshmy explains:

> "He gave individual Gods, colour, *rasa* and *bhāva* for each note. He contends that *Sa, Pa* and *Ma* came from Gods, *Ga* and *Ni* from Man, *Ri* and *Dha* from *Ṛṣis*. '*Sa*' had the colour of the lotus petal, '*Ri'* parrot green, '*Ga*' of gold, '*Ma*' of jasmine white, *'Pa'* of Dark, '*Dha'* of yellow and

'*Ni*' of multi-coloured. The deities for *svaras* are *Brahma, Agni, Bhāratidēva, Śiva, Indra, Ganēsa* and *Sun*."[19]

Matañga refers to only two *grāmās: Ṣaḋja* and *Madhyama grāmas*. It is from the *grāma* system that the *Mūrcchanā, jāthi, tāna*, and *rāgas* were evolved. He says *Mūrcchanā* is an ascent while tāna is a descent. According to him *Mūrcchanās* are those, which express *rāgabhāva* in its full form. He described 49 *Śādava* and 35 *audava Mūrcchanās. He defines Alankarās* as musical excellences that figure in songs. He lists 33 *Alankarās* and also stresses the importance of *alamkārās*.

"Matañga has defined the word *rāga* in three different ways and they are:

a). svara-vārna-viśeṣena dhvanibhedena vā punah /
rajyate yena yah kaścit sa rāgah sammatah satām //

b) Yo'sau Dhvani-viśeṣastu svaravarna – vibhusitah /
rajjako janacittānānm sa ca rāga udāhrtah //

c) ityevam rāga-śabdasya vyutpattirabhidhiyate /
rajjanajjāyāte rāgo vyutpattih-samudā 'hrta

"From the above *ślokas* or definitions we come to know that the word *rāga* has been derived from the root '*rañj*' – 'to tinge' or 'to impress.' Just as a sheet of white cloth can be tinged with some colours, in the like manner, the minds of men and animals get tinged as it were, with the pleasing vibrations of sweet sounds (tones) of music."[20]

V. *Sangīta Ratnākara* of Śārańgadēva

The 13th century A.D. presents the most significant account of Indian music theory after the *Nātya Śāstra: 'Sangīta Ratnākara* of Śārańgadēva, written between 1227 and 1247 A.D. in Deogiri in Central India.

Dr. Bhagyalekshmy says:

"The purpose of writing this work seems to be multifaceted. The author himself states the following

> reasons for writing this work for liberating every one from the 3 kinds of pain: physical, psychological and natural calamities, to uphold the eternal *dharma* for obtaining fame as well as to achieve liberation. In this book, the author has tried to consolidate the entire aspects of *Sangīta* in its 3 fold aspects: *Gīta, Vadya* and *Nṛitya.* Further he has tried to interpret more clearly the facts presented by *Bharata* in his *Nātya Śāstra.*"[21]

He classified music broadly as *Mārga* and *Dēśī. Mārga* is *Gandharva Sangīta,* which was serious and devotional and was discovered by *Brahma. Dēśī Sangīta* was popular and regional based on region, culture, local traditions, folklore.

According to Selina Thielemann,

> "Unlike the *Nātya Śāstra*, which is a treatise on drama with reference to music in a number of chapters, the *Sangīta Ratnākara* takes music per se for its subject-matter. It discusses exhaustively the various aspects of music such as notes, scale, melody types, meter and musical form. The systems of *Dēśī -rāgās* and *Dēśī-tālas* are fully developed, and with the chapter on *prabandha* (composition; chapter IV), for the first time, a comprehensive account of musical form is provided. The contemporary music practice points out the changes that had occurred since the *Nātya Śāstra.*"[22]

He stressed the importance of *Gīta*. Śāraṅgadēva defines *Nāda*, traces its origin, its production and greatness. He says that *Nāda* is the very essence of music. *Nāda* manifests letters, letters constitute the word, and words make a sentence. In music *Nāda* is a primordial concept. It is of two types: *Āhata* and *Anāhata*. He explains the origin and production of *Nāda* in human body. The *Ātman* desirous of speech impels the mind, which stimulates the fire inside the body. This in turn emanates the air in the navel that rises upward gradually and manifests the *Nāda* in the navel, heart, throat, cerebrum and the mouth. The term itself is a coordination of air and fire inside our body. The places of *Nāda* produced seem to have led to emergence of voice registers or *sthāyis:* Navel – *Aumandra,* Heart – *Mandrā,* Throat – *Madhya,* Head - *Tāra,* Mouth – *Athitāra.* The different varieties of *Nāda* are: *Atisūkşma, Sūkşma, pushtā, apushtā* and *kṛthṛma.*"[23]

He describes the *śruti* with the varieties. He gives many definitions for *śruti.* A *śruti* indicated the tangible interval that can easily be identified. *Śruti* is the minutest pitch that is pleasing to the listener's mind. *Śruti* by itself was colourless and obtained only when it took the status of a *svara* figuring in *rāga.* It is believed that the 22 *nadis* placed obliquely inside the body leads to the 22 *śrutis,* each successively rising higher in pitch. In order to demonstrate the 22 *śrutis,* *Śārańgadēva* conducted an experiment on *Veeṇā* having 22 strings named *Dhruva* and *Chala Veeṇā.* He proved that the concept of *śruti* is objective and that only 22 *śrutis* are possible in an octave. He fixed the 22 *śrutis* among *Sapta svaras* in this way: *Sa – 4, Ri – 7, Ga – 9, Ma – 13, Pa – 17, Dha – 20, and Ni – 22.*

Śārańgadēva says, the seven *svarās, Şaďja, Ṛşabha, Gāndhara, Madhyama, Pañcama, Dhaivata,* and *nişāda* resulted out of the *śrutis.* He distributed *svaras* among *Śruti jātis: Diptā, Āyāta, Karuṇā, Mridu* and *Madhyā.* Śārańgadēva gives description about *grāma, Mūrcchanā, jāti, tāna* etc., He defines *grāma* as a group of tones which form the basis for *Mūrcchanās.* According to him, there are three *grāmas: Şaďja grāma, Madhyama grāma* and *Gandhara grāma. Pañcama* will be located in its 4th *śruti. Brahma, Vişṇu, Maheśvara* were considered the presiding deities for these 3 *grāmas.* They are to be sung in forenoon, midday and afternoon during winter, summer and rainy season respectively. He describes *jāti* as the forerunner of *rāga.* It is a scale of 7 notes or heptatonic scale. *Śārańgadēva* gives definitions about *varaṇās, alankāras* etc., they are four types: *Sthāyi, Arohi, Avarohi* and *Sanchāri. Sangīta Ratnākarā* on a whole is an authoritative work in which facts and techniques on music are arranged and presented in a scientific and systematic manner."[24]

VI. *Sangīta Makaranda* of Nārada-II

The single manuscript of '*Sangīta Makaranda*' was discovered and published as early as 1920 A.D. The work is of much importance, because it serves as a link between '*Bṛihaddeśi*' of Matańga, and '*Sangīta Ratnākarā*' of Śārańgadēva. '*Sangīta Makaranda* follows more or less the lines of '*Dattilam*' of *Dattila* or *Brihaddeś* of Matańga.[25]

It is noteworthy that *Nārada* in his *Sangīta Makaranda* ('nectar of music'), develops a system of male and female *rāgas* not found in the *Sangīta Ratnākara* and other classical treatise, which draws an out line for the later *rāga-rāgiṇis* system that became prominent in the writings of North Indian authors.

> "According to Nārada, *Nāda* is the primordial sound generated from '*Ākāṣa*', which is one of the five elements (*Ākāṣa, Pṛthvi, Jala, Agni and Vāyu)* and it is the first and foremost of them. Its property is 'sound' or '*Śabda*'. *Nāda* means a living 'being', which is always felt and is omnipresent with manifest and unmanifest forms. Unmanifest sound is named as '*Anāhata* ', which means 'without striking'. The sound that is produced without any striking is eternal, causeless and unmanifest. The other type of *Nāda* is '*Āhata* ', caused by striking or by any artificial natural vibration that can be explained. Music is based on this *Nāda*. *Yogis*, sages and great souls attain the salvation through great mental concentration upon *Anāhata Nāda*."[26]

Nārada describes 22 *śrutis* as the basic unit for music. *Nārada* defines *svarās* and their association with family caste, colour, *ṛśis*, deities, *gothras*, constellation, *Rāsi*, *Graha*, *Rasa*, etc., *Nārada* defines *alankāras* as combinations of notes for developing a *rāga*. In the chapter of *rāgas*, he enumerates 93 different *rāgas*. It was the *Nārada* who for the first time gave the classification of *rāgas* into Masculine (*Puruśa*), Feminine (*Sthree*), and Neuter (*Putra*), categories. The arrangement of topics is highly systematic and scientific. From the content and style of presentation, this work may be assigned to a pre-*Sangīta Ratnākara* period. The work enables one to understand in a nutshell the technicalities of music prevalent during *Nārada* time.[27]

VI. Chaturdaṇḍiprakāśika of Veṇkatamakhi

"*Chaturdaṇḍiprakāśika* of Veṇkatamakhi is ascribed to 1620. *Veṇkatamakhi* was the son of the eminent musicologist and scholar Govinda Dikśitar who wrote the authentic work *Sangithasudha*. Veṇkatamakhi's *Chaturdaṇḍiprakāśika* was a Bible for musicologists at that time. He is addressed as the *Pāṇini* of *Carnātic* music. This work was written Sanskrit and consists of 10 chapters. But the last part of the 9th and the whole of 10th chapter are missing. He traces the origin of *svaras* as follows: 'As *Lord Nataraja* sounded his *Damaru*, *svaras*, such as *Sa*, Pairs *of ri, gu, ma* sounded from one side and *Pa*, pairs of *dha, ni* from the other side thus giving rise to 12 *svaras*. He defines *alankāras* of *sapta tālas* like *Druva, Matya, Rupaka, Jampa, Triputa, Ata*, *Ēka*, and *Jampāda* or *Ādi tāla.*"

While coming to the *rāgas* we get description about the scheme of 72 *mēlakarthas*, which is a creation of his own, covering a sequence of *rāgas* of the past, present and future. These 72 *mēlakartha rāgas* are grouped under 12 *chākrās*, each *chakra* comprising with its six *mēlās*. The names of the *chākrās* are *Indu, Nētra, Agni, Veda, Bana, Rutu, Riś, Vāsu, Brahma, Disi, Rudra*, and *Āditya.* The first half which includes *chākrās*, I to VI and *Mēlās* 1-36, the *suddha* madhyama occurs as constant note, and in the second half, which includes *chākras* VII to XII, and *Mēlās* 37 to 72 the *pratimadhyama* occurs as a constant notes, known as *prati madhyama Mēlās*. He also gives the 10 qualities of *rāga* as *graha, amsa, tāra, mandra, nyāsa, apanyāsa sanyāsa, vinyāsa, bahutva* and *alpatva. Veṇkatamakhi* established a system of procedure and rules for *rāgas* and *prabandhas* based on the careful study of the system of music prevalent before and during this time. His work '*Caturdaṇḍiprakāśika*' serves as a guideline for studying both the theory and practice of music.

"In spite of the introduction of the seventy two *mēlakarthās* or *thātas*, only nineteen out of them were practiced during Veṇkatamakhi's time. The tonal forms of most of the *rāgas* of the South Indian system were also different from those of the North. The various *pādam, kṛti* or *kîrtanam, varnam, rāgamālika, pallivi*, contributed by

Purandaradāsa, kṣetrajña, Tyāgarāja, Syāma Sāstri, Muthusvāmi Dikṣitar, Svāti Tiurnal and others, enriched of the South Indian music."[28]

Śruti

"In '*Nāradiya Śikśa*' Nārada does not mention the *śruti*. He neither enumerates their number nor defines the term else where in proper manner. He uses the term *Śruti* and its varieties *Dipta, Āyata, Kaurna,* etc., in connection with *Sāmagāna. Bharata* opines that in an octave, *Sthāna or Saptak*, there are only 22 *śrutis* and gives priority to *svara. Dattila* places *śruti* prior to *svaras* and *grāmas* and he does not mention their name. He follows the same *śruti* divisions in the formation of notes, i.e., four, three and two *śruti* accordingly while describing the two *Grāmas, Ṣaḋja and Madhyama. Mataṅga* discusses in length about *Śruti*: the cause and relationship between *śruti* and *svaras*. According to him, there is only a single basic *Śruti (Nāda)* that arises out of the navel because of the friction caused by fire and wind. It passes upwards like smoke spreading up in ascension. This sound of *śruti* takes the form of twenty-two *śrutis* accordingly. *Mataṅga* opines that there are two types of *śrutis*, the one forming the note and the other present in between the notes."[29]

"Nanya Bhupāla is the earliest author, who describes about the five types of *śruti* in *Śrutyadhyāya* of '*Bharata Bhāshyam*'. *Nanya Bhupāla* gives the types of *śruti* after *Nārada* of '*Nāradiya Śikśa* '. He classifies the five types of *śruti* allotted to each of the seven notes. The division as follows:

1.	*Ṣaḋja* has four *śrutis*	*Dipta, Āyata, Mridu* and *Madhya*
2.	*Ṛṣabha has three śrutis*	*Karuṇa, Madhya* and *Mridu*
3.	*Gandhara has two śrutis*	*Dipta and Āyata*
4.	*Madhyama* has four *śrutis*	*Dipta, Āyata, Mridu* and *Madhya*
5.	*Pañcama has* four *śrutis*	*Mridu, Madhya, Āyata,* and *Karuṇa*

6. *Dhaivata* has three *śrutis* *Karuṇa, Āyata*, and *Madhya*

7 *Niṣāda* has two *śrutis* *Dipta* and *Madhya*

Such classification has something to do with the *Rasās* accorded to the notes by the ancient authors. Giving the meaning of the names can elucidate this:

1. *Dipta*	Illuminated and bright
2. *Āyata*	Vast and wide
3. *Dipta*	Delicate, soft and tender
4. *Karuṇa*	Pathos
5. *Madhya*	Medium and central.

The Names of 22 Śrutis

"The names given to twenty-two *śrutis* are meaningful and suggest the nature of *śruti*. *Nārada* of *'Nāradiya Śikśa'*, *Bharata, Dattila*, or *Mataṅga* does not give the names of the *śruti*. In '*Sangīta Ratnākarā* ' of *Śāraṅgadēva*, which is proved to be the work prior to *Nanya Bhupala's Bharata Bhāshyam*,. The names of twenty-two *śrutis* occur at the earliest. *Nanya Bhupāla* gives the names of *śruti*, which are followed by all the authors of the later period including Śārañgadēva.

They are:

> *1). Thevra 2). Kumudvati 3). Manda 4). Chandovati 5). Dayāvati 6). Ranjani 7). Rathika 8). Roudri 9). Krodha 10). Vajrika 11). Prasārini 12). Preeti 13). Marjani 14). Kšti 15). Rakta 16). Sandeepini 17) Ālapini 18). Madanti 19). Rohini 20). Ramya 21). Ugra 22). Kṣobhini.*"[30]

But *Nārada* of '*Sangīta Makaranda*' does not give these names. His names of the twenty-two *śrutis* are utterly different from others. They are the earliest and original name of *śruti*.

They are:

> *1) Siddha 2). Prabhāvati 3). Kāntha 4). Suprabha 5). Sikha,*

6). Deeptimati 7). Ugra 8). Hlādi, 9). Nirviri 10). Dhira 11). Sarpsaha, 12). Kśthi 13). Vibhoothi 14). Mālini 15). Chapala 16). Bala 17). Sarvaratha 18). Sāntha 19). Vikalini 20). Hridayaonmālini 21). Visārini 22). Prasoona."[31]

Origin of Svaras

Music exists in the nature by itself. The early man imitated the cries of different animals and notes of birds while trying to express his emotions through singing. It is always accepted in India, that nature is the mother of invention of all existing forms art. Music too has its roots in nature. "Śāraṅgadēva explains how *svara* is of the form of *Nāda. Svara* is present in the consciousness, which is desirous of expression, in the form of *Nāda.* Through the great charm of the voice, or *Veeṇā* or *vamṣa, Nāda* stamps its impression on the listener's consciousness. It is this *Nāda* (which is not yet manifest), which is the soul of *gīta.*

The sound in which it is actually externalized, '*dhvani*', is merely the vehicle of the expressive consciousness. *Dhvani* or the sounds, which we actually hear, can be produced even accidentally. The sound, which is produced by accidentally plucking an instrument, or even a sound, which is uttered involuntarily by a human being, cannot be called *svara.* The first may be sound of a definite pitch and resonance, and the second may come from a human being, and yet they are not *svara* because the expressive intention, which is of the form of *Nāda,* is absent. Unless the *cittavṛtti* of the form of *Nāda,* the desire to create *gīta,* is presented, the sound produced is not *svara.* The desire is in the human mind, it may be externalized through the human body, or through instruments (*Veeṇā* and *Vamśa*). So *gīta* can be said to be the first, present in the *Śarira Veeṇā'* and then only it reaches the '*Daravi Veeṇā'*. This idea seems to have been in *Śāraṅgadēva's* mind when he declares "Since *Nāda* manifests itself in the body, I shall speak of the body." He goes on to give a detailed account of the production of the human body. (*Piṇdotpatti*)"

"*So'yam (Nāda) prakāśate piṇide tasmatpiṇḍo'bhidhitate.*"[32]

Starting from '*Nāradiya Śikśa* ' up to the concerned works at preset, the origin of seven notes (*Sa, Ri, Ga, Ma, Pa, Dha, Ni*) is accepted by one and all, as vividly pitched cries of birds and animals. *Nārada* of '*Sangīta Makaranda*' has named peacock, *chataka*, goat, heron, cuckoo, horse and elephant as the producers of the seven varieties of sound pitch which are utilized as the basis for fixing of the seven notes respectively. *Matañga* and *Śārañgadēva* differ from *Nārada* of *Sangīta Makaranda* and name, '*Dardura*' (frog) instead of '*Aśva*' (horse) for the note *Dhaivata*. Another *Nārada* of *Nāradiya Śikśa* names the cow as uttering the '*Ŗṣabha*' instead of '*Chataka*'.

Nanya Bhupāla of *Bharata Bhāṣyam* follows *Sangīta Makaranda* in accepting the horse as the producer of *Dhaivata*, but he discards '*Chataka*' bird and names the bull (*Riṣabha*) as producing the note '*Ri*'. As a rule, later writers follow '*Sangīta Ratnākara*' of *Śārańgadēva*.

"About the assumption of materialization, imitation or production of sound notes from the cries of animals and birds, it cannot be said how far it is scientific or justified. However, this much can be accepted that the different cries mentioned by authors are definitely not of a similar pitch. They are certainly higher and may be lower according to different birds or animals even of the same species. Moreover no experiments have been attempted to record the cries of the said animals and birds and justify the facts."[33]

Bharata of *Nātya Śāstra* and *Dattiala* (son of Bharata), of *Dattilam*, are silent about the origin of the seven notes generated in the physical organism. They admit the emanating of three octaves '*Sthānas*' from heart, throat and head. The authors of later period, who have mentioned the points about the seven notes, are Nārada of '*Sangīta Makaranda*', Nārada of '*Nāradiya Śikśa*', Nanya Bhupala of *Bharata Bhashyam*, and Śārańgadēva of *Sangīta Ratnākara*. The different aspects of seven notes are discussed in the following order in '*Sangīta Makaranda*' of Nārada. The *Vansha* or lineage gets the priority over other factors in the present work. There are four type of *Vanśas: Dēva, Pitru, Ŗṣi,* and *Asura*.

1. *'Sa', 'Ga',* and *'Ma'*	*Dēva,*
2. *'Pa'*	*Pitru* [forefathers)
3. *'Ri'* and *'Dha'*	*Ṛṣis* (seers)
4. *'Ni*	*Asura* (demonic) ancestry.

Śārañgadēva follows the same order, while Matañga leaves *'Ma'.* Nanya Bhupāla handles this point with a little difference. He believes that particular note pleases the divinity and so on, i.e., *Ṣadja* pleases the deities and *Ṛṣabha* pleases the sages, etc.

> "This lineage may fall in tune with the moods, the seven notes are capable of creating or evoking the response of the so-called superior classes. Probably, the qualities and powers of the divinities, ancestors, seers and demons might be imbibed in the notes. The point to note is *'Sa', 'Ga',* and *'Ma'*, get the superior lineage, i.e., *Dēva, Vanśa* and the three *Grāmas* are also in their name only."[34]

The caste attributed to the seven notes is fourfold, as was and is still practiced in some places. *Brahmin* said to be the high caste and capable of producing the priests and performing *Vedic* rituals. Generally the deification and the forms, colour, caste, discovering seers, meters and other factors have the *Vedic* origin. In Vedas, the *Vedic* hymns are provided with these aspects. Some aspects are attributed to the seven notes also by the ancient authors on music.

Kṣatriya	Warriors by caste with ruling capability
Vaiṣya	Business community
Śudra	Serving community

In *Sangīta Makaranda, 'Sa' and 'Ma'* are *Brahmins. 'Ri'* and *'Dha'* are *Kṣatriyas. 'Ni'* and *'Ga'* belong to *Vaiṣya* and *Pañcama* relates to *Śudras*. Matañga does not furnish this caste system but he mentions only about '*Kākali*' and *Antara* notes as being *Śudra. Nārada* of '*Nāradiya Śikśa*', *Nanya Bhupāla* of '*Bharata Bhāṣyam*', and Śārañgadēva of '*Sangīta Ratnākara*' believes that:

1.	*'Sa', 'Ma', 'Pa'*	*Brāhmaṇas*
2.	*'Ri'* and *'Dha'*	Kṣatriyas
3.	*'Ni'* and *'Ga'*	*Vaiṣyas*
4.	*Kākali'* and *'Antara'*	*Śudras*

In *Sangīta Makaranda*, *'Pañcama'*, which has four *Śrutis* (microtones), is accepted as belonging to the *Brahmin* caste by all others, gets pushed down to the lowest caste, i.e., *Śudra*. Nārada is very firm about this announcement of *'Pañcama'* caste and it is not at all a mistake. It might be, because in the older traditions, the term *'Pañcama'* was used as a synonym for casteless thing or individual. After *Vanśa* and Caste, the colour of the notes is mentioned in *'Sangīta Makaranda'*. It seems that seven is a very auspicious and important number in *Hindu* religion. There are seven notes, seven colours of radiation, main islands, sages, days in a week, seven oceans and seven *nādis*. The seven notes too have their own colours. They are. [15]

1. *'Ṣadja'*	Lotus or pink colour
2. *'Ṛṣabha'*	Light yellow colour
3. *'Gāndhāra'*	Golden colour
4. *'Madhyama'*	Bright colour
5. *'Pañcama'*	White or black colour
6. *Dhaivata'*	Yellow colour
7. *'Niṣāda'*	Mixed colour

Next comes the native lands or birthplaces of seven notes. According to Hindu Mythology, a part of eighteen *Purāṇas*, the world is divided into seven islands (*Dwipas*), separated by seven oceans. However, this concept may be compared with the seven continents and an equal number of oceans engulfing them. These seven *Dwipas* are: *1). Jambu 2). Śaka 3). Kuṣa 4). Kraunca 5). Śalmali 6). Śveta 7). Puṣkara.*

According to *Vedas* and *Purāṇas*, India is situated in the *Jambu Dwipa*. Nārada elucidates the particular *Svara* and its native *Dwipa*. This aspect of *Svara* is mentioned by Śāraṅgadēva. Nārada and Śāraṅgadēva, both are identical. The name of *Dwipas* and the corresponding *Svaras* related to them are:

1.	*Ṣadja*	*Jamubu*
2.	*Ṛṣabha*	*Śaka*
3.	*Gāndhāra*	*Kuṣa*
4.	*Madhyama*	*Krauncha*
5.	*Pañcama*	*Śalmali*
6.	*Dhaivata*	*Śveta*
7.	*Niṣāda*	*Puṣkara*

The seven *Ṛṣis* of the seven notes are mentioned after the native or birthplace of *Svara.* The seven names of *Riśis* mentioned in '*Sangīta Makaranda'* are very accurate and appropriate, as others have mixed the names of deities in the list. *Nārada* of *'Nāradiya Śikśa'* names six *Riśis* for seven notes. He attributes *'Dha'* and '*Ni*' to *Tumburu.* Other five notes have *Agni, Brahma, Soma, Viṣṇu* and *Nārada* respectively starting from *Ṣadja* to *Pañcama.* Nanya Bhupāla and Śāraṅgadēva follow Nārada of *'Nāradiya Śikśa.'* The names of the *Riśi* mentioned in '*Sangīta Makaranda'* are totally different from others. *Dakśa, Atri, Kapila, Vasishtha, Bhārgava, Nārada, Tumburu* to *Ṣadja, Ṛṣabha, Gāndhāra, Madhyama, Pañcama, Dhaivata, Niṣāda* respectively. The names of deities are given in '*Bṛhaddeśi', 'Bharata Bhāṣyam', Sangīta Ratnākara.*

1.	*Ṣadja*	*Agni*
2.	*Riṣabha*	*Brahma*
3.	*Gāndhāra*	*Śārada*
4.	*Madhyama*	*Śiva*
5.	*Pañcama*	*Viṣṇu*
6.	*Dhaivata*	*Bhāskara*
7.	*Niṣāda*	*Ganeśwara*

Nanya Bhupala and Śārañgadēva give similar names of deities, the only difference is that the deities of *Dhaivata* and *Niṣāda* interchange their places. Mataṅga's list of deities is not much different from the above list. His deities of *Ṣadja* and *Riṣabha* exchange their respective places and *Indra* instead of *Viṣṇu* governs *Pañcama.*[36]

> "*Matańga* says, that each of these syllables has an *Âgamic* significance. The five names that end with the short '*a*', *sa, ga, ma, pa, dha*, these five *svara* names are endowed with *Viṣṇu-bijā*. They are the *bijākṣaras* associated with *Viṣṇu*, and '*ri*' and '*ni*' ending with short '*i*', they represent the '*kama-bijā*' or '*śakti-bijā*.'' [37]

Rāgas

According to the definition of (*Bṛhaddeśī*), 'the *Bhāṣas*, and the *Antara-bhāṣas* were born of the *Vibhāṣas*, "*Grāma-Rāgodbhāsa Bhāsbhyaṣca Vibhāṣikah / Vibhāṣa bhyāśca Sanjātā tathā cāntara-bhaṣikāh/* [38]

"In the nomenclature of this definition, and in the feminine endings given to these early derivatives of the root *rāgas*, we have the seeds for the later classification of *rāgas* and *rāgiṇis*, picturesquely called as the wives of the *rāgas*, and the classification of *rāgas* and their derivatives picturesquely called as the sons (*putras*) of the *rāgas*. The three types of derivative *rāgas* mentioned by *Matańga*, have names with feminine endings. The differentiation of female melodies is first come across in the *Sangita Makaranda* of *Nārada*, who gives three classes of melodies under the headings of male *rāgas (Pumlinga-rāga)*, female *rāgas (Stri-rāga)*, and neuter *rāgas* (*napumsaka-rāga*). This classification is ascribed to *Brahma* and three groups are allocated to three different types of emotive values. The male melodies are assigned to the sentiments of wonder, courage, or anger; the female melodies to love, laughter and sorrow; the neuter melodies to terror, fear and disgust." [39]

The realisation of *Rāgas* is very deep and meaningful irrespective of the pattern, character and colour: music touches the sentiments of all human beings. The musical tunes create the melodic pattern in the spirit of ascents and descents maintaining harmonic relations in the context of the spirit of *alamkāras, Mūrcchanās, tānas* which tend to render music lively and vibrating with the new spirit. The microtones are equipped with aesthetic tones, sentiments and spirit and make celestial forms of the *Rāgas*, enriched with those qualities. Those who therefore come in contact with tunes of music, become absorbed in it and dark patches of their mind become slowly dispelled by the bright ones and their heart' becomes elevated too; in this way the self-effulgent light of the eternal *Ātman* gets kindled. Truly speaking the realisation of the knowledge or the *Ātman* is indeed the principal object of all music artistes and music lovers and the knowledge of music does indeed elevate the mind of the genuine *Sādhaka* of music for achieving something sublime and great.

Among the important landmarks of literature on music are the references to music in certain *Purāṇas*, such as *Markandeya Purāṇa*, *Viṣṇu Purāṇa, the Brahma Sutras* and other *Purāṇa* and epics of the early period. Each *Rāga* has its own particular form, which is recreated by the appropriate melody of tones. Melody is the essence of music. The following is an interesting one from the *Adbhuta Rāmāyaṇa* about *Nārada Ṛṣi,* which combines criticism with appreciation.

Once upon a time the great *Ṛṣi Nārada* thought within himself that he had mastered the whole art and science of music. To curb his pride the all-knowing Lord *Viṣṇu* took him to visit the abode of the gods. They entered a spacious building, in which were numerous men and women weeping over their broken limbs. *Viṣṇu* stopped and enquired of them the reason for their lamentation. They answered that they were the *rāgas* and *rāginis*, created by *Mahādeva*; but that as a *Ṛṣi* of the name of *Nārada*, ignorant of the true knowledge of music and unskilled in performance, had sung them recklessly, their features were distorted and their limbs broken; and that, unless *mahādeva* or some other skilful person would sing them properly, their was no hope of their ever being restored to their former state of body. Nārada, ashamed, kneeled down before Lord Viṣṇu and asked to be forgiven.[40]

Thus, we find how a *Rāga* could be responsible for bringing good as well as evil results to listeners. A *Rāga* when properly presented would produce good results and when done imperfectly would spell disaster. There was in that sense an excellent objective criterion of judging music in ancient India. That helped create a healthy tradition and thereby encouraged the development of worthy disciples who mastered, preserved and passed on this precious heritage to succeeding generations, of which India could well be proud. One significant point in the above story is that the *Bhāvya Rupa* of *Rāga* could put on a physical form in the shape of an image, beautiful or ugly; when a *Rāga* is correctly performed, the image is conceived to be beautiful and when it is mutilated or incorrectly sung the image cannot but be ugly. This idea inspired the mediaeval artists and painters to draw pictures of *Rāgas* and *Rāgiṇis* and to compose *Dhyānas* of them. "When a particular *Rāga* or *Rāgiṇi* is rendered accurately, it produces serial etheric vibrations which create the particular shape, said to be characteristic of it. The notes produced by certain musical instruments trace out on a bed of sand definite geometrical figures and rhythmical vibration gives rise to regular geometrical figures."[41]

Different *Rāgas* and *Rāgiṇis* are connected with visions of certain images, certain concepts of *Rupa*. The concept of *Rupa* is also connected with, a code of *mantra*. Different code *mantras* or *Bija-mantras* are there for invoking both in the *Brahmanical* and the *Buddhist tantras* the presiding deities or icons and they believe that firmly as the code mantras are properly recited. Gods and goddesses become incarnate according to the concept of the *tantra* cult. The *Bija-mantras* are the key-ziotes of worshipping the deities who often represent some specific *Rāga* or *Rāgiṇis*. The mystic word *A-U-M* represents the concept of *Praṇava*, the symbol of *Brahman*. Those who believe in abstract concepts do not have faith in any materialistic form of the god or the goddess and therefore they believe in the existence of a mysterious power of vitality in music. In the recital of songs based on some thought or feeling the spirit is caught in sound. The music becomes itself an independent topic for giving vent to one's feelings and it assumes a tune and a form, which is steady and fixed. It also contains a force, which offers a boon to the *sādhakas*.

The aspect of this speculation of an image of a *Rāga* or *Rāgiṇis* of music designs an idea of the prior formula of the *Rāgas* and *Rāgiṇis* also, and, therefore, the *Dhyānas* of *Rāgās* and *Rāgiṇis* are composed with colourful sophistications based on the imagination of the artist, for instance the painter also draws beautiful pictures of those images. The emotional sentiment and mood of the artist become enriched and elevated, and the light of the *Ātman,* which reflects different reactions of the mind illumines the 'entire realisation of the artist and thus superb feelings are conceived, designed and manifest in music and it has an effulgence of its own.

The art of music is also developed from the causal state into the gross from of music through the medium of gradual progress. The *rāga* is the norm or 'matrix' of Indian music. The ancient seers, musicologists, musicians and scholars laid the foundation for music and left great amount of knowledge in the realm of music.

Swāmi Prajñānanda says: "The conception of a *rāga* is very deep and meaningful in Indian music. It gets into the softest corner of the minds of men, irrespective of caste, creed and colour. The tones create the melodic patterns with their colourful ascents and descents and with harmonic relations, together *alamkāras, mūrcchanās, tānas* and ten essentials, which bring life into music. According to the Psychology of music, the microtones and tones are surcharged with aesthetic sentiments and moods, and they make the skeletal forms of the *rāgas* be impregnated with those qualities."[42]

Abnormal powers have been ascribed to music. It is said that *Muthuswām Dikṣitār* brought rain by singing the *rāga, Amritavarshaṇi.* Chanting the *Varuṇajapa* was bringing rains. The *rāga Meharanjani* also is considered capable of bringing about cloud-formation in the sky and subsequently rain. *Nāgavarali* subdues snakes. There was an authentic source that the late *Nāgasvaram Vidvan Sivakozhundu* could draw out cobras from their holes and make them swing their hoods rhythmically in tune with the music of his *nāgasvaram.*

There was a traditional story about the *rāga Deepak.* Gopal Naick was an expert musician in court of the great Akbar. One day Akbar was asking Gopal Naick whether he really believed in the mysterious powers attributed to music and particularly about the alleged power of *Deepak* to kindle fire. Gopal Naick affirmed his belief in those powers. *Akbar* challenged him to demonstrate the power of *Deepak* to produce fire. Gopal Naick said to Akbar that he could prove it but the moment he sang the essential part of the *rāga* he would be consumed by fire. Akbar could not believe but he suggested a demonstration with adequate safeguards against fire, and suggested him to stand neck-deep in the river *Jumna* and sing. Gopal Naick was intent on removing the doubts in the mind of the Emperor regarding the powers of music. So he agreed and started singing *Deepak rāga* standing neck-deep in the river. The story goes that when he fell into the proper mood and sang the characteristic phrases of the *rāga*, his body burst into flames and was reduced to ashes in an instant and the ashes were washed down the stream. That was how Gopal Naick met his end.'[43]

Srinivasan says: Musical expression, as any art expression, is fundamental in human beings and its appeal is universal. All art is in essence an expression of the inner being in man, and music, the queen of the arts, is especially so. It is fundamentally related to the aesthetic and super-intellectual aspects of life. Just as spoken words express our inner thoughts however inadequately, music expresses some of the indefinable, subtle experiences of human nature in a way that it alone can do. The mode of achievement of this may be vague and may escape our analysis, but then in the very nature of things it ought to escape such analysis."[44]

So when men, women and children come in contact with tones and tunes of music, they are absorbed, and their dark deposits of the minds are slowly replaced by the bright ones, and their hearts are purified so as to receive the self-effulgent light of the immortal *Ātman*. The prime object of Indian music is, therefore, to get the blessed boon of the Divine knowledge that makes men free from the chain of delusion forever and ever.

Sāma: The Root Concept of Mūrcchanās, Jāti and Rāga

The *Sāma saptaka* began from '*ma*' and descended up to '*pa*', i.e., it was *ma, ga, ri, sa, ni, dha, pa*. When each of these notes became the keynote or modern *sa*, it produced different scales, producing notes of different intervals. In this way it contained the seed of the subsequent *Mūrcchanās, Jātis,* and *Rāgas.* To illustrate this point, a chart is given below wherein the formation of the different *Mūrcchanās,* or scales from different keynotes and the potentiality of *rāgas*, is shown:

Key note of Sāma	*The Scale of Mūrcchanā obtained from that key note*	*The name of the Mūrcchanā according to Bharata's Nātya Śāstra*	*The Mēla or Thāta according to Modern music*
Pa	*pa dha ni sa ri ga ma* *Sa ri ga ma pa dha ni*	*Śuddha Ṣaḍja*	Resembling Janupuri or Nata Bhairavi with *Pañcama of 12 śrutis*
Ma	*ma pa dha ni sa ri pa* *Sa ri ga ma pa dha ni*	*Matsarikrtā*	*Khamāj or · Karnātaka Hari Kambhoji*
Ga	*ga ma pa dha ni sa ri*	*Asvakārnāt*	*Kalyān (Yaman) or Karnātaka Kalyāni*
Ri	*ri ga ma pa dha ni sa* *Sa ri ga ma pa dha ni*	*Abhirudgaāt*	*Bhairavi or Karnātaka Hanumat Todi*
Sa	*Sa ri ga ma pa dha ni* *Sa ri ga ma pa dha ni*	*Uttarmandrā*	*Kāfi or Karnātaka Kharaharapriya*
Ni	*Ni sa ri ga ma pa dha* *Sa ri ga ma pa dha ni*	*Rajani*	*Bilaval or Karnātaka* Śankarābharaṇam with *Dha* of 4 *śrutis*
Dha	*Dha ni sa ri ga ma pa* *Sa ri ga ma ma pa dha ni*	*Uttarāyatā*	*Bhairavi with two Madhyamas and Without Pañcama*

"It will be clear from all the illustrations that *Sāma* music had really the seeds of our classical music and the claims of our old scholars in their texts that it was the origin of Indian Classical Music systems of North and South. In *Sāma* music the three *jātis – Audava, Ṣādava* and *Sampurṇa* have been mentioned which are in vogue even today. In *Sāma* music, five parts are mentioned namely *hinkāra, prastava, udgita, pratihāra* and *nicdhāna*. In the *Dhruvapada* which came centuries later five parts were sung but they were given different names i.e., *Tom-nom* or *ālāpa, Sthāyi*, or *Udgraha, Antara, sancāri* and *abhoga*."[45]

North and South Indian Music Systems

Indian music is divided into two fundamental stylistic traditions regarded as classical *Hindustani* music of North India, and *Carnātic* (*Karnātaka*) music of South India. Both terms refer to the geographic regions with which respective traditions are associated: '*Hindustan*', literally the 'land of the *Hindus*', denotes the (largely *Hindi*-speaking) area between the rivers Indus and Ganges; '*Karnātaka*', according to an earlier 13th century interpretation, refers to the southern part of the subcontinent between the rivers *Kṛṣṇa* in the North and *Kāveri* in the south, with the two Oceans towards west and east. Later on, the term *'Karnataka'* was understood as a linguistic derivation from '*Kannāda* ', i.e., the language spoken in the state of Karnataka (formerly Mysore-State) on the west coast of South India. The boarder line between the two geographic regions is drawn by the Central Indian Deccan Mountains, with Maharashtra, Madhya Pradesh and Orissa, constituting the southern border of the *Hindustani* area, while the states of Karnātaka, Andhra Pradesh, Tamil Nadu and Kerala form the Karnataka region. The geographic border marks the division of the subcontinent into its two principal cultural and linguistic spheres, with the *Indo-Aryan* tradition in the North and the *Dravidian* tradition in the South. It is known that a distinct musical tradition has existed in South India at least for the past two thousand years, determined by the survival of pre-*Aryan* languages and cultures; this tradition came under the influence of Sanskrit treatises on music since the first century B.C.[46]

Though the two systems differ from each other in their peculiar and characteristic treatment of *Rāgas* their fundamental principles are similar. Both the systems recognize that there are twelve notes in an Octave and use the same *śrutis.* Both the systems classify *Rāgas* under different *Mēlakartas* or *Janaka Rāgas*, and derivatives or *Janya Rāgas*. It is also very interesting to note that certain *rāgās* of the one system correspond to particular *Rāgas* of the other though under different names; for example, *rāgas Shubha Pantuvarāli, Hindola* and *Mohana* of *Carnātic* Music correspond to *rāgas Thodi, Mālcos* and *Bhupāli* of the *Hindustani* music respectively, which many such counterparts may be readily found in the two systems. Hindustani Classical music is based on the Ten *Thāts* of Prof. Viṣṇu Narāyan Bhakthande of Maharashtra, who studied music against all odds hit upon a plan to rejuvenate and resuscitate and reclassify the *rāgas* of Hindustani music spread over vast areas under different *gharanas* or schools of music; whereas South Indian Classical music is based on *Mēlakarta rāgas* of Venkatamakhi.

S. Mukund says: "Sri Tyāgarāja used many Northern *rāgas* that were adopted in the South for his compositions too, such as the above and others like *Hindusthani Kafi, Suddha Deschee, Saindhavee, Jingala* and many others. Sri Muthuswāmi Dikṣitār was in *Varaṇasi* for five years to study the Holy Scriptures. There, he was in touch with *Hindusthani* music and as he was learning music on the *Saraswathi Veeṇā*, he absorbed many *Hindustahani rāgas* and projected in his *kṛitis* (and in *Veeṇā* play), *rāgas* like, *Rāmakali, Dwijawanthee,* Dēśī *Thodi,* or *Subha Panthuvarāli, Māhuri, Hamerkalyānee, Yamunakalyāni,* etc. thus blending the Northern *rāgās* to suit Southern music."[47]

Music as Part of the Daily Ritual Cycle in Hindu Temples

The new feature in the evolution of the *rāga* was the introduction of the time-theory. *Bharata* does not mention this aspect at all but Śārańgadēva while defining the *Grāma rāgas* clearly specifies the time theory governing them. The significant point is that the musical structure and aesthetics forms began to be associated with the diurnal and nocturnal cycles, and some inscrutable relationship established between the intrinsic expressive quality of the *svaras* and the particular time of day and night. This indicates the relaisation of the integration of sound and light in nature and how it is correlated in music. This in itself may open out a new field of research. In this age of highly technological specialization, it may not be difficult to scientifically investigate the exact correlation between the *svara* and varying degrees of light and shade. The time-theory came and is still lingering in the North but has disappeared altogether in the South.[48]

A rich and flourishing musical tradition has evolved from the *Vaiṣṇava* temples in both North and South India, with the association of music with divine worship. The significance of music is the vital and motivating element of the divine service in the Hindu tradition.

Daily ritual worship in the *Vaiṣṇava* temples, referred to as *Aṣṭāyama seva,* follows the division of the day into eight consecutive periods (*astāyama*). These periods were defined as comprising three hours each, viz., 3 to 6 am, 6 to 9 am, 9 to 12 pm, 12 to 3 pm, 6 to 9 pm, 9 to 12 am, and 12 to 3 am. The three-hour periods remain relevant at the back of the daily sequence as well as for the designation of *rāgas.* The daily ritual sequence in a *Vaiṣṇava* temple is determined by the daily routine in the life to *Kṛṣṇa*; it begins from *mangal*, when the deity is awakened in the early morning and ends with *sayāna*, when the deity retires for the night. At the time of the respective watches, the shrine is open for *darṣana*, i.e., the deity can be seen and worshipped. The exact hour for the watches is defined by the liturgical prescriptions of the individual temples and *sāmpradāyas*."[49]

The basis of Carnatic music is the system of *rāgas* (melodic scales) and *tālas* (rhythmic cycles). There are seven rhythmic cycles and 72 fundamental *rāgas.* All other *rāgas* are considered to have stemmed from these. An elaborate scheme exists for identifying these scales, known as *Mēlakarta Rāgas. Carnatic* music abounds in structured compositions in the different *rāgas*. These are songs composed by great artists and handed down through generations of disciples. While the improvised elaboration of a *rāga* varies from musician to musician, the structured portion is set. These compositions are extremely popular, with a strong accent on rhythm and lively melodic patterns.

Three saint composers of the nineteenth century, Tyāgarāja, Muthuswāmi Dikṣitār and Śyāma Śāstri, have composed thousands of songs that remain favorites among musicians and audiences. The learning of Carnatic music is blended in devotional path. The compositions of Saint Composers, like, Purandaradas, Tyāgarāja, Muthuswāmi Dikṣitār, Śyāma Śāstri, and others included in the system of music learning and all the compositions of South Indian Classical Music propound the various philosophical and religious thoughts of these composers, in worshipping their beloved deities. The *rāgas*, which all the composers rendered in devotion, became popular and divine and make the people learn Carnatic music in spiritual aspect.

REFERENCES

1. Suresh Chandra Dey, *The Quest for Music Divine*, p. 2.
2. Dr. M. Vijaya Lakshmi, *A Critical Study of Sangeetha Makaranda*, p. 25.
3. Swāmi Prajñānanda, *A Historical Study of Indian Music*, p. 43.
4. Dr. M. Vijaya Lakshmi, *A Critical Study of Sangeetha Makaranda*, p. 25.
5. Gautam, M.R., *Evolution of Rāga and Tāla in Indian Music*, p. 1.
6. *Nāradiya Śikśa*, Mysore edition.
7. Swāmi Prajñānanda, *A Historical Study of Indian Music*, p. 43.
8. Swāmi Prajñānanda, *op. cit.*, p. 44.
9. Vijaya Lakshmi M., *op. cit.*, p. 30.
10. *The Nātya Śāstra of Bharatamuni*, English Translation by a Board of Scholars, Rāga Nritya Series no. 2, Delhi, 1951).
11. Selina Thielemann, *The Music of South Asia*, pp. 21-22.
12. Swāmi Prajñānanda, *op. cit.*, p. 57.
13. *Nātya Śāstra, Kavyamāla*, ed., Bombay, I.16-17.
14. Mukund Lath, *A Study of Dallilam: A Treaties on the Sacred Music of Ancient India.*
15. Dr. Bhagyalekshmy. S., *Lakśaṇa Granthas in Music*, p. 48.
16. *Ibid*, p. 54.
17. Sharma Prem Lata and Beohar, *Bṛhaddeśī of Matañga*, (Text, translation and commentary), Vol. 1.
18. Swāmi Prajñānanda, *Historical Development of Indian Music*, Pp. 84-85.
19. Dr. Bhagyalekshmy S., *Lakśaṇa granthas in Music*. 1991, p. 55.
20. Swāmi Prajñānanda, *A Historical Study of Indian Music*, p. 118.
21. Dr. Bhagyalekshmy.S., *Lakśana granthas in Music*, p. 70.

22. Selina Thielemann, *The Music of South Asia*, p. 25.
23. Dr. Bhagyalekshmy, S., *op. cit.*, p. 70.
24. *Sangīta Ratnākarā of Śārańgadēva, with Kalānidhi of Kāllinātha and Sudhākara of Simhabhupala, edited by S.Subrahmanya Sastri, 4 vol. Madras, 1947-57.*
25. Dr. Vijaya Lakshmi. M., *A Critical Study of Sangīta Makaranda*, p. 75.
26. *Ibid*, pp. 75-78.
27. Dr. Bhagyalekshmy., S, *Lakśaṇa granthas in Music*, p. 79-80.
28. Swāmi Prajnānānanda, *A Historical Study of Indian Music*, p. 13.
29. Dr.Vijaya Lakshmi. M., *A Critical Study of Sangīta Makaranda*, pp. 82-86.
30. Dr. Vijaya Lakshmi. M., *A Critical Study of Sangīta Makaranda*, p . 87.
31. Dr. Bhagyalekshmy. S., *op. cit.*, p. 58.
32. Ramanathan, N., *Musical Forms in Sangītaratnākara*, p. 49.
33. Dr. Vijaya Lakshmi. M., *op. cit.*, p. 99.
34. *Ibid*, p. 100.
35. *Ibid*, p. 102.
36. *Ibid*, p. 104.
37. *Matańga and his work Bṛhaddeśī, Elements of Yoga and Tantra in Bṛhaddeśī and its influence in later Authors*, Vimala Musalgaonkar, Edited by Prem Lata Sharma, Delhi, 1995, p. 11.
38. *Bṛhaddeśi.*, p. 105.
39. Gangoly. O.C., *Rāgas and rāgiṇis, A Pictorial and Iconographic Study of Indian Musical Modes,Based on Original Sources*, p. 70.
40. Popley H.A., *The Music of India*, p. 7.
41. Suresh Chandra Dey, *op. cit.*, p. 12.
42. Swāmi Prajnānaanda., *A Historical Study of Indian Music*, p. 13.
43. Srinivasan. R., *Facets of Indian Culture*, p. 67.
44. *Ibid*, p. 68.
45. Goutam, M.R., *op. cit.*, pp. 27-28.
46. Selina Thielemann, *op. cit.*, p.18.

47. Mukund. S, *Sangeetha Lalithya Lahari, the Waves of Elegance in Music*, p. 47.
48. Goutam, M.R., *op. cit.*, p. 11.
49. Selina Thielemann, *op. cit.*, p. 18.

6

Devotional Music of South India

The Meaning of Bhakti Sangīt or Devotional Music

Indian music is described as devotional. The inherent spirituality is the first and basic criterion of Indian Music. It possesses a special character of its own and it differs from music of other countries in its structure, temperament and method of improvisation. Indian Music emerged directly from the *Vedas*, the ancient treasure of hymns conceived by seers through divine vision.

The beginnings of Indian music are lost in the beautiful and fanciful legends of gods and goddesses who were supposed to be its authors and patrons. The goddess *Sarasvati* is always represented as the goddess of art and learning, and she is usually pictured as seated on a white lotus with a *Veeṇa*, lute, in one hand, playing it with another, a book in the third hand and a necklace of pearls in the fourth.

The technical word for music throughout India is the word *sangīta*, which originally included dancing and the drama as well as vocal and instrumental music. The God *Śiva* is supposed to have been the creator of this threefold art and his mystic dance symbolizes the rhythmic motion of the universe.

Swāmi Prajñānanda states:

"The music that evolved in India and imbibed the spirit

> and atmosphere of spiritual India is known as Indian Music."[1]

Music is highly regarded as one of the channels for the development of an intimate relationship between God and Man. *Bhakthi* as a word and as a phenomenon touches every Indian in every part of the country.

Suresh Chandra Dey says:

> "The revelation of God is obviously to emphasize the special liking of the Supreme Lord for His devotees who are very fond of music and thus engage themselves in the musical chanting or *Samkīrtana* of the holy name of God."[2]

Traces of *Bhakti* (devotion) are found in Indus Valley civilization, in *Harappa* and *Mohenjadaro*. The scholars found big buildings, which are identical to temples also found traces of existence of *Śiva* idols, *Nāga dēvatās*, animals, trees, stone idols and these are identified as worshipping deities of that time.

The first and most significant move on the religious plane was the birth of the *Bhakti* tradition in India towards the end of the *Gupta* Period. In the *Śvetaśvatara Upaniṣad* (1200-600 BC), this could be traced to the Vedas. *Bhakti* flowered into a philosophical thought-stream by 400 AD. *Bhakti-Sangīt*, devotional music, as it is known today is a musical response to religio-cultural needs.

Swāmi Prajñānanda says:

> "Indian music breaths spirituality. It brings Heaven down to the earth, and uplifts the mind of every earthly being. The history of Vedic India reminds us of the spiritual legacy of the sacred *Sāman* chants. The adept chanters of hoary antiquity used to sing the *Sāmans*, in praise of *Agni*, *Varuna*, *Indra*, *Mitra*, and other Gods, and although they aimed at material prosperity on the surface, yet their main object was to attain spiritual illumination. Music of India has preserved that solemn tradition and ideal, all through

> the ages, and so the authors on music have laid the greatest emphasis upon its spiritual side. They say that practice of music is a '*Sādhana*', which unfolds the grand mystery of human life."[3]

The existence of relationship between God and devotee is not of now it is there since the Vedic times i.e. about 5000 years back. This relationship is considered to be devotional. *Bhakti* has proved attractive over a period of two thousand years as the devotional path brought together feelings and forms easily recognizable, generally acceptable and nearly pleasurable.

Dr. S. Radhakrishnan says that the *bhakti* is the means to attain salvation.

> "We have had in our country from the time of the *Ṛgveda* down to our own days a long line of torch bearers who stress the primacy of spiritual values, who point out that even as the human being is above the animal, the spiritual man is above the human. The exponents of pure abstract speculation find their way into the minds of men through song and poetry. The attainment of life in God is achieved more easily by *Bhakti* than by other means. The poets, singers and saints with their passionate devotion to the ideals of beauty, harmony freedom and aspiration have has the strongest impact on society."[4]

Supporting this viewpoint, Selina Thielemann says:

> "The divinity of sound, and music, is derived from the capacity of the sounding reality to establish a direct contact between man and the Supreme Being. According to the concept of *Bhakti*, bliss is not found in complete detachment and merging with an attribute less energy, but in the sensual experience of the divine. Indian Music as the aesthetic manifestation of *bhakti*, therefore, is not exclusively spiritualized and meditative in its nature - as often assumed by outsiders, but it is indeed very lively

> and sensual, manifesting itself in beauty as an artistic response to the living presence of the divine."[5]

Bhakti-Mārga enjoys with the doctrine of *avatārās*, (divine incarnations), which provided comprehensive basis for development of an intimate relationship between God and man.

Definition of 'Bhakti' or Devotion

In India, religion is more a direct experience than a code of conduct. From an early age different systems or *Mārgas* (paths) have been prescribed for attaining liberation, bliss and heaven. However, the different *Mārgas* were not contradictory and in some respects they supplemented each other; for example proficiency in *Jnāna-yoga, Rāja-yoga* and *Bhakthi yoga* are demanded from the highest *sādhakas* (devotees).

According to Selina Thilemann:

> "The chief tenet of *Bhakti* is a personal, an emotional relationship between man and God, a relationship that exists not only on an abstract, transcendental plane, but one which can be experienced by the human senses as concrete reality."[6]

The word *Bhakthi* is derived from the Sanskrit *Bhaj* by the application, which expresses an action and means among other things, service, devotion, attachment, loyalty, worship and homage. The Indian equivalent to the term *Bhakti* is, to honour, to adore, to worship.

According to Robert Leopold Simon,

> "The words *bhakti* and *bhajana* are associated with an approach to God in which the relationship of the worshipper to the deity is based upon varying attitudes of love. The beginning of this loving, adorational, mystical approach to God can be found at the dawn of Hinduism as early as the *Rgveda*."[7]

Bhakti may be best defined as 'devotional religion' and is characterized by the perception of the relationship between God and man as intrinsically personal and determined by loving devotion to the chosen divinity.

Peggy Holroyde observes:

> "The God of Indian devotion - *bhakti* - who responds to the same eternal needs of the human heart as exist anywhere else, never detaches himself wholly from this immanence in the world. He is personal and endowed with feelings only in the eyes of popular piety; to thought he reveals himself both far beyond and within at the same time; the universe is his manifestation rather than his creation, he reveals it as much as he hides it; and each man is in himself in some sort of a manifestation of God."[8]

The Concept of Bhakti in *Rāmāyaṇa* and *Mahābhārata*

In the two great Hindu epics, *Rāmāyaṇa* and *Mahābhārata* we find the historical evidence of the *bhakti* approach to God. Over the length and breadth of India, in every city and village, in every temple, math and home, tales from the epic *Rāmāyaṇa*, are told and retold on the following beliefs:

1) *Rāma*, the king has been the example to all, *Rājas* and subjects; for proper behaviour and administration of laws.

2) *Rāma* and *Sita* exemplify the ideal man and woman, husband and wife; their devotion to duty, endurance and fidelity under difficult conditions are the models by which Hindus pattern their lives.

3) The concept of the profound love and fidelity of brothers for each other is exemplified by *Lakshmaṇa*.

4) The relationship of *Rāma*, seeking to recover his wife, *Sita*, who had been abducted by the demon *Rāvaṇa*, represents the Supreme Being intent upon pursuing the human soul until He recovers it. *Sita* represents the individual soul yearning for reunion with God.

5). The role of *Hanumān*, chief of the monkeys, who demonstrates his devotion to *Rāma* by risking his armies, his life in order to save his beloved *Rāma* and *Sita*.

In the *bhajana Sāmpradāya* tradition in South India great emphasis is placed on the role of the devotee of God; *Hanuman* is looked to as the divine preceptor who exemplifies the highest devotional ideals.'[9]

Mahābhārata

The epic *Mahābhārata* retells the stories of the Great War during the second millennium B.C. between the *Kurus* and *Pāndavas*. The important aspect of *Bhajana Sāmpradāya*, which emphasizes salvation through the repeating of the names, and attributes of God, is first mentioned in the *Mahābhārata*. The *Sahasranāma* (thousand names) *Stotras* (prayers), the most important of which concerns *Dēvi* (Goddess), *Viṣṇu*, and *Śiva*, contains a catalogue of one thousand names and attributes of the deity.

> "The *Bhagavad-Gītā* comprises one chapter in the *Mahābhārata;* it contains within it, the central themes upon which contemporary Hinduism revolves; it is one of the most authoritative sources, indeed, the quintessence, of all Hindu ethics and doctrines and clearly indicates the path of *bhakti* if one is to reach Him."[10]

The work is written as a dialogue between The *Lord Kṛṣṇa* and *Arjuna*, one of the five sons of the King, *Pāndu*. The dialogue begins with *Arjuna*, telling *Kṛṣṇa* that although he believes in his cause he cannot kill his kinsmen and comrades; he asks *Kṛṣṇa* for advice as to what to do. *Kṛṣṇa's* answer embodies the foundations of Hinduism.

"*Ye yathā mām prapadyante tāms tathai' va bhajāmy aham!*
Mama vartmā' nuvartante Manuṣyāh parthā sarvaśah"/ [11]

"In whatever way men identify with Me, in the same way do I
carry out their desires; men pursue My path in all ways."

"Sam 'ham sarvabhutesu na me dveṣyo' sti na priyah!
Ye bhajanti tu mam bhakytā mayi te teṣu cā' py aham" [12]

"I am same to all beings; to Me there is none hateful, none dear. But those who worship Me with devotion, they are in Me and I also am in them."

"Mayy āv śya mano ye mām nitya Yukāt upāsate!
śraddhaya parayo' petas te me yuktatama matah"//[13]

"Those who have fixed their minds on Me, and who, ever steadfast and endowed with supreme *Sraddha*, worship Me - them do I consider perfect in *Yoga*."

The Concept of Bhakti in Vedas and Purāṇas

The concept of *Bhakti* is already evident in *Ṛgveda*. The beginning of *Bhakthi* may be traced in the hymns of the *Ṛgveda*.

" All my hymns in unison praise *Indra*: as wives embrace their husbands so do my thoughts embrace *Indra* the divine bestrew of gifts. For the sake of a favor they cling to the liberal God (*Indra*) as wives do their lords or as a woman does her handsome lover." [14]

'In another hymn, *Indra* is addressed as a friend and it is said that there is no limit to his friendship and he gives cows to those who want cows, and horses to those who want horses.'[15]

The writing and assembling of the largest collection of all Sanskrit writings, the *Purāṇas*, was an important factor, which emerged along with the rise of *bhakti* movement during the early middle ages. There are eighteen major *Purāṇas* set forth in some 400, 000 verses. These are comprised of legends and didactic literature on themes dealing with all of the important Hindu deities, concerned with *bhakti*. They are divided into three groups of six each, six related to *Brahma*, six to *Viṣṇu* and six to *Śiva*. Of all the *Purāṇas*, the *Viṣṇu* and *Bhāgavata Purāṇas* are important for *Vaiśnava*. The *Suta Samhita*, associated with the *Skanda Purāṇa* is important for *Śaivites*. All three expound the doctrine of *Advaita*, which propounds non-dualism (the oneness of universal soul and individual soul).

The Bhāgavata Purāṇa

The *Bhāgavata Purāṇa* is the most important of all in its impress on *Bhakti* worship. Book VII is a long narrative related by *Nārada*, a great devotee of God, on the life of *Prahlāda*, another of the great devotees of God who sung about in present day *bhajana* rituals

"*The Bhāgavata Purāṇa,* a philosophical text of the 9th Century A.D. forms the theological basis of the *Vaiṣṇava* branch of Hindu religion. The Tenth Book of the *Bhāgavata Purāṇa*, in which the life Lord *Kṛṣṇa* is narrated, contains five chapters explicitly referred to as '*Gītā*', 'song of the *gopī s*'.

> "It is stated: "Being fully practiced in meditation one attains *bhakti-yoga* in a short time, which indicates that *bhakti* is not a means to an end but the end itself." [16]
>
> 'Nine components of *bhakti* are enumerated as *Śravana bhakti, kīrtana bhakti, smaraṇa bhakti, pādasa sevana bhakti, archana bhakti, vandana bhakti, dāsya bhakti, sakhya bhakti* and *ātmanivēdana bhakti*.'[17]

Robert Leopold Simon says, 'Many of the song texts, themes from main dramas (loosely called 'operas in India today'), ritual dances, land many of the symbolic acts connected with *bhajana* have come from the *Bhāgavata*.'[18]

The main source for a vast output of musical works concerned with *bhakti* has sprung form the *Bhāgavata*, especially from chapter X. An important clue is available in the very nature of the *Vaiśṇava* kind of *Bhakti* in *Bhāgavata Purāṇa*, a basic work, which laid down nine modes of devotion.

They are listed as:

> "To listen to his name, to do his *Kīrtana*, to touch his feet, to worship him, to offer respects to him, to accept his servitude, to be intimate with him and to open ones heart to him."[19]

The *Bhāgavata Purāṇa*, which forms the theological basis of *Vaiṣṇavism,* provides numerous indications, for the performance of music, dance and dramatic enactments as part of the ritual service. It gives an elaborate list of prescriptions for the performance of *sevā* (worship).

"Sāngopāngām sa-pārshadām tām tām murtim svamantratah, pādhyarghyācamaniyadhyaih"[20]

(One should perform the worship of the Lord) inclusive of all his limbs and attendants, (worshiping) each image with its own mantra appropriate to it, by means of offering water to wash his feet and for rinsing the mouth etc., bathing and decorating him with cloth ornaments.

"Gandha-mālyākshata-sragbhir dhupa-dipophahārakaih, sangam sampujya vidhivat stavaih stutvaa named dharim"[21]

(One should worship him) with perfumes, flower garlands, unbroken grains of rice, incenses, light and food offerings. Having greatly honored him with hymns and songs of praise, (one should) bow to the Lord).

Components of Bhakti

Sri *Nārada-bhakti-Sūtra* defines eleven components of *bhakti*. They are *Guṇa, Rûpu, Pûja, Smaraṇa, Sakhya, Kānta, Vātsalya, Mādhurya, Ātmanivedana, Tanmaya* and *Virah*. Although *bhakti* is only one; this has been defined based on the liking and interest of the devotees.

"They are of the form of attachment to Him in different capacities or roles:

a). Attachment to the Lord's qualities or *Guṇas* and to His Form or *Rupa*.

b). Attachment to three acts of devotion towards the Lord, viz., Worship or *Puja*, constant memory or contemplation, i.e., *smaraṇa* and surrendering oneself to Him, (*Ātmanivedana*).

c). Attachment in four roles, as servant, *Dāsya*; as friend, *sakhya*; as child, *vātsalya*; and as beloved, *Kānta Śakti*,

d). Two stages of Divine Love in its climax, viz., seeing in and becoming one with Him, *Tanmaya Śakti;* and inability to bear His separation, *Aviraha.*[22]

Five Forms of Bhakti (Pañca Vidha Bhāva bhakti kalpane)

The components of *bhakti* has been narrated from *Nārada -bhakti-Sūtra* and *Srimad Bhāgavata* and out of these components or aspects Five forms has been derived in order to explain the nectars of *bhakti* to elicit more knowledge from the *Haridāsa Sāhitya*. This is called *pañcha Vida Bhāva*. This five division of *bhakti* is only to exercise and to get more mileage out of it. The five forms of *bhakti* is: 1.*Dāsya Bhāva* 2. *Sakhya Bhāva* 3. *Madhura Bhāva* 4. *Vātsalya Bhāva* 5. *Śānta Bhāva* .[23]

Bhakti Sangīt or Devotional Music in South India

All *Haridāsas* amazingly versatile compositions are illustrative of the above modes of approach to *Paramāthma* through *bhakti*. These modes of approach are favored because of the difficulty of *Jnāna Mārga*, wherein God is conceived as *Nirguṇa* and *Nirākāru*, remote and transcedental. In the 14th verse of *Gītā*, Lord *Kṛṣṇa* says that the location of both *Manas* and *Buddhi* in *Paramāthma* is adequate for the realisation of the Divine. Thus, *Bhakti Mārga* is unique in transcending *Karma Mārga*, *Jnāna Mārga* and *Yoga Mārga* and the easiest mode of approach to reality.

The words *bhakti* and *bhajana* are associated with an approach to God in which the relatioship of the worshipper to the deity is based upon varying attitudes of love. The beginnings of this loving, adorational, mystical approach to God can be found at the dawn of Hinduism as early as the *Ṛgveda*. We find in the *Bhāgavatha Purāṇa* the doctrine of *bhakti* crystallized into a set of loving attitudes and acts, the performance of which would aid the worshipper in the attainment of God. God is conceived of as being personalized; He (and She) is in human form, worshipped in representations of stone, bronze, paint, and photographs. Indeed, the supplicant's attitudes regarding the human, living aspects of the deities during worship, dictate the unique qualities of Hindu religious rituals. *Bhajana* as a word and as a phenomenon touches every Indian in every part of the country. Music as one of the channels was explored to bring into being and keep alive this relationship. The relationship is an intrinsically personal one, and it serves to constantly evoke and maintain the feeling of spiritual oneness.

Swāmi Prajñānanda says

> "Music of India, whether Northern or Southern, is, a divine art. It constitutes the object of a psycho-material principle, and creates an objective beauty of the subjective divinity, that inspires the artists to attain a vision of the transcendental beauty."[24]

In the history of South India religion is the growth of an intense theism marked by a fervid devotion (*bhakti*) to personal god which found expression in numerous popular devotional hymns; these hymns were collected and edited in a canonical form at a later time, and continue to be regarded as among the most precious treasures in the heritage of the country. The period of this development may be said to have lasted from the sixth century to about the end of the eighth century A.D. It was heralded by notable changes in the political map.

The *Śātavahana* power came to an end in the third century and the break-up of their empire led, as often in the history of India, to the rise of a number of smaller kingdoms in the different parts of the *Deccan*. The close of the *Sangama* age, which may have lasted well into the fifth century A.D., was followed by a dark period of well over a century. A *Pāndyana* copper plate charter of the ninth century A.D., the *Velvikudi* grant, mentions that during this dark period, perhaps towards its close, there occurred a political revolution as a result of which several kings lost their thrones religious endowments were abrogated, and much disorder and oppression ensured. Much later, *Tamil* literary tradition avers that *Accuta* captured and imprisoned the three 'crowned rulers' of the *Tamil* land – the *Cēra*, *Cola* and *Pāñdya*, and some songs about him are quoted y *Amitasāgara*, a Jain grammarian of *Tamil* in the tenth century A.D. Possibly *Accuta* was himself a *Buddhist*, and the political revolution which the *Kalābhras* effected may have been provoked by religious antagonism.[25]

Because of a reaction against asceticism, and also on account of the *Buddhist* refusal to acknowledge either the authority of the *Vedas* or the existence of the soul, in the sixth century A.D, saint leaders, worshippers of *Śiva* and *Viṣṇu* taught complete surrender by way of *bhakti* or personalized Gods. Those who worshipped *Śiva* were *Nāyanārs*, (leaders) and *Viṣṇu* were *Ālvārs* (divers into the divine).

With the union of *Aryans* with the non-Aryans to the religious ideas of *Vedic Aryans* had to be modified. The mechanical and elaborate religion of sacrifices could not satisfy the religious aspirations of multitudes and therefore, religious ideas of non-Aryans came to be amalgamated with the *Vedic* religion and this gave rise to the conception of theistic religion and therefore, by the end of Vedic Period god *Viṣṇu* rose to importance and become the personification of sacrifices.[26]

Similarly the *Vedic* god *Rudra* was gradually amalgamated with pre-Aryan Father God *Śiva*. Thus the germs of theism though a *non-Aryan* institution, completely absorbed the Indian religious life.[27]

The *Nāyanārs* and *Ālvārs* were poets and musicians, and used fervent devotional songs to convey their spiritual messages. An important feature of these new *bhakti* cults was the use of the *Tamil* vernacular in their song texts, rather than the traditional *Sanskrit*. This is due in part, to the fact that not all of the poet- singers were learned in *Sanskrit*, the study of which was reserved for that small minority of the upper castes.

Nāyanārs or Nāyanmars

'The soul thrilling hymns of galaxy of saints are known as *Nāyanārs* or *Nāyanmars* saints who have composed devotional hymns in praise of Lord *Śiva*. The *Śaiva* saints are supposed to be sixty-three in numbers.[28]

In the collection called *Tirumurai*, the complete works of the *Nāyanārs* are included. *Tirujnāna Sambandamurti (Sambandār)*, *Tirunavukkarasu (Appār)*, and *Sundaramurti (Sundarār)* are the three most notable of the *Nāyanārs*. Their compositions are compiled in the *Tevaram*, which is a part of the *Tirumurai*, and comprise the first seven of the total of twelve books. Songs from the *Tevaram* presently comprise a total of 795 (*Sambandār* 384, *Appār* 311 and *Sundarār* 100). The songs were written in melody types called pans, which were accompanied rhythmically.

The maintenance of the tradition of singing the songs from the *Tevaram* correctly has been the responsibility of the *Oduvars*, professional musicians retained by the temples who, for the last thousand years, have faithfully passed down the musical traditions. Songs from the *Tevaram*, considered to be the holiest of *Śaivaite* writings, are still performed regularly in temples, other religious institutions, and homes and have been included in *Tevaram bhajanas* since medieval times.

Appār, (7th century A.D) the oldest of the three *Tevaram* saints, like other poet singers, made innumerable pilgrimages to sacred temple shrines, composing a great portion of his works at the temples. The allusions to specific temples incorporated into the following verses:

"Viṣṇu, spouse of Lakṣmī, and
Four-ways facing Brahma,
Searched the heights and depths, but
Thy feet could never see.
Yet, only lord who in Athihai dost dwell,
Formless, in Thy grace, grant the Sight of them to me."
"All other worlds his sceptre swayed, but when Kailasa he would rule
Thy crushing foot presumption paid, O stamp me with Thy sacred bull,
White as Himalya's snowy hill. Accept me, O our truth divine,
There where the moon our soareth stillGroves of Tunganaimadam's Tamilnadu Shrine."[29]

The songs embrace a wide range of devotional lyrics ranging from idyllic comparisons with *Śiva*

"As the veeṇā's pure sound,
as the moonlight at even
as the south wind's soft breath, as

the spring's growing heat,
as the pool hovered over by whispering bees,
so sweet is the shade at our Father-Lord' feet."

The tradition of uttering the names and attributes of God is observed in the following text:

"O Lord abiding at Arur! O Lord with
A thousand feet resembling a thousand
Lotuses! O Lord with a thousand
Shoulders resembling golden hills!
O Lord with a thousand beads
Resembling a thousand suns!
O Lord who like to have a
Thousand names!

It is observed in the following lines that it is not necessary to perform the rituals in order to reach God; all that is required is that one spends his time thinking about God.

"Why chant the Veda, here the Śāstras lore?
Why daily teach the books of righteousness?
Why the Vedaṇgas six say o'er and o'er
Release in theirs, and theirs alone,
Whose heart
From thinking of its lord shall
Ne'er depart."[30]

Sweeter than honey is that lord of *Sambandār*, a younger contemporary of Appār, lived for only sixteen years and was held in great veneration by *Śaivites*. It was believed that he was chosen by *Śiva* to be a miracle worker; and through his miracles to lead the people back to *Śiva*. It was in vogue that he was suckled by *Pārvati* (*Śiva*' concert) and that at the age of three he began to sing his praises of God. Many of his texts allude to the attributes of *Śiva* in one sacred place.

milk-white ashes; He is indeed the sweet sugarcane;
He blesses his devotees with the bliss that makes them melt;

He abides on top and abides at numberless Shrines,
though transcending
The very heavens he has a Victorious form that the world
Might worship; that lord of mine who tore an elephant
And wrapped himself in its Hide and abides at Acchirappakkam. "[31]

Third of the *Tevaram* poet-singers, *Sundarār*, (9th century A.D.) was born in *Tiruvannainallur,* but was associated with *Tiruvarur, Tanjore* district, Tamil Nadu, which later became sacred because of musical *bhakti* movement. Like the other poet-singers, *Sundarār* made pilgrimages to the *Śaivite* shrines and dedicated songs to the residing deities. *Sundarār's* works are concerned with seeking release from the clutches of charming women, freedom from the bounds of birth and absorption into the infinite *Śiva.* *Sundarar* is said to have sung 38 thousand poems in praise of God, enshrined in the various temples of Tamil Nadu. Only 100 poems out of these were available in the tenth century and these run into 1026 verses set to music. These were actually sung by him during his visit to the temple for worship and even to this day these hymns continue to be sung."[32]

The God himself stopped the marriage of *Sundarar* arranged by his parents. It is said that an old *brahmin* appeared, when the marriage ceremony was going on, and produced documents executed by *Sundarar's* grand father pledging himself and all his progeny in eternal bondage to the old man. When asked to show him house, the old man took *Sundarar Tirvannai Nallar* to the innermost sanctum of the local shrine and there he disappeared. *Sundarar* immediately realized that the old man was the Lord himself, who granted *Sundarar* the melodious voice to sing Lord's praises. *Sundarar* sang the following song in praise of *Śiva.*

"Pitha, Piraisudi,
Permana, arulala,
Ninakkiren Manathjunnai,
"Vaitha ennai Thenpal
Vennai nallore arul thuraiul
Atitha, Unnakku allay ini
Allenenalame"[33]

(A song in praise of Lord Śiva the mad man the one whose forehead is adorned with crescent moon and whose consort *ummai* is always by his side, such a Lord *Śiva* blessed the poet with this *Darśan* at Thiruveni Nallur. Now without the aid of this Lord his devotee cannot do anything.)

In the song which is called '*Tiruttondattogai*' he has enumerated the names of all the sixty-three *Śaiva* saints and this song was elaborated in the 12th century into a large epic of over four thousand verses by the saint-historian *Sekkialr*." [34]

Thirujnana Sambandhar has composed eighty four hymns and each is called '*padigam*', which consists of 10 stanzas with an eleventh containing the author's name. It is said that Divine wisdom was bestowed upon him at the age of three. The seven miracles, like saving the princess from a dangerous ailment and bringing back to life a young merchant, which had happened in his life, lend support to the view that Saint Sambandhar was the 'Son of God.'

The hymns of the *Nāyanārs* or *Nāyanmars* are sung and are meant to be sung. Twenty-three melody patterns (called pan) have survived to this day. They are appropriate to various parts of the day and night and are expressive different emotions. The practice of singing in temples is referred to in the hymns of the *Nāyanmars* and in due course their own hymns came to be sung. Kings and rich devotees made endowments for paying the singers known as *oduvars*. Even on a conservative reckoning, the singing of *Tevaram, Tiruvachagam* and other hymns has been in vogue for more than a thousand years. At the conclusion of the worship in the temples, these hymns are sung I n the traditional way. It is also usual for *bhajan* parties to accompany the deity in a procession, singing these hymns. Like the *Divyaprabandham* of the *Alvars*, these hymns are the cherished possession of the *Tamils.*[35]

Ālvars

Vaiṣṇavite Ālvars represented the second of the two main thrusts of Hindu orthodoxy. They focused their adoration on *Viṣṇu* as the supreme deity. Like the *Nāyanārs*, the *Ālvārs*, moved from one temple to another singing of their intense love for God. Great spiritual leaders, both men and women, emerged out of all strata of society, *Nāyanārs* and *Ālvārs*, both were inspired by the same spirit of *bhakti* never considering differing sectarian outlooks. In this religious revival movement, between 6th and 9th centuries, poet-singers of these both groups borrowed from one another.

Thirumangai, (8th century A.D.), who was a petty king in the Cola Empire, was one of the most celebrated of the *Ālvārs*, following *Poygai*, *Pudam*, and *Pey* (6th century). He turned to religious thought after meeting and falling in love with a beautiful *Vaiṣṇava*. girl. As she insisted that she would marry only a *Vaiṣṇava*. Thirumangai immediately became *Vaiṣṇava*. She put a condition that before she would marry him he must feed 1,008 *Vaiṣṇavas* daily for one year. He did this willingly for one year and married her. "For the sake of the love of the woman, *Thirumangai* began to develop love for God. To fulfill his promises to his beloved, he stole money from his overlord, for which he was imprisoned. His six works comprised 2000 of the total 4000 verses of the *Divyaprabandha*.

"His work anticipates the passionate love symbolism of Jayadēva's *Gīta Govinda*. He often uses the imagery of the parted lovers suffering the pangs of separation:

"Golden hued as tender mango
Shoot was once my delicate one.
And now she is sickly pale.
Her bracelets have dropped
Down her withered arms. Even
Her pearl necklace and the delicious
Sandal paste burn and bruise her
Love -smitten heart.
And the moon that wraps
The whole world in a veil of
Tender, mellow light, sends
Through her only a wave

Of scorching flame. Her
Heart goes walling with
The distant moaning sea.
Why deniest Thou her
Thy grace still, oh my Lord?"[36]

The *Ālvārs* considered themselves as the brides of their eternal lover; the relationship between the individual soul and that of the Lord is expressed in terms of love. The *Bhakti*-movement had its first impact in the *Tamil*-speaking regions of India. It received canonical status in the 9th century with the establishment of its earliest religious formation, the Sri *Vaiṣṇava Sampradāya* founded by *Nātha Muni* (824-924 A.D.) of *Srirangam* in Tamil Nadu. *Nātha Muni*, the first teacher of the *Sri Vaiṣṇava Sampradāya*, collected the hymns of the *Ālvār* poets into a book and introduced them to be regularly sung in the *Vaiṣṇava* temples of *Srirangam*. The performance of music, especially song, is given scriptural authority in *Vaiṣṇava* theology. Later on, *Vaiṣṇava Bhakti* spread all over the country through saint-poets and philosopher-devotees. These indications refer to daily worship in the *Vaiṣṇava*temples all over India.

Srinivasa Raghavan says: "The works of the *Ālvārs* are as rich poetical record, intense and personal, of what Leibniz called 'Philosophia Perennis, 'the metaphysic that recognizes a divine reality substantial to the world of things and lives and minds, the psychology that finds in the soul something similar to, or even identical with divine reality, the ethic that places man's final end in the knowledge of the Immanent and transcendent ground of all beings."[37]

The work of the *Ālvārs* is known as the *Nalayira Divya Prabandham* (the Divine Four thousand). The works of the various *Ālvars* are as under:

1	*Periyalwar*	*Tiruppallandu, Periyalwar Tiruymozhi*
2	*Andal*	*Tiruppavai, Nachiyar Tirumnozhi*

3	*Kulasekhara*	*Perumal Tirumozhi*
4	*Tirumazhisai*	*Tiruchanda Viruttam, Nanmukan Tiruvantadi*
5	*Tondaraippodi*	*Tirumalai, Tiruppalli Ezhuchi*
6	*Tiruppan*	*Amalanadippiran*
7	*Madhurakavi*	*Kanninum Chiruttambu*
8	*Tirumangai*	*Periya Tirumozhi, Tiruneduntantakam, Tirukkuruntantakam,*
		Tiruvezhukkootrirukkai, Chiria Tirumadal, Periya Tirunadal
9	*Poigai*	*Mutal Tiruvantadi*
10	*Bhutam*	*Irandam Tiruvantadi, Moonram Tiruvantadi*
11	*Nammalwaar*	*Tiruvaimozhi Tiruviruttam, Tiruvasiriyam, Periya Tiruvantadei.*[38]

Every conceivable human relationship has been attributed to the God-devotee bond. These cravings or *Āsakti-s* provide intense and varied basis for the role-creation. These different dualistic relationships between God and devotees have unfailingly created places, atmosphere and occasions to express and channelize devotion. The process was more prominent in case of *Vaiṣṇavas* and hence the scope offered to performing arts was abundant.

The development of the *bhajana Paddathi* in South India was traced to the Tanjore District of three leaders, the *bhajana gurus*, *Sadāśiva Brahmendra* (*Bodhendra), Śridhara Venkates (Ayyaval)* and *Sadquruswāmi* (*Venkatarāma*). They were responsible for the Southern *bhakti* revival in the late 17th and early 18th centuries. They were all the followers of *Śankara* and wrote treaties and devotional songs based on *Advaita* Doctrines.

The *bhajana* ritual structure can be traced to Śankara because his *Advaitic* teachings form the basis upon which the *smarta* sect was founded. The *smartas* are the creators and carriers of the Southern orthodox tradition. This particular sect refers to the ritual structure as *Hari Bhajana Paddati*. This *Sampradāya*, practiced by *Smartas*, influenced other sects, regions in India and religious leaders and poet-singers from the North. This *Vaiṣṇava* influence continued by the way of the popular *Avatārās* of *Viṣṇu*, especially *Kṛṣṇa* and *Rāma* and *Anjaneya (Hanuman)* who assisted *Rāma* in rescuing *Sita* from *Rāvaṇa*.

Śankarāchārya is credited with saving *Vedic* religion from total destruction. It has been noticed that the desire to become a '*Sanyāsi*' and serve the people comes by the grace of God. Śankarachārya *was* one such who wanted to renounce the world even at an early age. He interpreted the Upaniṣadic sentence 'Thou art that' as 'I am *Brahm*' to mean that 'the spirit in man is identical with the Supreme Spirit'. His *Advait* Philosophy is, '*Brahma* alone is real. The world is *Māya* or unreal. The *Jiva* or the individual soul is not different from *Brahma*.[39]

Śankarāchārya has written number of *Stotras* or hymns in praise of various deities. The devotees sing these *Stotras* e.g., '*Kanaka Dharastava*' in praise of Goddess *Lakshmi* is learnt by heart and repeated on Fridays and *Punchmis*. *Sri Śankarāchārya* in his commentary on the *Gītā* (VIII, 19, XIV, 26) says that worship is *bhakti (bhajanam bhaktih)* and defines '*ananya bhakti*'[40] as non-experience of anything other than *Vāsudēva*.

In explaining '*Dhyāna*[41] Śankarāchārya says that meditation is a continuous and unbroken thought; like a line of flowing oil. Different illustrations are referred to by *Śankarāchārya*, to explain the nature of *Bhakti*, render it easy for the common man to understand or appreciate that *Bhakti* is a natural longing for the Lord and a passionate desire to become one with Him.

According to Sri Rāmānujachārya Dhāyna and devotion *(Bhakthi)* were interchangeable terms. Commenting on the first aphorism of the *Brahma Sūtra* he states: 'Meditation' means steady remembrance that is continuity of steady remembrance, uninterrupted like the flow of oil... steady remembrance of this kind is designated by the word 'devotion' *(Bhakthi);* for this term has the same meaning as *Upāsana* (meditation or worship). Thus according to him, continuous meditation or *Dhyāna* is *Bhakthi*, which is a synonym of *Upāsana.*

In Rāmānujachārya's system *Bhakti* has the highest place. The two systems of *Advaita* and *Bhakti* meet in *Vaiṣṇavism.* The followers of the both sects (*Vaiṣṇavism and Śaivism*) have no two opinions about the greatness and loftiness of Sri *Rāmānujachārya* because of his missionary tours, his organizing capacity, monuments affording the pattern of worship, and centres of study being run under hierarchy of priests, all have ensured permanence to *Vaiṣṇavism.*[42]

Sri Madhvachārya makes the supremacy of *bhakti* clear in his commentary on the Brahma Sūtra, where he observes that the soul's essential nature does not become fully manifested without *bhakti.*

> "Madhvācāhrya has an important place in the *Bhakti* cult because he broke away from the *Advaita* Philosophy of *Śankaracharya* (another great religious reformer of South) and also *Viśiṣtadvaita* of *Rāmānuja. Madhvāchārya* worked out his own system based on the *Bhakti* of *Bhāgavata Purāṇa.* He insisted that God is distinct from soul. He is distinct from matter. Individual souls are distinct from one another. They are different from matter and that one form of matter is different from another."[43]

According Sri Madhvāchārya *bhakti* and *jnāna* are practically synonymous terms. He writes, "*Jnāna* is often referred to *Bhakti.* Where the aspect of attachment is to be emphasized, their fusion is designated by the term *bhakti.* As mediacy and immediacy are integral parts of knowledge, similarly *bhakti* is particular kind of *jnāna.* Thus whenever the scriptures speak of *jnāna* as the means of release, *bhakti* is certainly indented. Sometimes the two are referred to separately."

The promulgation of regional languages and their preferred use as literary languages in place of Sanskrit is one of the principal features of the *Bhakti* tradition. Starting with the *Ālvārs* who wrote their poems in Tamil, the *Bhakti* movement, as it spread towards North, created a rich heritage of devotional poetry in Telugu, Kannada, Marathi, Gujarati,

Hindi, Bengali, and other languages. In the region of *Vraja*, the home land of Lord *Kṛṣṇa*, in Northwestern Uttar Pradesh, devotional literature in *Vrajabhāsha*-Hindi received its main inspiration during the 16th century with the works of poet-saints such as, *Suradasa, Sámi Haridāsa, Hita Harivamśa* and others.

Song Types

Bhajana

The word *Bhajana* is derived from the same verbal root *Bhaj*, which is a term to denote both a category of devotional song and a type of musical performance or ritual held by some South Indian Hindu communities. South Indian *Bhajana* ceremonies are based on *Śaivaite Bhakti*, devoted to Lord *Śiva*. It is this conception of *bhakti*, as propounded by Sri Madhva, which formed the basis of the *Haridāsa* movement or *Bhakti* movement. *Bhajana* as a word and as a phenomenon touches every Indian in every part of the country.

> "*Bhajana* means to sing the praises of, or to worship the Lord. It denotes: 1).a genre of devotional music; 2) a king of religious ritual; 3). An expression meaning, religious worship. In the first instance, as a genre of devotional song, there are several forms, some of which are performed only in a worshipful context, and others that are sung in the religious context as well as in concerts of classical music. The word *bhajana* also refers to a congregational ritual, i.e., the ritual itself is called '*bhajana.*' In this type, family friends, or groups organized for this purpose will meet periodically to worship together. The third meaning of the word *bhajana* has to do with an individual's approach to God. That is, one demonstrates one's devotion to and love for God through acts of ritual worship."[44]

In *Bhajana* rituals, there are six song types and they have specific functions within the rituals.

1. **Pundarikam:** It is a short responsorial song that indicates the beginning of a section of the ritual. There is no instrumental

accompaniment other than the drone and any *tāla* or *rāga*. The two tones sung are the intervals of the major third and fifth above the tonic.

2. **Śloka**: The *Śloka* is also an important musical type in *bhajana* rituals. *Ślokas* are composed in couplets or four-line stanzas and the number of syllables per line can be eight to twenty or more. Usually persons who have musical training will sing *Ślokas* and they maintain the melody, set in various *rāgas*. A leader or other solo singer, without melodic or rhythmic instrumental accompaniment, performs *Ślokas* in invocatory and meditative sections of the rituals usually. When a series of *Ślokas* are sung several members of the congregation take turns in singing.

3. **Nāmāvali**: It means, "a row of names." *Nāmāvali* song consists of names and praises of a deity for singing of the glories of God and repeating His names leads for achieving union with Him. The song text may be comprised of only two words, such as the names of a deity, *Nārāyana* and Hari. The *Nāmāvali* is the most used of all song types in congregational singing among all sects.

4. **Kīrtana:** The Sanskrit word *Kīrtana* means 'to sing the glories of the Lord'. It consists of two or more stanzas, usually the first of which acts as the refrain repeated between subsequent stanzas.

> "*Kīrtana* texts contain, inmost instances, excellent poetry; they have been composed by the great poet-saints and are in the South Indian tradition that goes back to the *Nāyanārs* and *Ālvārs*. The textual themes are often based on aspects of religious philosophy. *Kīrtanas* have been composed with the congregation in mind, being considered most important in performance. *Kīrtanas* are composed in a variety of *rāgas*, usually those that are commonly known; Adi is a common *Tāla*, but not exclusive. They are accompanied like *Nāmāvalis*, by all the musical instruments on hand and are sung solo, or in unison by the congregation, or responsorial."[45]

5. **Kṛitī**: The *Kṛitī* was developed from the *Kīrtana* and designed primarily as classical music, sung by trained musicians. It is just like a *Kīrtana* but when sung, the text will be broken into different phrases with classical twists. It is included in rituals by those who have perfect training in classical music. The saint-composer, *Tyāgarāja* was best known for his innovative style of rendering *Kṛitīs*.

6. **Aṣtapadi:** Each *aṣtapadi* will have eight stanzas and begins with an introductory stanza sung as a Śloka and solo, followed by the remaining stanzas sung like the *Kīrtana* without specific *pallavi*. *Jayadēva's Gītā Govinda* was composed in 24 *Aṣtapadis*. These are sung in each *bhajana* rituals and during the annual *Rādhā-Kṛṣṇa Kalyāṇam*.

Haridāsas and Bhakti

"Vaiṣṇava movement in Kannada began to exert strong influence from the time of *Krishnadeva Raya*. Before *Purandaradās*, he started composing his devotional songs *Narahari Tīrtha*, third in succession after *Sri Madhvāchārya*, had set the tradition of composing songs in *Kannada* in praise of *Viṣṇu*."[46]

Most of the Karnataka *Haridāsas* has recognized *Bhakti Mārga*, one of the four *Sādhanas* (paths), to liberation or reality, *Karma Mārga*, *Gnāna Mārga* and *Yoga Mārga*, as the easiest and most fruitful in their early life. *Bhakti* is the ultimate passion. Total surrender to the almighty is signal on the path of devotion. Based on the *Upaniṣads*, the *Purāṇas* and personal experience, the builders of the path of devotion have chosen to reach God by their master-servant, mother-child, preceptor-disciple (*Guru- Śiṣya*), *vātsalya* (friendly) and *madhura* (love) relationship. Love and devotion lead one to release from the trammels of worldly sufferings. The royal road starts with the directions in *Bhāgavatha Purāṇa* and the *Gītā*. The two scriptures, the *Srimad Bhagavad Gītā* and *Srimad Bhāgavata Purāṇa* are considered to be one of the basis of the *bhakti* philosophy of the middle ages. The *Gītā* as is well known is a part of the *Mahābhārata*, while the *Bhāgavata* is an independent work.

Haridāsas Lineage centered their affections on *Vittala* of *Pandharapur* as the patron deity of their order. There is evidence to show that Karnataka had cultural sway over *Pandharpur* and its neighborhood, where the worship of *Vittala* developed in ancient times, though the later days, the region passed under the political and cultural hegemony of Maharashtra mysticism. Even as late as the time of the great Maharastra saint *Janesvara*; *Vittala* of *Pandharpur* was still spoken of as the beloved deity of the Karnataka.

Haridāsas of Karnataka were the first to develop the cult of devotion to *Vittala* and make it a living faith and a powerful instrument of mass uplift through the aid of their soul-stirring music and *Bhajana* in the language of their province. Their example was subsequently taken up and carried further by the saints of the neighboring province of Maharastra like *Rāmadāsa*, *Tukarāma* and others. The *Dāsa Kuta* may therefore be regarded as the earliest movement of religious devotionalism in the Deccan, and then it spread to other parts of upper India and produced kindred movements.

The *Haridāsas*, moved by intense love and devotion for their own people in Karnataka, energized the impulse towards consolidation of Hindu forces against the threat of the monotheistic and Iconoclastic religion of Islam spreading slowly but inexorably in the Deccan and the South. Music teaches men not to be self-willed and fanciful, but to see the beauty of order, the usefulness of rule, and the divineness of Law. *Haridāsas* resorted to music as the medium of communication of sublime thoughts of the *Vedas* and the *Upaniṣads*, to impart instruction and to enlighten the people. It was firm conviction that God would manifest Himself when the soul craved His Company through music and dance. Of all modes of apprehension of God, music was the most effective and powerful.

According to *Haridāsas*, music and poetry *āṣitya* were twinborn and one would not exist without the other. *Purandaradāsa* says 'that *Dhyāna*, *Yagna* and *Archana* and *Kīrtana* are the forms through which *Purandara Vittala* bestows *Mokṣa* on the devotee'. *Sri Madhvāchārya* and followers of his *dvaita* philosophy regarded *Kīrtana* mode of approach to Reality as one of the nine forms of *Bhakthi*. The realization of *Parāmātma* through music and poetry, for the Lord, is the *Samagāna Priya* and both music and poetry are the *Sādhana* of *Ādhyātma Vikasa*. The *Haridāsas* sing the praises of *Hari*. *Bhakti* was enshrined in poetry and transmuted into living excellence by music for poetry and music was both dear to the Lord. Every *Haribhakta* was a composer, a poet and a devotee with soulful music.

The *Haridāsas* were the first saints in the world, to whom *Bhakti* through music was the only mode of attaining salvation. All these inclusive of *Sripādarāja, Vyasarāja, Purandara, Vadirāja* and *Kanaka* and other accept the religion of *Madhva* and his dualistic philosophy. *Purandara* was a devout follower of *Madhva* philosophy. His system *Bhajana* as described in the *Vedas* is called *Tāratamyapaddati*. The *dēvataratamya* or the order of merit in *Bhajana Paddati* is *Vināyaka, Pārvati, Śiva, Sesha, Garuda*, and *Bhārati* wife of *Vāyu*, *Gāyathri, Sarswathi*, *Vāyu Mukhya Prāṇa, Brahma, Lakshmi* and *Sri Hari Sarvottama*. According to the *Paddathi* the first invocation starts from *Mangalacharane, Dēvataratamya, Darṣana Kutohala*, *Avahāna, Agaman, Karna Yachane, Stotra, Dvaita Bhakti Prameya, Sri Kṛṣṇa Leela seva*, Moral teaching, *Dēva rnamas, Suladis, Ugabhogs, Mangalānd* finally *Harivana Seva*.

Tāllapāka Annamāchārya

The great *bhakti* movement and its accompanying musical expression, though originating in the south, seems to have moved clockwise around India, into Karnataka and Maharashtra, then through the Punjab, East to Bihar and the Eastern provinces, then down the east coast, and into the south once again. The second half of the 16th and first half of the 17th centuries brought to fruition in great part, the essential formation of the present-day *bhajana* ritual structure (*paddhati*), as performed by the orthodox groups. This task was begun by a family consisting of three generations of poet-singers from the village of *Tāllapākam*, whose activities were centred in *Tirupati* at the *Venkateśwarar* temple. The date of birth of *Annamāchārya* popularly known as *Annamayya*, ranges from 1408 to 1424; the latter of the two may be the more accurate. *Annamāchārya's* importance lies in the fact that he began many of the conventions that were to be continued and developed by those who came later. It was *Annamāchārya* who first codified the *bhahana* tradition. He is credited with establishing musical forms that are in present use; the terms, *pallavi, anupallavi, carana,* and *citta svara* have been attributed to him. [47]

'Believed to be an *amṣa* of the Lord's sword *Nandaka, Annamāchārya* was born with devotion to *Venkateśvara*. Even as a child he would not eat unless it was given to him as His *prasāda*, nor would he go to sleep unless the lullaby was also about Him. Born, as he was with a gift for poetry and song, the boy *Annamāchārya* would improvise songs on *Venkateśvara*, and sing and dance in ecstasy. Absorbed as he was in the thoughts of God, he found attending to domestic chores and intolerable interference with his pre-occupation. So he ran away to *Tirupati*. By the time he could do the first steep climb of the *Tirumala* Hills, he could do the first steep climb of the *Tirumala* Hills, he felt exhausted and slept on a stone. Then he dreamt of *Alamelumanga*, *Venkateśvara's* consort, who told him that if he had climbed the sacramental hill with unshod feet, he would not have been tired. Then she gave him the *prasāda* of the temple and assured him that he would see the Lord. *Annamāchārya*, as he woke up from the dream, composed extempore a *Śataka* in Her praise. Double enthused, he proceeded and reached the temple where, as he beheld the Lord, he burst into a song of ecstatic praise. He has a few songs, which capture something of his thrill during his first visit to *Tirumala*.'[48]

Although propitiated other deities like *Rāma*, *Kṛṣṇa*, *Narasimha* and *Vittala*, he viewed them all as forms of *Venkateśvara*, the Ultimate reality. His songs are, his outstanding achievement. He regarded them as 'flower-offerings' to God and himself a mere instrument singing His praise at His behest. While, through his songs, he exhorts and persuades others to seek God in *Venkateśvara*, the primary urge behind them is the felt creative need to give expression, as poetry and song, to his own inextricable involvement in *Venkateśvara*. They are, in a sense, literally *samkīrtanās* since they all praise Him. In them

Annamāchārya prays and praises *Venkateśvara*, makes love to Him, converses, argues and quarrels with Him, meditates on His many attributes, confesses his failures and apprehensions, sues for His grace, and surrenders himself to Him. Traditionally *Annamāchāryas's* songs are classified into *Ādhyātma* and *Sṛingāra Samkīrtanās*, although they are not necessarily mutually exclusive.

> "All saints share the common experience of devotional ecstasy. So are the songs of *Annamāchārya* and they can be described as a sincere devotee's call to Divinity. His contributions are at once musical, religious and philosophical. The Highest Supreme, Lord *Venkateśa* for *Annamāchārya*, stands exalted above everything and his *Samkīrtanās* testify to appropriateness of blend of the mystical and bhakti aspects. The highest fulfillment of human existence, as *Annamcharya* has conveyed through his songs, is surrender to the Lord of Seven Hills. He has show that spiritual perfection is within reach of everyone."[49]

Among the songs of *Annamāchārya* available now, the *Sṛngarasamkīrtanās* outnumber the *Adyatmasamkīrtanās* by several thousands. In adopting *madhurabhakti*, which had already an established tradition, he was partly attempting to sublimate his own sensual nature of which he was acutely aware. He speaks for himself and for others who similarly long for God, and view spiritual life in terms of *rakti* rather than *virakti*.

Some songs describe *Alamelumanga's* love for *Venkateśvara*. In *Alaruluguriyaga*, (in *Śankarābharaṇam*) *Annamāchārya* recreates verbally every graceful gesture and movement of *Almelumanga's* dance before *Venkateśvara* meant to please Him. *Palukutenelatalli* (in *Sālanganāta*) describes how the 'Mother of honey-sweet speech' pleases Him by every art of love and finally possesses Him by surrendering Herself to Him. From such songs *Alamelumanga* emerges as the proto-type of all seekers of union with God, just as *Venkateśvara*. Himself remains the *Puruṣottama* to be loved and sought incessantly.

'The *rāgas* used by *Annamāchārya* in his songs are only about a hundred. A good many of them, such as *Abali, Amarasindhu, Kondamalahari, Sourāṣtragujjari,* etc. have become either rare or obsolete now. Of the well-known *rāgas*, which are in use now and used frequently by him are *Mukhāri, Śankarābharaṇam, Kāmbhoji, Devagāndhāri, Āhiri, Śri, Kedāragoula, Bhairavi* etc., *Annamāchārya* takes his place in the tradition of Karnataka music as a great *Padakarta*.'[50]

Purandaradāsa

'Sri Purandara is the founder of *Carnataka* Music and his songs range from the most homely to the most philosophical. It was *Purandaradāsa,* who, more than 400 years ago, gave form to the system of training in music that is being followed. His original name is Srinivasa Naik. He initiated the practice of starting music lessons and formulated graded exercises. Purandaradāsa was born in Purandargad near Pandharpur, around 1400 A.D. In fact the learners of Karnataka music will start his composition first.

Purandara selected *Māyamālavagowla Rāga* for it enabled the later development of the 72-*Mēla* schemes. He has won the unique place in history of being the father of Modern Carnatic music. Sri Purandara was in a way, the founder of *Kīrtana* form which it its melody is based on technical compositions like *Gītā* whose purpose is to elucidate *Rāga* forms and *Tāla* patterns. The emphasis in the *Kīrtanas* is on its aesthetic excellence and that is why it is considered as the most important part of Carnatic classical music. Purandaradāsa have composed some five lakh songs. Popularly called *Dēvanamas.*

Dwarakanath says,

> "Using the simplest of words with baffling dexterity, he adopted the conversational style for his songs in which we find the impassioned pleas, urging the people to follow virtuous ways."[51]

Sri Purandaradāsa had not merely perfected thousands of musical patterns and evolved the thrilling technique of Carnatic Music, but had preached the message of the Vedanta to the millions who were not familiar with Sanskrit. through the medium of Kannada in a striking and successful manner.

Nagarāja Sharma asserted that:

> "The tunes and the language of *Purandara* are unsurpassable in their direct psychological appeal to diverse personalities, attracting irresistibly children, the young, the adult, and the old alike. Every mood, passion and emotion, ranging from the ridiculous to the spiritual sublime have been portrayed by *Purandara* with uncanny sympathy and insight."[52]

Purandara's theism is grounded on belief in the supremacy of the Lord, *Sri Mahā Viṣṇu (Narāyana, Vittala,* etc.) who alone is the saviour of the finite selves. The doctrine of *Karma* has found striking expression in many pieces. The great master composers who came after Sri *Purandara* faithfully followed the tradition and form which *Purandara* established. The *Rāga* and *Tāla* aspects are followed by composers like *Dikshitār* and *Śyāma Śāstri* and the purely *Rāga* aspects by composers like *Kṣetragna*. But it was *Tyāgarāja* who brought out in the fullest measure all the three aspects viz. *Rāga Bhāva* and *Tāla* of the tradition, founded by Purandara.

Bhadrāchala Rāmadās

Rāmadās was a renowned composer who dedicated his life in spreading the spiritual path, during 16th century as an ardent follower of his deity, *Rāma* and declared that his poetry and compositions are for his God alone. *Rāmadās* whose name was *Gopanna*, was the son of *Linganna Mantri* who belonged to the place called *Nelakondapalli* in the former *Nizam's* dominion. Because of his *Rāma-Bhakti*, this *Gopanna* came to be known as *Rāmadās*. *Rāmadās* followed spiritual path to such an extent that he saw *Rāma* in all beings and things, a state of which he himself expressed in one of his songs;

"Antha Rāmamayam, Ee jagadantha Rāmamayam in Varāli rāga."

There was a practice of the Nizam of Hyderabad, making a grant for the conduct of the festival of the temple of *Rāma* at Bhadrachalam. *Rāmadās* was appointed as Tahsildar for the firka of Bhadrāchalam and he directed the revenues of his division for the renovation of the temple of *Rāma* without remitting the revenues to the Central Treasury. *Rāmadās* was arrested and thrown into the prison in Golconda. He was imprisoned for 12 years and during this period he composed most of his moving songs on *Rāma,* his deity. In a song in *Nātakurunji rāga,* he asks *Rāma,* why He was not saving when he was in this much suffering and agony.

"Edunnādo Bhadrādrivāsudu, Edunnādo nāpali Rāmudu Edunnādo"

"*Rāma*, why don't you speak?" "Are your words pieces of gold?"
"Even in my dreams I never forget your name."

He sang in *Ānandabhairavi rāga, Rupaka tāla,*
"Paluke bangara māyena Kodandapani Kalalo ni nāmasmarana maruvā chakkani thandri." [53]

One night, *Rāma* and his brother *Lakshmaṇa*, in disguise of two servants under *Rāmadās,* enter the palace of *Tani Sha*, remits the entire dues that *Rāmadās* owe to the *Padshah's* exchequer. The dues of several years were paid in gold at that time of night. The appearance and disappearance of these two persons who cleared all the debts of *Rāmadās* revealed to *Tani Shah* that the two servants are none other than *Rāma* and *Lakshmaṇa*, the deities of *Rāmadās.* Immediately *Tani Shah,* reported the miraculous *darşana* to *Rāmadās,* expressed his gratitude to *Rāmadās* and sent him back to *Bhadrachalam* with enormous money to continue his devotion and service to *Rāma. Rāmadās* congratulated *Tani Shah* as he was blessed and had a privilege of seeing *Rāma* face to face.

His innumerable songs, composed on his favourite God, *Rāma* gained a noteworthy place in the tradition of *Rāmabhaktas. Śataka Stotra* (*Dāśarathi Śataka* in Telugu) is considered as one of the best compositions. In his *Prahalada Bhakti Vijaya*, Sri *Tyāgarāja* showed his admiration towards *Rāmadās* and followed his ideas and expressions in several songs. In his *Kīrtana, 'Kṣirasāgara śayana'*, Tyāgarāja mentions how *Rāma* freed *Rāmadās* from the prison.

"Dhirudu Rāmadāsuni bandhanamu thirchinadi vinnānura."

Rāmadās gained a noteworthy place in the tradition of the galaxy of *Rāmabhaktas*. His songs on *Rāma* spread all over the country. His life, his sufferings and his obtaining in the end the blessings of *Rāma*, became a common story among the people."[54]

The tradition of taking to music for God realisation is as old as the idea of the existence of God Himself. The songs of the saint-singers were written in vernaculars and had the quality of being rendered musically not only in folk tunes but also as classicalised Music. The history of the evolution and development of music tells us that through the devotional songs of these saint-singers there was not only a musical mass awakening but also a religious revival.

REFERENCES

1. Swāmi Prajñānanda, *Historical Development of Indian Music*, p. 19.
2. Suresh Chandra Dey, *The Quest for Music Divine*, p. 73.
3. Swāmi Prajñānanda, *Historical Development of Indian Music*, p. 403.
4. Dr. S. Radhakrishnan, Foreword, *The Spiritual Heritage ofTyagaraja*, p. iii.
5. Selina Thielemann, *Singing the Praises Diviine*, p. 16.
6. Selina Thielmann, *Singing the Praises Divine; Music I the Hindu Tradition*, p. 17.
7. Robert Leopold Simon, *Spiritual Aspects of Indian Music*, p. 4.
8. Peggy Holroyde, *The Music of India*, p. 36.
9. Robert Leopold Simon, *Aspects of Indian Music*, p. 10.
10. *Ibid*, p. 11.
11. Swami Chidbhavajnanda, *The Bhagavat Gītā*, IV,: 11, p. 281.
12. *Ibid.*, p. 517.
13. *Ibid.*, p. 642.
14. The Ṛgveda., X. 43.1.

15. The Ṛgveda., VI. 45. 26.
16. Ganesh Vasudeo Tagore, (*Srimad Bhāgavata*, II, I.21) (*The Bhāgavata Purāṇa* Translated and annotated, Motilal Banarsidass, Delhi, 1979.
17. *The Bhāgavata*, (VII, 5.23).
18. Robert Leopold Simon, *Spiritual Aspects of Indian Music*, p. 34.
19. Ganesh Vasudeo Tagore, (*Srimad Bhāgavata*, II, I.21) (*The Bhāgavata Purāṇa* Translated and annotated, Motilal Banarsidass, Delhi, 1979
20. *Ibid.*
21. Selina Thielemann, *Singing the Praises Divine., Music in the Hindu Tradition*, p. 20.
22. C. Rāmānujachariar, Prof. V. Raghavan, *The Spiritual Heritage of Tyāgarāja*, p. 164.
23. C. Rāmānujachariar, Prof. V. Raghavan, *The Spiritual Heritage of Tyāgarāja*, p. 164.
24. Swāmi Prajñānanda, *Historical Development of Indian Music*, p. 403.
25. Dr. Annapurna.L., *Music and Temples: A Ritualistic Approach*, p. 3.
26. Sircar. D.C., *Studies in the Religious Life of Ancient and Medieval India* , p. 12.
27. Shantheela Sathianathan, *Saints of South India*, p. 136.
28. Robert Leopold Simon, *Spiritual Aspects of Indian Music*, p. 18.
29. Robert Leopold Simon, *Spiritual Aspects of Indian Music*, p. 19.
30. Robert Leopold Simon, *Spiritual Aspects of Indian Music*, p. 20.
31. Robert Leopold, *Spiritual Aspects of Indian Music*, p. 21.
32. Arunachalam. M, *Tamil Saints-9*, p. 227.
33. Arunachalam. M., *Tamil Saints-9*, p .227.
34. Bharati Shuddhanand, *Alvar Saints and Acharyas*, p. 2.
35. Devasenapathi. V.A, Nayanmars, *Devotional Poets and Mystics*, Part–1, Publication Division, Ministry of Information and Broadcasting, Government of India, New Delhi, 1978, p. 25.
36. Robert Leopold Simon., *Spiritual Aspects of Indian Music*, p. 28.
37. Srinivas Raghavan. A, *Ālvars, Devotional Poets and Mystics*, Part–1, Publication Division, Ministry of Information and Broadcasting, Government of India, New Delhi, 1978, p. 45.

38. Srinivas Raghavan. A, *Ālvars, Devotional Poets and Mystics*, Part–1, Publication Division, Ministry of Information and Broadcasting, Government of India, New Delhi, 1978, p. 25.
39. Shantsheela Sathianathan, *Saints of South India*, pp. 232-33.
40. Swami Chidbhavanananda, *The Bhagavad Gita*, XI: 54, Sri Ramakrishna Tapovanam, Madras, 1970, Page: 637
41. *Ibid.*, p. XIII : 24, 705.
42. Shantsheela Sathianathan, *Saints of South India*, p. 241.
43. Sharma. D.S., *Hinduism Through the Ages*, p. 42.
44. Robert Leopold Simon, *Spiritual Aspects of Indian Music*, p. 4.
45. Robert Leopold, *Spiritual Aspects of Indian Music*, p. 56.
46. Sastri Neelkanth, *A History of South India*, Third Edition, p. 403.
47. Dr. Annapurna. L., *Music and Temples A Ritualistic Approach*, p. 6.
48. Jayantha R.A. *Tāllapāka Annamāchārya*, Composers, *Cultural Leaders of India*, Ed, V. Raghavan, Publications Division, Ministry of Information and Broadcasting, Government of India, New Delhi, 1979, pp. 12-13.
49. SVK, *The Hindu Speaks on Music*, p. 52.
50. Jayantha R. A., *Tāllapāka Annamāchārya*, Composers, Cultural Leaders of India, Ed, V. Raghavan, Publications Division, Ministry of Information and Broadcasting, Government of India, New Delhi, 1979, p. 19.
51. Dwarakanath. G., *The Hindu Speaks on Music*, Ed p. 38.
52. Dr. Nagaraja Sharma. R., *Glimpses of Indian Music*, Ed, p. 157.
53. *Bhajana Ratnākara*, p. 44.
54. Dr. V. Raghavan, *Glimpses of Indian Music*, Ed, pp.11-16.

7

The Trinity of South Indian Music: Their Contribution

In the middle of the 17th century, Shivaji's father Shahji took charge of the Karnatak and Bangalore provinces and Shahji's second son Vyankoji (the step brother of *Shivaji*) defeated the *Nayak* kings then ruling over the Tanjore territory and 1673, established a dynasty that played the foremost part in the development of South Indian music. Every one of these Tanjore kings was a learned and versatile man and under their patronage the literature and fine arts flourished wholesomely. One more remarkable thing about these rulers was that, they, keeping to their liberalism, learnt the local art form of Carnatic music.

Deshpande says:

> "A few saint-singers flourished and were able to contribute so much to the art of music that this period is known as the Golden Age of Carnatic music. To quote an example of these rulers, interest and aptitude in music, we can refer to the works and contributions of younger *Shahji,* the son of *Vyankoji*, who was a man of letters and a trained musician. He was a poet and a play writer of a high order and his most important works published so far are his two operas or '*Gēya-Nātakas*' in Telugu and '*Pallaki Seva*

> *Prabandhan'*. The fact that these operas were being performed in the *Tiruvannur* temple in *Tanjore* district speaks for the loftiness and the greatness of the work." [1]

The hundred years from 1750-1850 are considered to be the golden age of Carnatic music. It was during this period that the three great composers, styled musical 'trinity' illuminated the musical horizon by their kṛitis and their devote lives. The three great saint-musicians, *Tyāgarāja, Śyāma Śāstri* and *Muthuswāmi Dīkṣitār* of *Tanjore* flourished in this period and the South Indian music of today is mainly as the result of the contribution of these three great musician composers.

The trinity was great devotees, poets and musicians, who gave a fresh life to South Indian music by their superb handling of the art. They were born in the same village, *Tiruvārur*, which has become thrice holy to all the lovers of music since then. The remarkable significance about the Trinity is that they were great composers and at the same time *bhaktas.*

Śyāma Śāstri (1762-1827)

Sri Śyāma Śāstri, who was affectionately called, '*Śyāma Kṛṣṇa'*, like other two members of musical trinity, was born in *Tiruvarur* in 1762. He received Sanskrit and Telugu education in his early years and in fact, he had no musical tradition in his family. When he was 18 and his family shifted to *Tanjore*, he got the real opportunity to step in to music. *Sangīta Swāmi*, a *sanyāsi*, led him into the higher aspects of music and *Śyāma Śāstri* got trained under him for a few months.

Parthasarthi. S. observes:

> "His devotion to *Sri Kāmākṣi* is increased by leaps and bounds and it is no exaggeration to say that the *Lokamāta* spoke to him and inspired the rich musical compositions that flowed out of his heart."[2]

He is said to have composed about 300 pieces consisting of *Kṛitīs, svara jātis*, *Varṇas* and *rāga mālikas.*

"*Śyāma Śāstri* was a genius whose contribution was choice and excelled in the few things he created. His *Bhairavi svarajāti* is one of the three epics of its class; his *Manji* will outlive all attempts on its life by *Bhairavised* renderings of the piece, in it, and his forte as it were, will continue to sway and rock us on the billows of ineffable bliss as that of few others can."[3]

His praise for the Goddess is exalted in a descriptive manner in these lines (in *Sāveri rāga*):

"Śankari! Śamkaru Chandramukhi!
Akhilandeswari! Śāmbhavi!
Sarasijabhāvavandithe! Gouri! Sree!"
Śankata Harini! Ripuvidarini!
Kalyāṇi! Sadānathaphaladayaki!
Haranāyaki! Thrijagajjanani!"
"Śyama Kriṣna Sodari!
Śaymalesa sodari!
Samaganalola! Bala! Sada thribhanjani!"[4]

He expresses his strong belief and faith to the Goddess in his *Kṛitī* in *Śankarabharana rāga:*

"Saroja dala nethri Himagiri Puthri-
Nee sdambhujambule sadā
nammi nā namma!
Subhamimma Shree Minākṛamma!"
"Parāku seyaka varadāyaki
Neevale dyvamu lokamulo galada!
Purāni Shukapāni Madhurakaraveni
sada Sivunaku Rani!
Kori vachina varikellanu
korke losagane birudu gada Amaba
Yathi Bhārama nannu brova
thalli krupala vala nethalajalanu!"
"Indu mukhi, karuninchumani
ninnentho vedu kontini!

Nayandu jagelavamma!
Mariyadukadu- Dayavathi neevu!"
"Sāmagana vimodini! Gunadhama!
Syāma Kṛṣṇa Vinutha! Shuka syāmalaDēvi! [5]

Śyāma Śāstri asked for the blessings of *Dēvi*, in the words, "*Dēvi brova samayamide*", when he was invited by *Bobbili Kesavayya* for a musical contest. He showed his intellectual caliber in presenting *Kāmākṣini* his *Kṛitīs* and in his *svarājathis*. He surrendered to his Goddess as "*Ninne Namminānu*" (*Todi rāga*), and he addressed Divinity as the Mother. It is the highest kind of innocent and sacred relationship in creation as the child seeks mother's affection and protection.

"Birāna varālichi brovumu
ninu nera nammithi ;
Purāri manoharini sree Kāmākṣi;
Thamasambu seyaka neevu karunanidhi gāva;
Paramukha nela vinu sarojamukhi!
Kamithardhadāyaki devi –
samkalpa lathikapuranimadhuravani
Śivuniranigada //
Śyāmakriahnasodari Gouri –
parameśwari girija -
anadarakshanambu salipithe vinanu // [6]

He prays for the Mother's grace in his *Kṛitī*, in *Purvikalyani rāga, Chāpu tāla:*

"Ninnu Vinaga mari dikkevarunnaru nikhilaloka Janani
nannu brochutaku;" [7]

"Ninu kirtinchi yetlâyunna
biddayani maruvaka
Ninnu ne madi dalachaganu
manninchi veravaku manarāda."

He says in Madhyamavathi rāga,

"Jagamu kapādina thalli gada, nenu needu bidda lālinchi."

The ideals of *Śyāma Śāstri* are well observed in his *Kṛitīs*.
In *Madhyamāvathi rāga,*

"Vemaru labinchi kritharthunda naitina?
In purva Kalyāṇi rāga,
"PaRāmalobhulanu pogadi pogadi athi pamarudai
Thirigi thirigi vesari sthiramuleka athi chapaludaithi."

Praising the fools, I became an ignorant and roaming all-around, I became an unstable man. In *Ānandabhairavi Kṛitī*, he says,

"Manavini vinuma, mariyada lerugani
dushprabhula kori vinuthimpaka varambosagi."

Let me not sing in praise of the rich. Please listen to my plea and protect me.[8]

He urges the Goddess to come and save Her son in *Ānandabhairavi Rāga:*

"Kuamara janani samāna mevarilanu --
Mānavathi shree Bruhannāyaki Devei"!
"Saroja mukhi! birāna neevu varālosagumani ninu vedithi;

"Himachala thanaya brochuta kidi
manchi samayamu rave Anba!
Purarihari Surendranutha
Purani para mukha Mēlane thalli"!

"The frequent vocatives O *Jagadamba, Janani,*
Amma and the plaintive *'Brovavamma'*,
'Mari veregati', *'Nammiti'*,

and the use of the address syllable "O" simply or in repetition will not fail to transport one to the presence of the Divine Mother or open up the inner fount of the tears of bliss."[9]

Śyāma Śāstri had a great mastery over the technique of *Carnatic* music and his contributions to this art are unique. *Ānandabhairavi* was given special charm and beauty and was enriched by him to remarkable degree. Two of his compositions viz. *Kāmākṣi Arnedinamu* in *Rāga Bhairavi* and *Kāmākṣi Arnedinamu* in *Yadukula Kambhoji Rāga* are supposed to be masterpieces. The largest number of *Syāma Sāstri's* are composed *Triputa* or *Misra Chāputāla*. .

Many of the folk songs and devotional songs, which are natural expression of human soul, are found to be naturally blending themselves into the *Tāla* of seven *Mātras*. Therefore it could be possible that *Śyāma Śāstri* gave importance to *Triputa Tāla*. Ancients considered seven as a mystic number is evident from the fact that a week is of seven days, there are seven colours, seven notes, seven *Ṛṣis*. It could be that because of this uniqueness of no. seven, *Śyāma Śāstri gave* special importance to *Triputa Tāla* of seven *Mātras*."[10]

The historical musical contest between *Śyāma Śāstri* and *Bobbili Kesavayya* in which the former sang a *Pallavi* in *Sarabhanandana tāla* as a counter to the *Pallavi* in *Simhanandana tāla*, sung by *Kesavayya*, and emerged victorious has been remembered in tradition.

Kesavayya was musician of fame from *Bobbili*. It was usual in those days for musicians of one *samstanam* (Princely state) to visit others and challege the musicians of these *samstanams* to a contest to prove their supremacy. *Bobbili Kesavayya* threw a challenge to the court-musicians of *Tanjavoor*. They met in a conclave and unanimously resolved that *Śyāma Śāstri* who was an adept in handling intricate *tāla*-measures should meet the challenger and save the honour and reputation of *Tanjavoor*. *Śyāma Śāstri* took up the challenge and prayed to his deity, the *Dēvi* Herself. *Śyāma Śāstri* sang '*Dēvi brova samayamide*' (Now is the time for you to protect me) in *Chintāmaṇi raga*, which is one of the two mythological gems, which yield anything desired like the *Kāmadhenu*. The lieteral meaning of the word

Chintāmaṇi can be taken as a gem of mental power, or a product of the creative aptitude.

The court assembled. It overflowed with an expectant surging crowd of music-lovers and musicians. *Bobbili Kesavayya* attired in all his pomp and splendour, was accorded a place of honour. King *Saraboji* was as keen as his subjects to witness their contest. *Śyāma Śāstri* took his seat in front of opponent. The contest commenced with *Bobili Kesavayya* singing a *rāga-ālāpana* (a creative elaboration of a melody-form) followed by *tāna* (graded exposition of a *raga* using the sol-fa syllables *tam, nam, anantam,* with rhythmic stress in *madyamakala* or aster speed).

He kept the audience spellbound by singing a difficult *pallavi* set in complicated *tāla, simhānandana. Śyāma Śāstri* was asked to render the same *pallavi*. Much to the delectation of the audience, *Śyāma Śāstri* handled with ease and charm. Following it up, he wove a pattern in *sarabānandana tāla* consisting of 79 *akṣarakāla* (units of time) in 24 *angās* (parts). This time-measure was a creation of the exponent himself. It was a marvelous performance on the part of *Śyāma Śāstri* to sing a complex *pallavi* with such skill and ease as he did. *Bobbili Kesavayyah* was bewildered and accepted defeat.[11]

Sambamoorthy. P explains the *akṣarakāla* of 24 *angās*:

"*Sarabhānandana tāla* comes to be known for the first time through *Śyama Śastri's Pallavi*. An *āvarta* of this *tāla* takes 19 -3/4 *mātras* or 79 *aksharakālas*. The 24 *angās* figuring in this *tāla* in their order are: *guru, laghu, drutam, laghu, laghu drutam, anu drutam, laghu virāmam, drutam, drutam, drutam, anudrutam, laghu drutam, laghu druta virāmam, laghu virāmam, drutam, anudrutam, drutam, anudrutam, drutam, laghu virāmam, drutam, druta virāmam, laghu, drutam.*[12]

Temple Kṛitis of Śyama Śastri[13]

The widely known *Navaratna-mālika kṛitis* of *Śyama Śastri*

They are:

Name of the *kṛiti*	*Rāga*	*Tāla*
Sarojadalanētri	*Śankarābharaṇa*	*Ādi*
Dēvi minanetri	*Śankarābharaṇa*	*Ādi*
IMarivērēgati	*Ānandabhairavi*	*Chāpu*
Nannubrovu	*LalitaLalita*	*Misralaghu*
Māyamma	*Āhiri*	*Ādi*
Dēvi ni pādasarasa	*Kāmbhoji*	*Ādi*
Minālochanabrova	*Dhanyāsi*	*Chāpu*

Some of the Well-known Compositions of Śyāma Śāstri[14]

Beginning Words	*Rāga*	*Tāla*
Ninne namminānu	Todi	Chāpu
Kanakasaila (Sanskrit)	*Punnāgavārali*	*Ādi*
Enneramum (Tamil)	*Punnāgavarāli*	*Ādi*
Brova samayamu	*Punnāgavarāli*	*Ādi*
Pārvati Ninnu	*Kalagada*	*Rūpaka*
Taruanmidamma(Tamil)	*Gaulipantu*	*Chāpu*
Triloka māta	*Pharaz*	*Chāpu*
Nilayatākṣi	*Pharaz*	*Chāpu*
Samkari Samkuru (Sanskrit)	*Sāveri*	*Rūpaka*
JananiNatajana(Sanskrit)	*Sāveri*	*Rūpaka*
Durusugakrupa	*Sāveri*	*Rūpaka*
Kamalamuna	*Sāveri*	*Rūpaka*
Brovavamma	*Manji*	*Chāpu*

O Jagadāmba	*Ānandabhairavi*	*Ādi*
Himāchalatanaya	*Ānandabhairavi*	*Ādi*
Pāhi Sri Girirajasute	*Ānandabhairavi*	*Rūpaka*
Phalinchu Kamākshi	*Madhyamāvati*	*Ādi*
Ninnuvina marigalada	*Ābheri*	*Rūpaka*
Akhilandesvari	*Kapi*	*Rūpaka*
Karuṇa judaninnu	*Srirāga*	*Chāpu*
Karuṇa Chudavamma	*Varāli*	*Ādi*
Ninnu vinagamari	*Purvikalyani*	*Misralaghu*
Sāminirammanave	*Ānandabhairavi*	*Ata*
Devibrovasamayamide	*Chinatamani*	*Ādi*
Talli ninnu near	*Kalyoṇi*	*Chāpu*

Different Rāgas rendered by Śyāma Śāstri in Devotional Aspect

The following are the *rāgas* rendered in devotional aspect:

Ābheri, Āhiri, Ānandabhairavi, Begada, Bilahari, Dhanyāsi Goulipantu, HamirKalyāṇi, Jaganmohini, Janaranjani Kalgada, Kalānidhi, Kalāvathi, Kalyāṇi, Kāmbhoji, Lalitā Madhyamāvathi, Manji, Mukhāri, Nātakuranji, Navanitham, Navarasakannada, Nilāmbari, Panthuvarāli, Phalamanjari, Pantuvrāli, Pharāz, Śankarābharaṇam, Sāveri, Srirāga, Todi, Varāli, Vasanta, Yadukulakāmbhoji.[15]

Besides the scholarly *kṛitis* in highly rhythmic setting, *Śyama Śastri's Svarajatis* constitute the magnificent contribution to *Carnatic* music. He is the architect of the concert type of *Svarajati*. His *Svarajatis* in *Todi rāga* is patent in each. The commencing notes of the *caraṇas* (stanzas) of his *Bhairavi svarajati*, '*Kamākṣi anudinamu*' have been so conceived by the composer to be in the ascending order pitch. The attractive *makutam* ending found in the *Yadukulakāmbhoji svarajati*, '*Kamākṣi ni pāda yugame*', adds a proper finishing to the piece. In the three *svarajatis*, the *pallavi* commences in the *mandrasthāyi* and this endows certain gravity, reflective of the meditative mood of the piece. The *mudra* '*Śyama Kṛṣṇa* ' is found in the last *caraṇa*.

Śyāma Śāstri is genius is seen not only in his kritis in the common *rāgas*, like '*Śankarābharaṇam*', '*Kalyāṇi*', '*Bhairavi*', etc. His pieces in rare *rāgas* like '*Manji*', and '*Cintāmaṇi*', are equally noteworthy. These *rāgas* do not see to have been handled by others and serve as models showing the distinctive features of the respective *rāgas*.[16]

Tyāgarāja (1767-1847)

Tyāgarāja was born on 4th May 1767 at *Tiruvarur* in the *Thanjavur* District of Tamil Nadu. He is the father of modern Carnatic music and regarded as the greatest among the music composers of South India. At the age of 13, he composed his first song '*Namo namo Raghavaya*' in *Dēsya Todi*, and became one of the musical prodigies of all time. Being a born musical genius from his very childhood *Tyāgarāja* became a devotee of *Nāda-Brahma* and devoted his time in learning. He had his training in music from *Sri Shanti Venkata Ramanayya*, one of the greatest masters of his time. [17]

Eulogising *Tyāgarāja*, Dr. S. Radhakrishnan says:

> "*Tyāgarāja* was person of great humility, utter self-effacement. He expresses the truths of the Upaniṣads and the *Bhagavad-Gītā* in a simple and appealing language. He addresses the Supreme as *Rāma*. The kingdom of God acquired through devotion is the greatest of all treasures: '*Rāma bhakti samrājyamu*. He brings *Rāma* before our eyes as he steps forward with his waving hair to bend the bow his pride. Religion is the *Sādhana* or discipline by which we make a whole of our being, when our thought, speech and action, *manas*, *vāk* and *kāya* work together. *Tyāgarāja* speaks of *Rāma* as an integrated person."[18]

The name *Tyāgarāja* means the prince of renouncers, of those who give up worldly desires. *Tyāga* or renunciation is the way to mental peace and freedom. So long as we are incapable of withstanding the snares of fear, greed ambition, vanity, we will have disquiet in our minds and violence in the world. In one of his songs '*Tera tiyagarāda*' *Tyāgarāja* says: "O Supreme Being, *Tirupati Venkata Rāmaṇa*, could you not remove the screen of pride and envy, which is taking a firm stand within me, keeping me out of the reach of *Dharma* and like.

About the contribution of *Tyāgarāja* T.S.Pardhasaradhi remarks:

> "*Tyāgarāja* exerted the greatest influence upon musical art in South India during the 18th and 19th centuries and revolutioned the very nature of *Carnatic* musics. His songs are accepted today as the only adequate interpretation of classical *Carnatic* music from both the musical and the *Sāhitya* points of view."[19]

Recognizing his extraordinary gifts and musical talents, *Rāma Brahman*, his father joined him under *Sonti Venkatasubbayya* who was the chief among the vidwans of *Thanjavur* in Tamil Nadu, and his son *Venkatarāma nayya.* As a boy *Tyāgarāja* learnt '*Rāma Shadakshari*' mantra from a saint *Rāmakrishnānanda.* On the advice of this *Guru*, *Tyāgarāja* performed *japa* of the *Nārada Mahāmantra* and soon he had a vision of *Sage Nārada* who was stated to have given him a treatise called the '*Svararnavam*'. As his fame was spreading in and around the area, his guru *Venkataramaṇayya* invited him to perform before the leading musicians of *Tiruvaiyaru.* The *Walajahpet* manuscript of *Tyāgarāja's* life records that he first sang '*Janakiramana*' in *Suddhasimantini rāga* and then '*Dorukuna ituvanti*' in *Bilahari rāga*. It was a proud occasion for his *guru, Venkataramanayya* and eulogized his performance and honoured him with his own medals.

"To those of Tyāgarāja's contemporaries who might have regarded his talent as mainly lyrical and devotional, the majestic sweep of the epic style displayed in the '*Pancharatna 'Kīrtanas*' must have come as blinding revelation."[20]

Every composition of *Tyāgarāja* overflows with the sentiment devotion *(Bhakti)*. The qualities of *Sāhitya* or literature wedded to the attractive *Sangītā* or music. *Tyāgarāja* says that *bhakti*, combined with the ambrosial *Rasa* of *Svaras* and *Rāgas*, is itself Heaven and salvation.

"*Svara-rāga-sudha-rasa-yuta-*
bhaktisvargapavargamura manasa."[21]

"Several times *Tyāgarāja* in his addresses to *Rāma* calls him a lover of music. In his *Varāli* piece, *'Ēti janmam idi'* and in the *Kāmbhoji* piece, '*Sri Raghuvara aprameya*, he calls *Rāma*, '*Sangīta-lola*', '*Gāna-lola*', in the *Sudha-simantini* piece *Jānkirāma* nā; '*Gita-priya*', in the *Kedarāgaula*, '*Divyanāma, Rāmuni maravakave*'.

In his *Srirāga Pancaratna*, he describes the Lord as reveling in the sacred music of the *Sāmaveda*- *'Sāma-gāna-lola*'. In an *Athaṇa* piece, he calls upon the mind to resort to the *upāsana* of music, which is dear to the Lord. '*Sripapriya sangitapasana ceyave, O manasa*! In his appealing *Todi* piece '*Ninu Vina sukahamu gana*, he describes *Rāma* as one who delights in the *Rāgas* of music, '*Rāga-rasika*'.

It is in the seven notes that the Lord lives and moves and has His being: *Saptasvaracāri* (in *Sriāppriya Rāga* in *Athaṇa*). If one can manifest the *svaras* precisely, each one of them would form a veritable ornament to God (*Susvarama yabhusa* in *Ni dayace Rāma* in *Rāga Yadukula Kambhoji*). In '*Sadhincene*' in *Rāga* Āarabhi, he refers to Rāma as the maintainer of the music tradition - *'Sangītasāmpradāyakudu'*.

In the beautiful piece '*Manamuleda*', so well set in music and words, *Tyāgarāja* says to *Rāma* that one so detached in heart like Him could not be found and His attitude towards a musician like *Tyāgarāja* was inexplicable in one who knows the appeal of music and is the father of the musician like *Kuṣa* and *lava*. He conceives *Rāma*, in an *Ārabhi* piece, as also in *Ni dayace Rāma* in *Rāga Yadukula Kambhoji*, and '*Tāla cinantane*' in *Mukhāri* as the very embodiment of the ambrosial *Rasa* of *Nāda*, *'Nādasudha-rasāmbilamunarakrtiyaye'* *'Nāda-Brahmānanda-rasakṛitī'* and *Nāda-Brahmānanda-rupa.*

"Tyāgarāja says that *Rāma bhakti* is the greatest kingdom one can wish for and the supreme *Brahmānanda* one should attain.

In *Suddabangala rāga*, *Ādi tāla*, he sings:
"*Rāmabhakti Sāmrajyame mānavula kabbeno manasa*" [22]

The rise of the *Bhakti* movement and the *Bhāgavata Sāmpradāya* popularized this path of musical devotion all over the country. The book of this school says that the devotees must do the worship of the Lord with song and dance as *Nitya-Karma.* This belief is elaborately set forth, with illustrative stories, both in the Linga Purāṇa and in the *Adbhuta Rāmāyaṇa.*[23]

Tyāgarāja's musical contribution is remarkable for its quantity and variety, as much as for its quality. The highest musical excellence is found in his compositions, which we have come to call *Kṛitīs,* in, which he captured and effectively picturised the essence of *Rāgas.*

Tyāgarāja is stated to have composed thousands of *Kṛitīs* but only about 700 *Kṛitīs* are available now. According to *Nārada's Bhakti Sūtras* there are eleven types of devotion in which '*kīrtana*' are treated as *Bhakti. Tyāgarāja* took up this path of devotion and made the *Kṛitī* the sole vehicle for all the species of music current in his time.

Tyāgarāja, a confirmed *Rāmabhakta* has sung on several other deities with equal devotional fervour and his songs addressed to *Rāma*, however, stand in a class of their own. A mystical rapture appears to have seized him at the very thought of *Rāma*, conversing with his *Iṣta Dēvata* on an equal plane, now pleading with Him as a devotee, now reproaching Him for His slighting him and now assuming the role of a *Nāyaki* and communicating his love for him."[24]

What if sages like *Vālmiki* and other poets have described you, Oh *Rāma* excellently and in a manner that true devotees of yours applaud? Could my yearning cease for that reason? I feel the appointed service of my life is to sing your glory.

"Ē Paniko janminchitinani nannencha valadu
Sri Rāma neSripati Sri Rāmachandra
Ni Chittamunaku teliyada ne Vālmikadi munulu narulu
ninnu Varninchiri nayasa diruna Melmiyai yundunu sadbhaktulu
Meccudure Tyāgarājanuta!ne" [25]

The songs and references cover every aspect of the art, musical criticism, elucidation of musical concepts, the best way to practice music, music as a help to spiritual effort and above all, music itself as *Yoga* and a *Siddhi*, a path and a realisation. In his *Srirañjani* piece:

"Sogasuga mridanga tālamu jatagurci
ninu sokkajeyu dhirudevvado"
in *Sri Ranjani rāga, Rûpaka tāla.*[26]

Tyāgarāja declares in the *Kṛitī*, that music is *yoga.* "Music which is composed of the seven svaras is a treasure for the great *tapasvins* (ascetics) who have cooled the *tāpatraya* (the world of involvement. *Mokṣa* is impossible for one who has no music in him.

"*Sri pāpriya Sangītopāsana Cheyave O' manasa. in Athāṇa, rāga, Ādi- Tāla.*"[27]

Tyāgarāja says that music, without devotion, would lead one astray, that music is something high that great sages and saints have practiced and that its real efficacy is known only to a person knowing the right and wrong and the worthlessness of worldly things, and one who has subdued his defects and the six inner enemies: passion, anger, avarice, delusion, elation, and intolerance.

"*Sangītā jnānamu bhakti vina*
Sanmārga mu galade? Manasa
Bhrngi Natesa SamiRāja Ghataja
Matanga Nārada dulupasinchu
Nyanyayamulu delusunu jagamulu
Mayamayamanī delusunu durguna
Kayajadi sadripula jayinchu
Kayamu delusunu, Tyāgarājuniki."[28]

It is not *Bhajana* as such but true *Bhajana* of the Lord that is the means of welfare in the hereafter-*Paraloka Sādhana*; such true *bhajana* is what one does without lust, avarice, delusion and other sins and it is such bhajana that is the effective antidote of the ills of mundane life and the Transmigratory cycle.

> *"Smaralobha mohadi pāpulanu*
> *smariyinchake Sri Rāmabhajana*
> *para loka Sādhaname manasa"* [29]

He propounds that until sunsets, everybody should worship Rāma. He sings in *Todi rāga, Chāpu tāla:*

> *"Proddu poyyeni Sri Rāmuni bhajimpave manasa;*
> *Niddura cheta konnallu,*
> *visaya buddhula cheta konnallu."* [30]

His *Vedantic* notion of ultimate reality of life is reiterated in following lines in *Manirang rāga, Ādi tāla,*

> *"Kānidi rādu surasurla kaina Ponidi podu bhusurula kaina."* [31]

According to *karma* theory of Indian Philosophy, one should get the result according to his deeds.

> *"Adigi sukahamu levaranubhavinchithi rā"* [32]

Tyāgarāja has chosen *Jñāna-Mārga* or *Jñāna-Yoga. Advaita* doctrine says revelation leads to liberation. In *Tyāgarāja's* words,

> *"Manta lēkunda vanta ela kādo,*
> *Jnānam lēkunda mokṣamu rādu."* [33]

"The *Prahlāda Bhakti Vijayam* does not depict the usual story of *Prahlāda* but contain *Tyāgarāja's* imaginary version in which even the *Narasimha* does not figure. Similarly, the *Nauka Charitram* describes as episode in which the *gopīs* of *Gokulam* take young *Kṛṣṇa* on a boating excursion on the *Yamuna.* How *Kṛṣṇa* humbles their pride and makes them surrender to Him unconditionally has been depicted in delightful verse and song."[34]

Another noteworthy feature about the music of *Tyāgarāja* is that it is full of '*Bhāva*', the *rāga* chosen for the song aptly conveys the emotion expressed by the *sāhityam* (lyric). In particular, the pieces of *Tyāgarāja* reflecting '*karunarasa*' are matchless for their excellence, and remind one of the poet's observations. 'Our sweetest songs are those that tell us of saddest thought'.

The emotion is portrayed in a variety of shades. To take a few examples; in "*Chalamēla ra*", *Tyāgarāja* implores *Rāma* not to be angry with him. In "*Manamuleda*" he charges him with lack of sympathy for his own men. In "*Noremi*", he blames himself for his unworthy conduct. In "*Erāmuni*" he gives himself up to despair. An infinite variety of shades of emotion are well brought out in these songs. Now the unique feature about *Tyāgarāja's* music is that the melody of his songs is itself suggestive of the meaning of the '*sāhityam*', the *rasa* and the *rāga.*" [35]

V. Gouri Rammohan observes:

> "*Tyāgarāja's* was a subjective intermixture of self-conversational, interrogative type. *Tyāgarāja* appeared to have been in direct conversation with *Rāma*."[36]

Tyāgarāja sings:

"Nannu vidachi kadalakura "(Ritigoula rāga)
which means 'do not leave me and go'[37]
"Nanu palimpaga nadachi vachithiva" (Mohana rāga),
means 'have you come walking to save me?[38]

"Bhaktuni Charitamu (Begada rāga, Ādi-Tāla)
describes the outstanding characteristics of a real *Bhakti.*

Tyāgarāja expressed his devotion by words and deeds, and he gave a deeper thinking and a cognitive structure to devotional aspects such as qualities of a devotee. He expressed his thoughts and feelings, about others who did not know the real devotional path. A number of his compositions stand as examples about such lamentations.

T.S. Pardhasaradhi observes:

> "*Tyāgarāja* was a great river into which the noblest traditions of music, *bhakti* and renunciation flowed. In the depths of his nature he was preoccupied with the mystery of God and the Soul's yearning for redemption. His vision and songs reveal the conception he formed of the attributes of God the redeemer."[39]

To illustrate the Nine Forms of *Bhakti*; K Vasudevacharya has drawn a comparative study of *Sri Tyāgarāja* and *Sri Purandra Dāsa* with their compositions respectively. It goes like this:

Comparative Study of Sri Tyāgarāja and Sri Purandara's Compositions on Nine Forms of Bhakti

Nine Forms of Bhakti	*Sri Purandara Compositions*	*Sri Tyāgarāja Compositions*
Śhrvanam	*Katha Śrvana mado*	*Rāmakatha sudhi*
Kīrtanam	*Harināma kīrtane*	*Aathade dhanyudi nāma Kīrtanapādu*
Smaranam	*Smaranavode salade*	*Smarane sukhamu*
Pādasevanam	*Bide ninna pādava*	*Sre Rāmapādama*
Archanam	*karāgaleradu ninnarchisali*	*Nāmakusum*
Vandanam	*Śarnu ninagembe*	*Vandanumu raghunandana*
Dasyam	*Dasana madiko*	*Dasoham*
Ātmanivedanam	*Matapitaru ninagande maridarenna*	*Swamtamani saroja munu samarpanamujeu*
Sakhyam	*Yandapikombhe*	*Athade.. salpamanayadu* [40]

Two special classes of *Tyāgarāja's* called '*Divyanāma-Kīrtānas* and *Utsava Sāmpradāya Kīrtānas* are more pronouncedly religious in affiliated to worship. The old type of musical form known as *Dvi Dhātu, Tri Dhātu, Chatur Dhātu Prabandhanas* are found in *Tyāgarāja's* compositions e.g., his *Divyanāma Kīrtānas* viz. '*Pāhi,*

Rām Chandra' and '*Shri Raghuvara Dasaratha'* in Śankarābharaṇa *Rāga'* are good examples of '*Dvi Dhātu Prabandhas'*. Similarly the *Kṛitī 'Sarasa Samādāhna'* in *Kapinārayani Rāga* is a good illustration of '*Tridhātu Prabandha*' and the *Kṛitī 'Amba ni Charanamu' Ānand Bhairavi Rāga* is a good place of the *Chaturdhātu Prabandha.*[41]

Shantsheela Sathianathan says:

> "In the compositions of this musical genius we are able to find that the South pursued the ancient traditions of musical forms, which were lost permanently in the musical forms of North India. All his life *Tyāgarāja* adored Lord *Rāmachandra* and poured forth all his music, as an ablation to this incarnation *Viṣṇu According* to his songs Lord *Rāma* had vouchsafed to *Tyāgarāja* that he would reveal himself and bless him with salvation."[42]

On the spiritual heritage of Tyāgarāja it is observed:

"Poetic fancies, learned allusions, moral precepts, enunciation of doctrines, high *Upaniṣadic* truths, condemnation of shame, hypocrisy and false paths, happy similes, worldly wisdom, popular sayings, and above all every shade and mood of religious, devotional and spiritual experience-renunciations of worldly good and the flattery of the rich, prayer, plaintive pleading, yearning, anguish, remonstrance, sportive rebuke, despair dejection, self-depreciation, faith, hope exhilaration, ecstasy of realisation, endearment, joy of service, surrender and dedication, satisfaction at his own devout life, gratitude. These make the songs of *Tyāgarāja*, an endless epic record of the mind of a great *Bhakta* which was, till the end, erupting like a ceaseless volcano."[43]

Pañcaratna refers almost exclusively to the groups of five *kṛitis*, composed by *Tyāgarāja*. He has six sets of *Kṣētra Pañcaratna kṛitis* to his credit on the presiding deities of five *Kṣēṭra,*

1). Tiruvaiyāru 2). Tiruvottiyûr 3). Govûr

4). Lalgudi and 5). Śrirañgam.

Tyāgarāja has to his credit a total number of 44 *Kṣētra kṛitis.*

Tyāgarāja's kṛitis may be broadly classified under the following heads:

1. *Kṛitis* in praise of *Narasimha, Rāma Laksmana Sīta, Hanumān, Śiva , Ambika, Gaṇapati, Subrahmanya, Tulsi, etc.,* The *Pañcaratna* group in the five *ghana rāgas*, *Nāta, Gaula*, Ārabhi, *Varāli* and *Srirāga.*
2. *Divya nāma Kirtanas.*
3. *Utsava Sāmpradāya Kīrtānas*
4. *Prahlāda Bhakti Vijayam* in five acts with 45. *Kṛitis* set in 28 *rāgas* and 132 verses in Telugu. 6.*Nauka Caritram* in one act with 21 *Kṛitis* set in 13 *rāgas* and 45 verses in Telugu.
5. *Prahlāda Bhakti Vijayam* in five acts with 45. *Kṛitis* set in 28 *rāgas* and 132 verses in Telugu.
6. *Nauka Caritram* in one act with 21 *kṛitis* set in 13 *rāgas* and 45 verses in Telugu.

Pañcaratnas comprise group of 5 *kṛitis*
each with greatness of the number five.[44]

1. *Pañcaratnas* denote the five functions of the universe *Śriṣṭi, Sthiti, Laya, Tirobhava* and *Anugraha. Lord Vināyaka* holds these *Pañcakriyas* in his five hands and hence is known as '*Ainkaran*'.
2. Our sensory organs are five in number called *Pañcendriyas.*
3. *Bhûtas* are five in number i.e., *Pañcabhûtas.* They are *Pṛthivi, Appu, Tēyu, Vāyu* and *Ākāśa.*
4. The five *Bijakṣaras* of *Mantraśastra* are *Om, Aim, Hrim, Klim* and *Saum.*
5. The possessor of *Pañcabanas* Goddess *Ambica* is called *Pañcabaneśvari.*
6. *Manmatha's banas* are five in number: *Aravinda, Asoka, Chuta, Navamallika* and *Nilotapala*

7. In *Smārta sāmpradāya* daily worship is done to five *dēvathas*. This *Pañcayatana pûja* is to *Śiva, Viṣnu, Sûrya, Gaṇapathi* and *Dēvi.*
8. *Pañcagavyas* consists of milk, curd, ghee, *gomûtra* and *gomaya.*
9. The reputed *Pańcapatras are chuta, bilva, amalaka, kuṣa, and apamarga*
10. *Pañcabhakaṣyas are Bhakṣya, Bhoja, Lehya, Chohya and Paniya.*
11. In *Karnataka* the *Pañcalinga darṣana* at *Tālakkadu* is held sacred
12. The five important rhythmic phrase groups in music - *Nāgabandha, Swastika, Alanga, Śudha* and *samaskalika* - are said to have emerged from the five faces of *Lord Śiva - Sadyojata, Vāmadēva, Aghore, Tatpruṣa* and *Iṣāna* respectively.
13. The notes of music scales are also believed to have emanated from *Lord Śiva's* five faces. *Tyāgarāja* makes this clear in the *carana* of his *Cittaranjani kṛiti*, '*Nādatanumanisam*'.
14. *Pañcamaha Śabda* refers to the music played during royal processions to the accompaniment of the five instruments - Trumpet, *Tambura*, Conch-shell, kettledrum and gong
15. Among the *Navagrahas*, the number ascribed to *Budha* is five. *Budha* means learned and He is the giver of wisdom
16. The *Pañcamukha vadyam* for which *Tiruvārur* is famous is a five-faced drum.

Temple Kṛtis of Tyāgarāja[45]

Tiruvaiyaāru Pañcaratnam:

The Tamil word '*Aiyāru*' means five rivers. *Tiruvaiyāru* is in the midst of five rivers, *Kāveri, Arasalār, Vennāru, Vadayār* and *Kadamurutti.* So the Lord of the place has taken the name *PańcanAdia (Pranatarthihara).*

Tyagaraja's Pańcaratna kṛitis on this deity are:

No.	*Kṛitis*	*Rāga*	*Tāla*
1.	*Sarivedalina*	*Āsāvari*	*Ādi*
2.	*Illalo Pranatārthi hara*	*Athāna*	*Ādi*
3.	*Ehi TrijagĀdiṣa*	*Sāranga*	*Chāpu*
4.	*Muchata Brahmādulaku*	*Madhyamāvati*	*Ādi*
5.	*Evarunnaru*	*Mālavasri*	*Ādi*

Tyāgarāja's two sets of *Pañcaratna kṛitis* on Goddess *Dharmasamvardhini* are:

No.	*Kṛitis*	*Rāga*	*Tāla*
1.	*Bāle Bālendu*	*Ritigaula*	*Ādi*
2.	*Amma Dharmasamvardhani*	*Athana*	*Ādi*
3.	*Vidhicakrādulaku*	*Yamunākalyāṇi*	*Rūpaka*
4.	*Śive pāhimam*	*Kalyāṇi*	*Ādi*
5.	*Karuṇa Judavamma*	*Todi*	*Ādi*

No.	*Kṛitis*	*Rāga*	*Tāla*
1.	*Innalla vale*	*Deśiyatodi*	*Chāpu*
2.	*Māravairi*	*Nāsika bhuṣani*	*Rūpaka*
3.	*Nannukanna talli*	*Kesari*	*Deśādi*
4.	*Parasakti*	*Sāveri*	*Ādi*
5.	*Nivu brovavale*	*Sāveri*	*Ādi*

Govūr Pañcaratnas:

These *Pañcaratnas* are all in the praise of *Lord Sundarēśa.*

No.	*Kṛitis*	*Rāga*	*Tāla*
1.	*Sambho mahadeva*	*Pantuvarāli*	*Rūpaka*
2.	*Korisevimparāre*	*Kharaharapriya*	*Ādi*
3.	*Sundarsvaruni*	*Śankarābharaṇa*	*Ādi*
4.	*Ivasudha nivanti*	*Śahana*	*Ādi*
5.	*Nammi vachina nannu*	*Kalyāṇi*	*Rūpaka*

Tiruvottriyûr Pañcaratnas:

These Pañcaratnas are all in the praise of Dēvi Tripurasundari.

No.	*Kritis*	*Rāga*	*Tāla*
1.	*Dārini telusukonti*	*Śudha Sāveri*	*Ādi*
2.	*Sundari ni*	*Kalyāṇi*	*Ādi*
3.	*Kannathalli*	*Sāveri*	*Ādi*
4.	*Sundari nannidārilo*	*Bēgada*	*Rūpaka*
5.	*Sundari Ninnu*	*Ārabhi*	*Miṣra Chāpu*

The *Śrirañgam Pañcaratnas* alone are on the *Vaiṣṇavite* deity, *Lord Rañganatha. Śrirangam* is the most celebrated among the '*Svam vyakta' Kṣētras.* In *Tamil Periya Koil* refers only to *Śrirangam* and the Lord is worshipped as *Periya Perumal.*

The five *kṛitis* are:

No.	*Kṛitis*	*Rāga*	*Tāla*
1.	*Jûthamurārē*	*Ārabhi*	*Rûpaka*
2.	*Vinarādana*	*Dēvagāndhāri*	*Dēsādi*
3.	*Rajuvedala*	*Todi*	*Rûpaka*
4.	*Karunajudavayya*	*Saranga*	*Ādi*
5	*O Rañgasayi*	*Kāmbhodi*	*Ādi*

Lālgudi Pañcaratnas

In this *Pañcaratna* Tyāgarāja composed the first two *kṛtis* on the Lord *Saptarṣisvara* and the next three on the Goddess, *Pravṛddya Śrimati.*

No.	*Kṛitis*	*Rāga*	*Tāla*
1.	*Iśa Pahimam*	*Kalyāṇi*	*Rûpaka*
2.	*Dēvasri*	*Madhyamāvati*	Triputa
3.	*Mahitha Paaruddhe*	*Kāmbhodhi*	*Chāpu*
4.	*Gathinivani*	*Todi*	*Ādi*
5.	*Lalithe Śripraviddhē*	*Bhairavi*	*Ādi*

Tyāgarāja's Pañcaratna Kīrthanas

As there were some critics who used to propaganda against *Tyāgarāja* that he was only a devotee of *Rāma* but not a Classical pandit, *Tyāgarāja* composed his firtst *Kīrthana* '*Jagadānandakāraka*' in *Nāta rāga, Adi tāla,* which expounded his great command and mastery over Classical Music. In his second *Kīrthana*, '*Dudukugala Nannelu dora koduku brochura*' in *Goula rāga, Ādi tāla, Tyāgarāja* critisised the arrogant nature of some Classical pandits in his time. In his third *Kīrthana, 'Sādhinchene O manasa', Ārabhi rāga, Ādi tāla* and fourth *Kīrthana 'Kanakanaruchira', Varāli rāga, Ādi tāla, Tyāgarāja* sang about the incarnations of *Sri Rāma* and expressed his ardent devotion towards his Deity. In his fifth *Kīrthana, 'Endaro mahānubhāvulu andariki vandanamulu', Sri rāga, Ādi tāla,* he expressed his deep respect and regard towards all the great people around him who were devotees of his favourite deity, *Rāma.*[46]

Tyāgarāja's kṛiti in *Hindola rāga* became popular and brought name to the particular *raga:*

> *"Sāmajavaragamana*
> *Sādhuhruthsārasābjapāla*
> *kālāthitha vikyātha!*
> *Sāmani gamajasudhāmaya gāna*
> *vichakṣaṅa guna sheela*
> *dayālavāla māmpālaya!*
> *Vedashiromathruja sapthasvara*
> *nādachaladeepa!*
> *Svikṛutha yâdavakula- Muralivādana*
> *vinodamohanākāra!*
> *Tyāgarāja vandaneeya."*[47]

There is a tradition that the Classical sigers starts their concert with *tāna varṇa* or *ata tāna varṇa* or a *Kīrthana* in praise of *Gaṇapathi. Tyāgarāja* coposed a *Kīrthana* in praise of *Gaṇapathi*. in *Souraṣtra rāga,* which is being presented in many concerts even now.

> *"Śri Gaṇapathi. nī sevimparāre –*
> *Śritha mānavulara Śri Gana!*

Vāgādhipādi supujalachekoni –
bāga natimpunu vedalina Śri!
Panasanāri kelādi jambuphalamulāraginchi
ghanatha rambuganu mahipai!
Ghallu Ghalluna nunchi anyamu
Hari charana yugayugamula!
Hridayāmbuna nunchi vinayamunanu
Tyāgarāja vinuthudu!
Vividha gathula Dithalāngumani vedalina Śri."[48]

Different Rāgas rendered by Tyāgarāja in Devotinal Aspect

The following are the *rāgas* rendered in devotional aspect:

Ābheri, Ābhogi, Āhiri, Amrithavarşini, Ānandabhairavi, Andhali, Āndholika, Ārabhi, Āsāveri, Athāna, Bahudāri, Bālahamsa, Bāngala, Begada, Bhairavam, Bhairavi, Bhauli, Bhavapriya, Bhinnashadja, Bhushavali, Bilahari, Brindavanaāsranga, Chakravāka, Chandrajyothi, Chārukesi, Chayanāta, Chenchukāmbhoji, Chittaranjani, Darbār, Desiyatodi, Devaāgndhari, Devakiriya, Devamanohari, Dipakam, Divyamālati, Gambhiravāni, Gānavaridhi, Gangeyabhushani, Garudadhwani, Goulipantu, Gouri, Gaurimanhohari, Ghanta, Gujjari, Garudapriya, Hamirkalyāṇi, Hamsānandam, Hindola, Hindolavasanta, Ishamanohari, Jaganmohini, Janaranjani, Jayantasri, Jenjhutti, Jhankāradwani, Jhingla, Jujahuli, Kaikavāsi, Kalākanthi, Kalgada, Kalānidhi, Kalāvathi, Kalyānavasantha, Kalyāṇi, Kamalāmonohari, Kāmbhoji, Kānada, Kanakāngi, Kannada, Kannadagoula, Kantāmani, Kāpi, Kāpinarāyani, Karnataka Kāpi, Keādra, Kedāragoula, Kesari, Khamās, Kharaharapriya, Kranavali, Kiravani, Kokiladwani, Kokilapriya, Kokilaravam, Kolahalam, Kuntālavarali, Kuranji, Latāngi, Madhyamāvathi, Malavasri, Mālavi, Malayamārutham, Mānavati, Mandāri, Manirang, Manjari, Manoranjani, Margahindola, Maruvadhanyāsi, Māyāmālavagoula, Mohana, Mukhāri, Nabhomani, Nādachintāmani, Nādanāmakriya, Nādatarangini, Nāgagāndhāri, Nāganandini, Nāgaswaravali, Nāgavarangini, Nalinakanti, Nāryanadeshakshi, Narāyani, Nasikabhushini, Nāta, Natakuranji, Navanitham, Navarasakannada, Nilāmbari, Panthuvarāli, Phalamanjari,

Pharāz, Pratapavarāli, Punnagavarāli, Purnachandrika, Purānalalitha, PurviKalyāṇi, Rāgapancharam, Rāmapriya, Ranjani, Ratnāngi, Ravichandirka, Revagupti, Rishmapriya, Ritugoula, Sahana, Sāma, Śankarābharaṇam, Sāramati, Sāranga, Sārangi, Saraswati, Saraswatimanohari, Sougandhini, Sāveri, Śdvidhamargini, Śanmukhapriya, Sidhasena, Simhendramadhyama, Simhavāhini, Sindhuramakriya, Srirāga, Sriranjani, Srutiranjani, Subhapantuvarāli, Subhoshini, Sudhabāngla, Sudhadesi, Sudhadhanyāsi, SudhaSāveri, Śudhasimantini, Sulini, Suprādipam, Surutti, Suryakantham, Svarabhushani, Svarāvali, Takka, Tivravahini, Todi, Umabharanam, Vāchaspati, Vāgadhisvari, Vakulābharanam, Vanaspati, Varāli, Vasanta, Vasantabhairavi, Vasantavarāli, Vardhani, Vegavāhini, Vijayasri, Vijayavasanta, Viravasanta, Vivardhini, Yadukulakāmbhoji, Yamuna Kalyāṇi.[49]

Tyāgarāja is verily the 'tone-poet of humanity'. With minimum means of execution, he has given maximum melodic expression. The *kṛitis* of *Tyāgarāja* couched in dignified prose though appear simple and tiny, assume, when rendered, a magnificent melodic proportion and each *kṛiti* leaves scope for being dealt and interpreted in a very exhaustive manner. His handling of rare *apurva rāgas* served to immortalize them. *Nalinakānti, Umabharanam, Candra jyoti* and many others live through his songs.

"The highly *rakti rāgas* have been defined by his *kṛitis* in a most ideal manner. The use of medium tempo, fewer words, employment of easy time measures and above all, a very clear picture of the *rāga* depicted in an impressive manner are considered the charm of his compositions. They have the fundamental resources to enchant, inspire and please the listeners. His *kṛitis* are profusely used in *Bhajans* and *Harikatha kālakṣepa.*[50]

"The infinite play of imagination and originality is evident in him more than in other composers. In fashioning a variety of expressive forms in well-known melodies or in newly invented melodies, "In several respects, the genius of *Karnataka* music may be in the perfecting of the form of composition called *kṛiti* and enriching it with inventive elements, in the poetry and philosophy of the text of the songs, in all these, he stands out as the foremost tone-poet and as the single complete example of the genius of *Karnataka* music at its best and highest."[51]

Muthuswāmi Dīkṣitār (1775-1835)

Muthuswāmi Dīkṣitār, the youngest of the musical Trinity of South Indian Music, was born in 1775 at *Tiruvarur* in Tamil Nadu. He visited different places of pilgrimage at a young age. When he was fifteen, he accompanied a saint called *Chidambaranātha Yogi* to Vāranasi to study philosophy. When he was in *Banarus,* one day *Chidambaranātha Yogi* took him to *Annapurna's* temple and told him that the Goddess had blessed him and advised him to worship her daily all through his life and taught him that she would liberate him from the cycle of birth and death. The next day, when he was going for a dip in the Ganges, the *Yogi* told him when he bathe in Ganges, he might find something and he asked him to bring that along with him. When Muthuswāmi Dīkṣitār was bathing he found a *Veeṇā* and on it was written *'Rāma'*. He brought it and gave it to the *yogi*. *Chidambaranātha*, his *guru*, blessed and gave it back to *Muthuswāmi Dīkṣitār,* saying that the Goddess Ganga had presented the *Veeṇā* to him and he would become a great *Vaiṇika* and *Vaggeyakāra* in future.[52]

He was true *Advaitin* and *Jñāni*. He was steeped in the *Vedānta* as interpreted by Śankarācārya and that may be summed up thus: 'The creator, the parabrahma, is one and omnipotent; He transcends name and form; all the deities worshipped are only manifestations of the *Parabrahman*; the object of their worship is to enable us to withdraw our minds from attachment to the material world and concentrate upon form conceived as divine; the *Saguṇopāsana (*worship of personal God) is but a step in the realization of *Nirguṇa Brahman* (Impersonal Absolute) within us.

'One day *Chengalvorāya (skanda)* presented himself before his devotee as a *Mahāpuruṣa* (noble being) and said to him "Friend! Open thy mouth." *Muthuswāmi Dīkṣitār* did so fully aware of the Divine presence before him. A piece of sugar candy was left in his mouth and the vision melted away before his eyes. All at once *Muthuswāmy Dīkṣitār* felt a new force swelling up from the inner most depths of his Being and all unconsciously, even as the sage *Vālmiki* of yore, burst forth into a hymn of praise. It manifested itself as *Kīrtana* in *Rāga Malavagowla* opening with "*Sree Nathadi Guru Guha jayavathi.*'[53]

The lyrical values and scholarly descriptions of his deity show in his each and every *Kṛitī* or *kīrtana*. The following *Kṛitī* in *Śankarābharaṇa rāga, Ādi tāla,* expresses his master presentation:

"Akṣyalingavibho svayambho –
Akhiālnda koti prabho - pahiṣambho;
Akṣara svarupa amitha prathāpa –
Arudha vruṣavahajaganmoha-
Dakṣha sikṣana daṣathara!
Suralakṣana vidhi vilakṣana –
lakṣana bahuvichakṣana sudhābhakṣana guru katākṣa vikṣana!
Badari vanamula Nayikā sahitha
-Bhadra kālika bhaktavihita –
madanajanakādi deva duhita māāy kārya kalana rahita-
Sadaya guruguhatata gunathitha
sadujanopetha śankara navaneetha hrudaya
vrutha thumburu Sangita –
Hrinkara sambhutha hemagirinadha –
sadashrita kalpaka mahiruhapadambujayuga radhagajathurāga –
padādi samyutha chaithrothsava sadāśiva sachidānanda // "[54]

"A scrutiny of *Muthuswāmi Dīkṣitār's* compositions shows that he was a zealous pilgrim with an insatiable thirst for visiting sacred places and singing the praises of the deities enshrined there. There is hardly any song, which does not describe a temple, the deity worshipped there and the traditions and customs prevalent, locally."[55]

Muthuswāmi Dīkṣitār's Kṣētra Kṛitis

Muthuswāmi Dīkṣitār composed his first song at Tiruttani, which is one of the six famous abodes of *Lord Muruga*. His *kṛiti* was followed by seven *kṛitis* on *Guruguha* in seven other *Vibhaktis:*[56]

No.	*Kṛiti*	*Rāga*
1.	*Manasaguruguha rûpam*	*Ānandabhairavi*
2.	*Sri Guruna*	*Pādi*
3.	*Guruguhaya*	*Sāma*
4.	*Guruguhadanyam*	*Bālahamsa*
5.	*Guruguhasya*	*Pûrvi*
6.	*Guruguhaswāmini*	*Bhānumati*
7.	*Sri Guruguhamûrte*	*Udayaravichandrika*

At Tirupati Dīkṣitār composed the songs '*Śesācalanāyakam*' in *Varāli rāga* and '*Sri venkatagiriśam*' in *Surati rāga* in praise of Lord *Venkateśvara*. In praise of *Vāyu Linga*, he composed the songs '*Kālahastiśa*' in *Huseni rāga* and '*Jnānaprasunāmbike*' in *Kalyāni rāga* in praise of the goddess at *Kālahsti*.

The compositions of Dīkṣitār at *Kānchipuram* in praise of the deities *Kāmākṣi, Ekāmreśvara, Varadarāja* and *Kailasanātha* are the following:

No.	*Kṛiti*	*Rāga*
1.	*Kāmākṣi mam pāhi*	*Śudhadeṣi*
2.	*Ekāmreśvaranāyikē*	*Karnātaka Śudhasāveri*
3.	*Ekāmranātham bhajeham*	*Gamakakriya*
4.	*VaradarājamUpāsamahe*	*Sāranga*
5.	*Kailasanāthena*	*Kāmbhoji*
6.	*Kailasanāthena*	*Vē*gavāhini

His influence is clearly reflected in many of his songs on *Lord Rāma*. In his composition, '*Rāmacandrena samrakṣitoham*' in *Manji rāga*, *Rāma* is described as the embodiment of the *Trimurti*. At *Tiruvottriyur*, he composed '*Ādipurisvaram*' in *Ārabhi rāga* in praise of the presiding deity '*Ādipurisvara*' and song '*Tripurasundari*' in *Sāma rāga* in praise of the goddess of the place.

At Chidambaram, where the Lord manifests himself as the *Ākāsha Linga, he* composed his next *Pañcabhūta kṛiti* '*Ānanda natana prakāṣam*' in *Kedara rāga*. Other songs composed by him at Chidambaram are:

No.	Kṛiti	Rāga
1.	*Śivakāmeṣvaram*	*Kalyāni*
2.	*Śivakāmeṣvaram*	*Ārabhi*
3.	*Kanakasabhāpatim*	*Mālavasri*
4.	*Govindarājam*	*Mukhāri*
5.	*Govindarājena*	*Mechabhauli*

In praise of goddess *Abhayāmba* at *Māyavaram*, he has composed *kṛitis* in different *vibhaktis* known as *Abhayamāba Navavarna kṛitis*.

They are:

No.	Kṛiti	Rāga
1.	*Abhayāmba jagadāmba*	*Kalyāni*
2.	*Abhayāmba mām*	*Bhairavi*
3.	*Girijaya Ajaya*	*Śankarābharana*
4.	*Abhayāmbikāyah*	*Yadukulakāmbhoji*
5.	*Abhayāmbikāyah*	*Kedaragoula*
6.	*Ambikāyah abhayāmbhikāyah*	*Kedaragoula*
7.	*Abhayāmbikāyam*	*Śahana*
8.	*Dākṣayani*	*Todi*
9.	*Abhayāmba Ninnu*	*Manipravala*

At his birthplace, *Tiruvārur,* where he stayed many years, he composed three groups of *vibhakti kṛitis* on the deities of the *Tiruvārur* temple. The most famous of these *vibhakti kṛitis* are the *Kamalāmba navavarna kṛitis.*

They are:

No.	Kṛiti	Rāga
1.	*kamalāmbike*	*Todi*
2.	*Kamalāmba samrakṣatu*	*Ānandabhairavi*
3.	*Kamalāmbam bhajare*	*Kalyāni*
4.	*Sri kamalāmbikāya*	*Śankarābharaṇa*
5.	*Kamalāmbikeyai*	*Kāmbhoji*
6.	*Śri kamalāmbikāyah*	*Bhairavi*
7.	*kamalāmbikayastava*	*Punnāgavarāli*
8.	*Śri kamalāmbikāyam bhaktim*	*Śahana*
9.	*Śri kamalāmbike ava ava*	*Ghanta*
10.	*Śri kamalāmba jayati*	*Āhiri*
11.	*Śri kamalāmbike*	*Śri*

The second group of *Vibhakti kṛitis* in praise of Lord *Tyāgarāja,* the presiding deity of the *Tiruvārur* temple.

They are:

No.	Kṛiti	Rāga
1.	*Tyāgarāja virājate*	*Athāna*
2.	*Tyāgarāja bhajare*	*Yadukulakāmbhoji*
3.	*Tyāgarāja Samrakṣitoham*	*Salagabhairavi*
4.	*Tyāgarāja namaste*	*Begada*
5.	*Tyāgarājodanyam*	*Darbār*
6.	*Śri Tyāgarāja bhakto*	*Rudrapriya*
7.	*Tyāgarāja kṛitya kṛitim*	*Sāranga*
8.	*Viravasanta Tyāgarāja*	*Viravasanta*

The third group of *Vibhakti kṛitis* is in praise of goddess *Nīlotpalāmba* of the same temple. They are:

No.	Kṛiti	Rāga
1.	*Nīlotpalāmba jayati*	*Nārāuanagaula*
2.	*Nīlotpalāmba bhajare*	*Ritugaula*
3.	*Nīlotpalāmbikāya*	*Kannadagaula*
4	*Nīlotpalāmbikāya*	*Kedaragaula*
5	*Nīlotpalāmbikāyah*	*Gaula*
6.	*Nīlotpalāmbāya stava*	*Māyāmālavagaula*
7.	*Nīlotpalāmbikāyam*	*Purvagaula*
8	*Nīlotpalāmbike*	*Chāyāgaula*

Kṛitis on five *Śiva Lingas:*

No.	Kṛiti	Rāga
1.	*Acaleṣvara*	*Bhupāla*
2.	*Hatakesvara*	*Bilahari*
3.	*Valmikeṣvara*	*Kāmbhoji*
4	*Anandeṣvara*	*Ānandabhairavi*
5	*Siddheṣvara*	*Gaula*
6.	*Nīlotpalāmbāya stava*	*Nilāmbari*

Mantra Śastra is an esoteric lore but even the common devotees irrespective of status and learning can derive its benefits if it comprises ordinary hymns and songs. *Dīkṣitār's Navagraha Kṛitis* are easily accessible versions of *Mantra* and *Tantra Śastras* and they are pertaining to different planets. *Dīkṣitār's Navagraha Kṛitis* on different planets:

No.	Kṛiti	Rāga	Tāla	Planet
1.	*Sûryamûrte*	*Saurastra*	*Dhruva*	*Sun*
2.	*Chandra bhaje*	*Asāveri*	*Marthya*	*Moon*
3.	*Angārakam*	*Surati*	*Rûpaka*	*Mars*
4	*Budhāmasrayāma*	*Natakuranji*	*Jampe*	*Mercury*
5.	*Brhaspate*	*Athāna*	*Triputa*	*Jupiter*
6.	*Sri Sukra*	*Pharaz*	*Ata*	*Venus*
7.	*Divākara*	*Yadukula Kambhoji*	*Eka*	*Saturn*
8.	*Smarāmyaham*	*Rāmamanohari*	*Rûpaka*	*Rahu*
9.	*Mahāsuram*	*Camaram*	*Rûpaka*	*Ketu*

Kṛitis on goddess *Minākṣi* and *Madhurāmba:*

No.	*Kṛiti*	*Rāga*
1.	*Minākṣi memudam*	*Gamakakriya*
2.	*Māmava Minākṣi*	*varāli*
3.	*Śri Minākṣi*	*Gouri*
4	*Śri Madhurāpuri*	*Bilahari*
5.	*Kādambari Priyāyai*	*Mohana*
6.	*Madhurāmba Samraksatu*	*Devakriya*
7.	*Madhurāmba Bhajare*	*Stavarāja*
8.	*Śri Madhurāmbikaya*	*Atāna*
9.	*Śri Madhurāmbikāyai*	*Kalyani*
10.	*Madhurāmbaya*	*Begada*
11.	*Madhurāmbikayam*	*Desi Simhārva*
12.	*Madhurāmba jayati*	*Pharaz*

Dīkṣitār's Kīrtana in *Hamsadhvani rāga, Ādi tāla*, gives importance for *Bhajana:*

"Vāthapi Gṇaapathim bhaje ham-
Vāthapi Gṇaapathim bhaje;
Vāraṇasyam vara pradam sree!
BhuthĀdi samsevitha charaṇam -
Butha bhouthika prapancha bharaṇam;
Veetharagiṇam vinuthayogiṇam
Vīsva kāraṇam vighnavāraṇam!
Purkāumbha sombhavamunivara –
prapugitham thrikona madhyagatham –
Murāri pramukhādi sevitham –
mulādhara kshetrāsthitam –
parādii chatvarivāāgthmakam –
praṇavāswarupa vakrathundam –
Nirantharam nitāla Chandra khandam –
nija vāmakara - vidhruthekshudandam –

karāmbhujapasha bijapuram –
kalushaviduram bhuthākaram –
anādi guruguha thoshita bimbam –
Hamsadwani bhushita herambam //"[57]

Muthuswāmi Dīkşitār's style of writing was more descriptive, highlighting the characteristics of his deity.

"*Nilakantham Bhajeham - sathātham - nirājasnĀdinutham;*
Bālakuchamba - sahitham - bālachandra sevitham.
śeela guruguha pujitham - srikadambavananadam //
Akşaya rupakkhanda - kaverithirotharabhimukham –
panchamukha -rakşitha bhakta pramukham –
naşkathra shekharam - namrupa vichithram –
dakşakaramishvaram - kedara goula priyakaram –
dakinaşkashipuram - dandithakamathripuram –
dakşadhvaraharam haram dayakaram kamalakaram //"[58]

He praises and worships *Dēvi Sarasvathi* in his *Kṛitī,* in *Āarabhi rāga, Rūpaka tāla:*

Sri Sarasvathinomostute - varade vara dēvathe -
Sripathi gouri guruguhavunuthe - Vīdhiyuvathe;"[59]

"*Muthuswāmi Dīkşitār's Navavarņa Kṛitīs* and *Navagaraha Kṛitīs* have caught the wide attention of musicians. *Dīkşitār's* compositions of *Navavarņa Kṛitīs* are significant for the following reasons:

1. The nine *Kṛitīs* were composed in nine *vibhaktis* or cases.
2. The nine segments are supposed to be occupied by nine goddesses and each goddess illustrates particular rasa or emotion.
   a) *Aştadala*' padma signifies *Karuna rasa* (pathos).
   b) *Bupura*' signifies '*Sringara*' *rasa* (erotic)
   c) *Śodasadala' padma* signifies '*Vira' rasa.* (heroic).
   d) *Chaturdasara* signifies '*Bhayānaka' rasa* (fear)

e) *Bhahirdasara'* signifies '*Bhibhatsa*' *rasa* (horror)

f) *Antardasara*' signifies '*Roudra' rasa* (anger)

g) *Aṣtakona chakra'* signifies '*Hāsya' rasa* (ludicrous)

h) *Trikona*" signifies '*Vismaya*' or '*Adbhuta' rasa* (wonder)

i) *Bindu*" signifies '*Śānta' rasa* (peace)

Bhāvanpaniṣad mentions the significance of the nine *āvaraṇas*, dwelled by different *Dēvatas* who are active in various aspects of life activities."[60]

On Muthuswāmi Dīkṣitār R. Srinivas observes:

> "Muthuswāmi Dīkṣitār's Kṛitīs we find that there is no trace of incompleteness in the musical moulds adopted by him. The beginning phrases of the *Kṛitīs* are enough to reveal the *Rāga,* in its entirety its fullness, its essence, its uniqueness i.e. all its *Rāgas*, possibilities are there. Some of *Muthuswāmi Dīkṣitār 's* musical edifiecs like '*Bālagopala'* in *Bhairavi Rāga*, *Shri Subrahmanya Namasto'* in *Kambhoji Rāga*, *Akṣay Ling Vibho* in *Śankarabharana Raga*, are eternal monuments. His *Kṛitīs* have the excellence of *Sahityam* also. His compositions are mostly invocations to various deities, which have a deeper significance to students of *Mantra Shāstra, Tantra Shāstra* and *Yoga Shāstra*."[61]

A *Kṛitī* need not necessarily be a medium of giving moral or intellectual instructions or of narrating stories or dilating abstruse philosophies, therefore, the *Kṛitīs* of *Muthuswāmi Dīkṣitār,* which speak simply of the ways along which the inspired soul seeks and makes contact with the Over soul in its multifarious manifestations speak of his super personal attitude.[62]

Dīkṣitār was a multifaceted genius. He was a profound scholar, a poet and composer of the highest order, a master-singer, a natural mystic- one can not easily comprehend how these various elements came to be combined in one individuality in one life.

Different Rāga rendered by Muthuswāmi Dīkṣitār in Devotional Aspect

The following are the *rāgas* rendered in devotional aspect:

Ābheri, Ābhogi, Āhiri, Amrithavarshini, Ānandabhairavi, Andhali, Ārabhi, Āsāveri, Athāna, Bālahamsa, Begada, Bhairavam, Bhairavi, Bhauli, Bhogachyanāta, Bhupāla, Bhushāvali, Bhavāni, Bilahari, Brindavanaāsranga, Chamaram, Chaturangini, Chayagoula, Darbār, Doutapanchamam, Desisimhārāvam, Devaāgndhari, Devakiriya, Devamanohari, Dhanyāsi, Dharmavāti, Dhunibhinnashadja, Dvijavanti, Gamakakriya, Gunasamavarali, gangeyabhushani, Goula, Gourivelavali, Chanta, Gitapriya, Geyahejjuji, Gopikavasanta, Gundakriya, Goulipantu, Gouri, Gujjari, HamirKalyāṇi, Hamsadwani, Hindola, Hindolavasanta, Huseni, Ishamanohari, Jaganmohini, Jenjhutti, Jhankārabhramari, Jivendhika, Jyothi, Kalāvathi, Kalyāṇi, Kamalāmonohari, Kāmbhoji, Kānada, Kanakāmbari, Kannada, Kannadabangla, Kāpi, Kasiramakriya, Kedāra, Kedāragoula, Khamās, Kirānavali, Kiravani, Kumbhini, Kumudakriya, Kuntālam, Kurunji, Kusumakaram, Lalitha, Lalitpanchama, Madhyamāvathi, Malahari, Malavapanchama, Malavasri, Mangalakaishika, Manirang, Manji, Manohari, Manoranjani, Mārgadesi Mārgahindola, Maruva, Māyāmālavagoula, Mechabhouli, Megharanjani, Mohan, Nabhomani, Nādanāmakriya, Nādatarangini, Nāgagāndhāri, Nāganandini, Nāgaswaravali, Nāgabharanana, Nāgagāndhārai, Nāgavarāli, Nāmadesi, Nārāyanadeshākshi, Narayanagoula, Natanārāyani, Naritigaula, Nasamani Nāta, Natabharanam, Nātakuranji, Nilāmbari, Nishāda, Nāyaki, Navaroj, Pādi, Panthuvarāli, Purnapanchamam, Purvagaula, Purvavarāli, PurviKalyāṇi, Purvi, Rāgamālika, Rāmamanohari, Rasamanjari, Ratipriya, Ravikriya, Revagupti, Ritigaula, Rudrapriya, Rupavati, Sahana, Sailadesākahi, Saindhavi, Sāma, Samanta, Śankarābharaṇam, Sāranga, Saraswatimanohari, Sougandhini, Sourāshtra, Sāveri, Subhapantuvarāli, Sudhadesi, Sudhadhanyāsi, SudhaSāveri, Sudhavasanta, Sumanapriya, Surutti, Sumadyuti, Syāmalam, Takka, Tarangini, Todi, Vamsāvati, Varāli,

Vasanta, Vāgavāhini, Vasanta, Vegavahini, Viravasanta, Yadukulakāmbhoji, YamunaKalyāṇi [63]

Dīkṣitār's contributions to music are immortal in nature. He was a prolific composer and a peerless composer of group *Kṛitīs, Navagraha Kṛitīs, Pañchalinga sthala Kṛitīs, Vibhakti Kṛitīs.* His pieces are set in high-flown *Samskṛta* couched in a highly dignified and learned style. They are replete with descriptions of gods and goddesses, *Kṣetramahima*, coupled with *Upaniṣadic* truths. Being a Devi *Upāsaka*, we find in his songs addresses to the Goddess, the truths dealt in *tāntric* and *māntric* philosophy.

"Rhetorical beauties abound in his pieces. He is primarily *Vainika* and hence he has follwed the intrumental mode of *rāga* expression in his songs. He adopted a slow and *vilambita kāla*, and helped him to create living forms of exquisite beauty, noted for their originally par excellence. Each song reads like an elaboration of the *rāga* in its entire form. His compositions are mostly for the richness and beauty with which the *rāga* forms are portrayed."[64]

One finds Tyāgarāja, Dīkṣitār and Śyāma Śāstri, the Trinity o. South Indian classical music, to be true followers of Hindu philosophy, who showed concern for the inner-self and were equally balanced and self-disciplined. They followed the four stages of life, which bind a man's life into a whole according to the Hindu philosophy.

They felt that the four stages, *Brahmacharya* (The stage of the student), *Grihasta* (house holder), *Vanaspathi* (retiring thinker), *Sanyāsi* (forsaking all possessions and emotional entanglements to contemplate on God), are very much necessary for a man to prepare himself for divine path. They followed music as their path for self-realization, which meant God -realization and composed and sang for their favorite Gods in the attainment of Salvation.

Peggy Holroyde promptly says:

> "The long tradition of South India has been such that music was never separated from its religious context in the actual temple; all the great composers were devotees of God in the same way."[65]

"The strong belief and unflinching faith in a personal loving God, combined with a metaphysical view of creation on a cosmic scale is the dominating and all-pervading theme which swells up through the sacred music of the composer-saints such as Purandaradasa, *Tyāgarāja, Svami Tirunal, Muthuswāmi Dīkṣitār* and *Śyāma Śāstri* of South India, *Saint Tukaram, Eknath and Jnāna Das* of Western India, *Guru Nanak, Saint Kabir, Sur Das, Goswami Tulasai Das*, and *Mirabai* of Noth India, *Vidyapati, Jayadēva, Chandi Das, Ramprasad, Kamalakanta, Swami Vivekananda, Rabindranath Tagore, Rājanikanta, Atulprasad, Kazi Nazrul* and *Salabega* of Eastern India."[66]

REFERENCES

1. Deshpande, Vamanrao., *Maharashtra's Contribution to Music*, p.5.
2. Parthasaradhi. S., *Glimpses of Indian Music*, p.200.
3. *The Hindu Speaks On Music*, Compiled by the Editor, p.33.
4. Pardhasaradhi N. C., *Compositions of Śyama Śastri*, p.71.
5. Sundarm Iyer., *Śyāma Śāstri Kṛitīs*, p.45.
6. Iyer & Vidya Sankar., *Kṛitīs of Śyama Śastri*, p.61.
7. Pardhasaradhi. N. C., *Compositions of Śyama Śastri*, p.158.
8. Parthasaradhi. S., *Glimpses of Indian Music*, p.203.
9. *The Hindu Speaks On Music*, Compiled by the Editor, p.34.
10. Shantsheela Sathianathan., *Saints of South India*, Vol-I, pp.215-216.
11. Vidya Shankar., *Shyama Sastry*, p.22.
12. Sambamoorthy, P., *Composers, Cultural Leaders of India*, Government of India, p.50.
13. Annapurna. L, *Music and Temples A Ritualistic Approach*, p.157.
14. *Ibid.*, p.158-159.
15. Gouri Kuppuswami, *Index of South Indian Music*, pp.913-914.
16. Annapurna. L, *Music and Temples A Ritualistic Approach*, p.156.
17. Ram Vani Bai., *Glimpses of Indian Music*, p 125.
18. Radhakrishnan., S, *Foreword to The Spiritual Heritage of Tyagaraja*, p. iv.
19. Parthasaradhi. T.S., *Glimpses of Indian Music*, p.219.
20. *Ibid.*, p.219.

21. Rāmānujāchariyar and Raghavan. V., *The Spiritual Heiritage of Tyāgarāja*, p.59.
22. Parthasarathi., *Sri Tyāgarāja Kṛitīs*, p.150.
23. Sri Ramanujachari, *Music in the Adbutha Ramayana*, Journal of the Madras Music Academy, Vol, XVI, pp. 65-73.
24. Parthasaradhi. T.S., *Glimpses of Indian Music*, p. 223.
25. Ramanujachariar & V. Raghavan., *The Spiritual Heritage of Tyāgarāja*, p.141.
26. Prof. Gowri Kuppuswamy & Dr. Hariharan. M. *Index of Songs in South Indian Music*, p.585.
27. Ranga Ramanuja Iyengar, *Kṛitī Mani Malai*, Vol iii, p.333.
28. Ramanujachariar and V. Raghavan., *The Spiritual Heritage of Tyāgarāja*, p.50.
29. *Ibid.*, p.88.
30. Parthasarathi. T.S., *Sri Tyāgarāja Kṛitīs*, p.19.
31. Ranga Ramanuja Iyengar., *Kṛitī Mani Malai*, Vol iii, p.211.
32. Prof. Sambamoorthi, *Indian Songs*, Vol. IV, p.22.
33. Prabhala Janaki., *The Echo of Vedanta in Tyāgarāja's Musical Compositions*, pp.141-142.
34. Parthasaradhi. T.S., *Glimpses of Indian Music*, p. 223.
35. *The Hindu Speaks on Music*, compiled by the Editor, p.5.
36. Gouri Rammohan., V, (Ph.D, Thesis) *A Comparative and analytical study of the lives and works of Tyāgarāja, Muthuswāmi Dikshitār and Śyāma Śāstri-The Musical Trinity*, Chapter IV, p.46.
37. Parthasaradhi. T.S., Sri *Tyāgarāja Kṛitīs*, p.531
38. *Ibid.*, p.205.
39. Parthasaradhi. T.S., *Glimpses of Indian Music*, p.224.
40. Vasudevacharya. K., *A Comparitive Study of Sri Tyāgarāja and other Vaggeya Karas*, p.33.
41. Goswami. O., *The Story of Indian Music*, p.14.
42. Shantsheela Sathianathan., *Saints of South India*, p. 214.
43. Ramanujachariar and V. Raghavan, The Spiritual Heritage of *Tyāgarāja*, Madras, 1957, P: 5.
44. Dr. Annapurana. L., *Music and Temples A Ritualistic Appraoch*, p.148.

45. Dr. Annapurana. L. *Music and Temples A Ritualistic Appraoch*. pp.149-152.
46. Satyanarayana Nookala., *Sri Tyāgarāja Pañcaratna Kīrthanamulu*, p.1.
47. Jampana Kumaravarma., Vartha Telugu daily, Prabhathavartha cultural, 24th June, 2006, Visakhapatnam.
48. *Ibid.*
49. Prof. Gowri Kuppuswamy & Dr. Hariharan. M., *Index of Songs in South Indian Music*, pp.915-920.
50. Dr. Annapoorna. L., *Music and Temples A Ritualistic Approach*, p.146.
51. Raghavan. V., *Composers, Cultural Leaders of India*. Publications Division, Ministry of Information and Broadcasting, Government of India, p.20.
52. Mangal Gowri. N., *The Divine Heritage Of Muthuswāmi Dīkṣitār*, Ph.D.Thesis, Submitted to Andhra University, Visakhapatnam, p.12
53. *The Hindu Speaks on Music*, Compiled by the Editor, p.24.
54. Sundaram Iyer, *DīkṣitāKṛitī Mani Malai*, Vol-XII, 1959, p. 35.
55. Parthsaradhi. T.S., *Glimpses of Indian Music*, Ed. by Gowry Kuppuswami, p.98.
56. Annapoorna. L., *Music and Temples: A Ritualistic Approach*, pp.167-175.
57. Kṛitī Mani Malai., *RangaRāmānuja Iyengar*, Sabarmati, Vol-V, p.400.
58. Tachur brothers., *Gayaka Parijatha*, II series, p.21.
59. Tachur brothers., *Gayaka Lochanam*, IV series, p. 9.
60. V. Gouri Rammohan, A Comparative and analytical study of the lives and works of Tyāgarāja-Muthuswāmi Dīkṛitār and Śyāma Śāstri - The Musical Trinity, Thesis, 1999, Chapter IV, p. 60.
61. Shrinivas R., *Facets of Indian Culture*, p.107.
62. Shantsheela Sathianathan., *Saints of South India*, Vol. I, p.217.
63 Gouri Kuppuswami., *Index of South Indian Music*, pp. 884-888.
64. Annapurna. L, *Music and Temples: A Ritualistic Approach*, p.162.
65. Peggy Holroyde., *Indian Music*, New York, 1972.
66. Suresh Chandra Dey., *op.cit*, p.102.

8

Summary and Conclusion

Philosophers and scientists alike have always experienced great difficulty in their attempt to describe what music is. They have had even greater difficulty when they tried to understand why music should have such a profound impact, emotional, spiritual, upon many who hear it — an impact often referred to as, "meeting the moment in music".

The main object of studying Indian music as a synthesis between philosophy and religion is to bring out the facts that how Indian Music, especially, in Religio-cultural activity, plays a dominant role in establishing the spiritual path as a means to attain salvation. India had a rich cultural heritage, particularly in the field of music, in which singers and saints found an excellent means of realizing God. Music is the language of human souls and it is the one and only medium, which can easily convey human feelings direct to the Divine realm.

We learn from the Hindu mythology that Lord Viṣṇu, in the form of a fish, known as Matsyāvatāra, brought from the bottom of the Ocean the four *Vedas*, which were lying hidden there and handed those four *Vedas* to the human beings whom he created later. Lord *Viṣṇu* also taught the human beings all about the proper use and value of these four *Vedas*, which were afterwards, compiled as the *Ṛgveda*, the *Yajurveda*, the *Sāmaveda* and the *Atharvaveda*. *Vedas* were primarily and essentially meant for ritualistic ceremonies. The *Sāmaveda* was the source of music, and it was meant to sing. Large number of tunes came into use as *Samans* which are believed to be the original sources of later Indian music. It is said that there were a thousand ways of singing the *Samans*. As found in the *Chhāndogya Upaniṣad*. *Samans* were addressed to different elements of nature like the cloud, the seasons, the tree, the plant, the animals, etc.

Vedic music is the earliest instance of the deep relationship established between religion and music in India. Many features of this music later percolated in various ways and in different proportions into different kinds of Indian music, including Hindustani Art music. The *Ṛgveda* relied on recited hymns (*richa*). The musical chanting of the *Sāmaveda* employed more notes (finally settling on seven notes), and is said to be the source of the later secular and classical music. In fact, the word *sāma* itself is a compound expression and includes two entities: the first component '*sa*' refers to hymns, i.e. *richa*, and the second component, '*ma*' refers to the musical notes.

The tones used in the *sāmagāna* were five, six and seven and they were in downward movement emphasizing on the harmony between speech, tune and rhythm. The people to please the presiding deities of different *Vedic* sacrifices or *Yajñas* to get benedictions of brilliance, power, beneficence and wisdom used these *Vedic* songs. It is only from this *sāmagāna*, that seven notes were evolved which formed the basis not only for the *rāga* system of India, but also what is known as world music.

The singing of *sāma* was accompanied by the *veeṇā* in accordance with a procedure that connected body-movements, gestures and correct intonation in singing. Seated properly, the singer was to touch the middle phalanx of the fingers of the right palm with the right thumb according to the pitch of the note intended. A disciple learnt this procedure by imitating his preceptor in pitch, intonation as well as in finger movements.

As the early Indian music was based on ritual and *mantra*, correct pronunciation was of great significance. Often, even a slight mispronunciation signified 'death' instead of 'life'! And yet, music makers in the *Sāma-gāna* did not hesitate to bring about changes in the words of the *mantras* they sang! Freedom was so liberally enjoyed that rules were made to regularise these deviations because they added to the quality of music produced.

The *Gurukul* system dates back to the *Vedic* period. In the *gurukul* system of education, a pupil or *Śiṣya*, after his initiation (sacred thread ceremony), lived in the house of his *guru,* or teacher, and studied the *Vedas* and other subjects under his guidance, for a period of 12 years. *Gurus* were expected to teach everything they knew to the disciple. The institution was accessible only to the upper classes. The *gurukuls* were well supported by the kings who considered them as their bounded duty to make them financially sound viable.

After the Vedic music, *Gandharva* or *Mārga* music evolved, and then the formalized regional or Dēśī music enriched the treasury of Indian classical music in the form of *rāgas* and gītis.

Since the ancient times, Indian Music had a very clear differentiation in the different forms of music in use and had recognized the different aspects of music and the ways of expressing with the specific tone and rhythm to bring the desired equilibrium or desired emotions. The music of the peasants was different from that of the intellectuals. The music of the stage was different from that of the temple and the music for entertainment was different.

The Classical Period

The *Rāmāyaṇa* and the *Mahābhārata*, were originally secular in character, describing the heroic deeds of kings and noblemen, and most of them are not recorded in history. Subsequently, religious matter was added, including the very famous sermon *Bhagavad-Gītā* ("Song of the Lord"), and song celestial which is the most important religious document of *Hinduism;* and most of the heroes of the epics were identified as incarnations of the Hindu deities. The legends were probably sung and recited by wandering minstrels and bards even before the advent of the Christian Era, in the same way as they still are. The stories were also enacted on the stage, particularly at the time of the religious festivals. The earliest account of drama is to be found in the *Nāṭya Śāstra* ("Treatise on the Dramatic Arts"), a text that has been dated variously from the second century BC to the fifth century AD and even later. It is virtually a handbook for the producer of stage plays dealing with all aspects of drama, including dance and music.

Theatrical music of the period apparently included songs sung on stage by the actors, as well as background music provided by an orchestra (which included singers) located offstage, similar to an orchestra pit. Melodies were composed on a system of modes, or *jātis*, each of which was thought to evoke one or more particular sentiments (*Rasa*) by its emphasis on specific notes. The modes were derived in turn from the 14 *Mūrcchanās* - seven pairs of ascending seven-note series beginning on each of the notes of two closely related heptatonic (seven-note) parent scales, called *Ṣaḍjagrāma* and *madhyamagrāma*. A third parent scale, *gāndharagrāma*, was mentioned in several texts of the period and some even earlier but is not included in the system laid in the *Nāṭya Śāstra*.

Mediaeval Period

In the next significant text on Indian music, the *Bṛhaddeśī*, written by the theorist *Matañga* about the tenth century AD, the *grāma-rāgas* are said to derive from the *jātis*. In some respects, at least, the *grāma-rāgas* resemble not the *jātis* but their parent scales. The author of the *Bṛhaddeśī* claims to be the first to discuss the term *rāga* in any detail. The *rāgas* of this period seem to have been named after the different peoples living in the various parts of the country, who suggest that their origin might lie in folk music.

The mammoth thirteenth-century text *Sangītaratnākara* ("Ocean of Music and Dance"), composed by the theorist Śārañgadēva, is often said to be one of the most important landmarks in the history of Indian music. It was composed in the Deccan (South-Central India) shortly before the conquest of this region by the Muslims and thus gives an account of Indian music before the full impact of Muslim influence. A large part of this work is devoted to *mārga* - that is, the ancient music that includes the system of *jātis* and *grāma-rāgas* - but Śārañgadēva mentions a total of 264 *rāgas*. Despite the use in both the *Bṛhaddeśī* and the *Sangītaratnākara* of a notation equivalent to the Western tonic sol-fa (with syllables, as do-re-mi...) to illustrate the *rāgas*, modern scholars have not yet been able to reconstruct them with assurance.

Seven Svaras and Suras

In Indian music it is traditionally known there are seven *svara*s or *suras*. These seven svaras are Ṣađja, *Riṣabha*, *Gāndhāra*, *Madhyama*, *Pañcama*, *Dhaivata*, and *Niṣāda (*or *Nikhāda*). Seven abbreviated forms of these are *Sa- Ri- Ga- Ma- Pa- Dha- Ni* or seven *Sargams*. These seven are *Śuddha svaras* and there are five more flat or sharp *svaras*, known as *Vikṛta svaras*. It is said that the *sargam* or the seven principal *svaras* have been primarily devised according to the voices and sounds of seven animals and birds. Among the seven *svaras Sa Ri Ga Ma Pa Dha Ni.* the *Sa* or *Ṣađja*, resembles the sound of the peacock. *Ri* or *Ṛṣabha* is similar to the sound of the bull; *Ga* or *Gāndhādra* is like the sound of the goat. *Ma* or *Madhyama* is like the sound of the "*Kraunca*" bird, *Pa* or *Pañcama*, is like the sound of the cuckoo; *Dha* or *Dhaivata* is like the sound of the horse, i.e. neighing of the horse, *Ni* or *Niṣāda* is like the sound of the elephant. Or, it can be said in other words that the seven *'svaras'* or the '*sargam*' have been culled or borrowed from the sounds of these animals and birds.

The first *Svara 'Sa'* comes out from the action of six parts of a human body: the nose, the throat, the chest, the palate, the tongue and the teeth-all these six parts of the human body are at work to reproduce the correct intonation of the first *Svara 'Sa'*, so the name for this '*Sa*' is *Ṣađja*,. According to Nārada, however, it is called *Ṣađja*, because the other six notes *Riṣabha* etc. proceed from it.

The sound which rises from the umbilicus, i.e. the navel sound, comes out through the throat and the head, thus it often appears to be like the sound of a bull and this sound is known as *Ṛṣabha*. In the same way the navel sound coming out through the throat and the head gives the touch of fragrant breeze before the nose and that *Svara* is called *Gāndhāra*. Incidentally it may be mentioned that unless one is a genuine type of devotee for practising the recitals of music, instrumental or vocal, he or she cannot realise the touch of the sweet breeze or anything like that.

The navel sound is called the *Madhyama Svara*. This *Madhyama Svara* originally rises from the umbilicus, then the sound passes through the chest and the throat and again goes back to the umbilicus. This is the type of *Madhyama Svara*. The *Pañcama Svara* moves about in five places of the body, i.e. in the umbilicus, the chest, the heart, the throat and the head. The *Dhaivata Svara* rises from the forehead of the human body. Since the *Dhiman* or the wise people would give vocal recitals of songs following this particular type of *Svara*, it is called *Dhaivata Svara*. And finally the seventh *Svara* or *Ni* is that one in which all these previous six *Svaras*, i.e. *Sa Ri Ga Ma Pa Dha* are absorbed or intermingled, i.e. *Nisanna*, so the seventh *Svara* is called *Niṣāda*.

It is but natural that religious music and secular music have mutual repercussions in any country and India was no exception to this, In fact, in the opinion of scholars, *Vedic* music and secular music developed side by side in India and the latter borrowed the elements of the former in a great measure. There is, therefore, nothing wrong in saying that the music of the *Vedas* inspired the popular music of India.

Different *Rāgas* and *Rāginis* are connected with visions of certain images, and concepts of *Rupa*. The concept of *Rupa* is also connected with, a code of *mantra*. Different code *mantras* or *Bija-mantras* are there for invoking both in the *Brāhmanical*, the *Buddhist tantras*, the presiding deities or icons and they believe that firmly as the code *mantras* are properly recited. Gods and goddesses become incarnate according to the concept of the *tantra* cult. The *Bija-mantras* arc the key-ziotcs of worshipping the deities, which often represent some specific *Rāga* or *Rāgini*. *Patanjali* stated that the mystic word *A-U-M* represents the concept of *Pranava*, the symbol of *Brahman*. Those who believe in abstract concepts do not have faith in any materialistic form of the God or the goddess. Therefore they believe in the existence of a mysterious power of vitality enveloping in music. In the recital of songs based on some thought or feeling the spirit is caught in sound. The music becomes itself an independent topic for giving vent to one's feelings and it assumes a tune and a form, which is steady and fixed. It also contains a force, which offers a boon to the *sādhakas*.

The aspect of this speculation of an image of a *Rāga* or *Rāgini* of music designs an idea of the prior formula of the *Rāgas* and *Rāginis* also. Therefore, the *Dhyānas* of *Rāgas* and *Rāginis* are composed with colourful sophistications based on the imagination of the artist, for instance the painter also draws beautiful pictures of those images. The emotional sentiment and mood of the artist become enriched and elevated, and the light of the *Ātman* which reflects different reactions of the mind illumines the 'entire realisation of the artist and thus superb feelings are conceived, designed and manifested in music. It has an effulgence of its own.

The Islamic Period

In the beginning of the fourteenth century the great poet Amir Khusru, who was considered to be extremely proficient in both Persian and Indian music, wrote that Indian music was superior to the music of any other country. Further, it is stated that, after the Muslim conquest of the Deccan under Malik Kafur, a large number of Hindu musicians were taken as captives by the royal armies and they settled in the North. Although orthodox Islam considered music as illegal, the Sufi doctrines, accepts music as a means for the realization of God. This enabled Muslim rulers and noblemen to extend their patronage for the development of this art.

At the courts of the Mughal emperors Akbar, Jahangir, and Shah Jahan, music flourished on a grand scale. Apart from Indian musicians, there were also musicians from Persia, Afghanistan, and Kashmir in the service of these rulers; nevertheless, it appears that it was Indian music that was most favoured. Famous Indian musicians, such as *Swāmi Haridas* and *Tansen,* are legendary performers and innovators of this period. After the example set by *Amir Khusru*, Muslim musicians took an active interest in the performance of Indian music and added to the repertoire by inventing new *ragās, tālas*, and musical forms, as well as new instruments.

The Muslim patronage of music was largely effective in the north of India and has had a profound influence on North Indian music. Compositions in the various dialects of *Hindi, Braj Bhasha, Bhojpuri*, and *Dakhani*, as well as in Urdu and Persian were introduced. A new approach to religion was, in any case, sweeping through India at about this time. This emphasized devotion (*bhakti*) as a primary means to achieve union with God.

The Islamic Sufi movement was based on an approach similar to that of the *bhakti* movements gained many converts in India. Sufism is a mystical school of Islamic thought which seeks the truth by direct personal experience. In Arabic, this mysticism is known as '*tasaww*''. The difference between Sufism and Islam is simple. All Muslims believe that every man is on a path leading to God. The mainstream Muslims believe that it is only possible to reach God after one's life; Sufis believe that God can be found during one's life too.

A manifestation of these devotional cults witnessed the growth of a new form of mystic-devotional poetry composed by wandering mendicants who dedicated their lives for the realization of God. Many of these mendicants have been sanctified and are referred to as poet-saints or singer-saints, since their poems were invariably set to music. A number of devotional sects sprang from all parts of the country, Among them, some Muslim, some Hindu, and others merging elements from both were found. These sects emphasized the individual's personal relationship with God. In their poetry, man's love for God was often represented as a woman's love for man and, specifically, the love of Rādha for Lord Kṛṣṇa. In the environment of the royal courts, there was a less idealistic interpretation of the word love, and much of the poetry, as well as the miniature painting, of the period depicts the states of experience of the lover and the beloved.

This attitude is also reflected in the musical literature of the period. From early times, both *jātis* and *rāgas* in their connection with dramatic performance were described as evoking specific sentiments (*rasa*) suitable for accompanying particular dramatic events. It was this connotational aspect, rather than the technical one, that gained precedence in this period. The most popular method of classification was in terms of *rāgas* (masculine) and their "wives", called *rāginis*, which was extended to include *putras*, their sons, and *bhāryas*, the wives of the sons. The *rāgas* were personified and associated with particular scenes, some of which were taken from Hindu mythology, while others represented aspects of the relationship between two lovers. The climax of this personification is found in the *rāgamāla* paintings, usually in a series of 36, which depict the *rāgas* and *rāginis* in their emotive settings.

The Modern Period

With the collapse of the Mughal Empire in the eighteenth century and the emergence of the British as a dominant power in India, the subcontinent was divided into many Princely States. Music continued to be patronized by the rulers, although the courts were never again regained their past glory and splendour.

Musically, there has been a continuous evc lution from the Islamic period to the present, and both North and South Indian classical music continued to expand. South Indian music has clearly been influenced more by theory than the North. In North Indian music, theory has had little influence on performance practice. This can be ascribed to the language problem, an especially significant influence exerted on the many Muslim musicians in North India, who were not able to cope with the Sanskrit musical literature. Thus, no attempt had been made to systematize the music, and the gap between performance and theory was widened until the present century. *Viṣṇu Nārayaṇa Bhaktānde*, one of the leading Indian musicologists of this century, contributed a great deal towards reducing the gap. Being both a scholar and a performer, he made much effort to collecting and notating representative versions of a number of *rāgas* from musicians belonging to different *gharānas* (family traditions).

To achieve perfect happiness even in this worldly life through the methods of concentration and undivided meditation to experience truth in the very depth of this world performance of music happens to be the only successful media. India had a rich cultural heritage, particularly in the field of music, in which singers and saints found an excellent means of realising God.

Music is the language of human souls and it is the one and only medium, which can easily convey human feelings directly to the Divine realm. It is a unique and unchallengeable medium that gives the singer supreme delight and transports him to sublime heights, to a state of bliss and godliness. Music melts the hardest of hearts and draws every living being with its magical notes, transporting the listeners to the unknown region of enchanting sound harmonies far beyond the trammels of this world. It makes the singer lose himself in the ecstasy of his own melody, plunging him into a "*Bhāva samādhi*", a state of intensely elevating meditation.

Indian Classical Music is much more than a mere sensate music, which only pleases the ear and ends there, but it is idealistic expressing mystic significance of life and fills the human mind with the Divine thoughts. They gratify the soul of the listeners. The *rāgas* create a consoling and transcending attitude of the human mind, elevate the listener to an ethereal plane and purify the knots of the mind through devotion, and the Supreme sacrifice.

It is stated that the *Ātman* happens to be the basic source or *adhisthāna* of the spirit of music as per the description of the philosophy of music. The sublime tune of the absolute music, which has no such audible sound or colour in essence, represents a song eternally and thus the phenomenal music with the basic raw-materials of tone, tune, rhythm, grace, etc. manifests itself; the absolute music is abstract and not objective in form. It is visual as well as audible through phenomenal music as it has been stated in the philosophy of music. The absolute music is indeed the quintessence of the sound in melody. The absolute music can be realised through the medium of the spiritual mind and that is celestial too. The spiritual *Sādhana* is indeed inseparable from the solid pattern of realising the eternal spirit of music. The purest form of *Sādhana* can raise the musician to the mystic truth of philosophy and in that stage the musician could be in direct communion with the heavenly bliss and he could achieve an immediate awareness of the absolute truth and tranquility.

Folk, Classical, and Popular Music

The wide field of musical phenomena in India ranges from the relatively simple two- or three-tone melodies of some of the hill tribes in central India to the highly refined art music heard in concert halis in the large cities. This variety reflects the heterogeneous population in terms of race, religion, language, and social status. In the villages, music is not just a form of entertainment but is an essential element in many of the activities of daily life and plays a prominent part in most of the rituals. These include life-cycle events, such as birth, initiation, marriage, and death; events of the agricultural cycle, such as planting, transplanting, harvesting, and threshing; and a variety of work songs. Much of this music could be described as functional, for it serves a utilitarian purpose; for instance, a harvest song might well give thanks to God for a bountiful harvest, but underlying this is the idea that singing this song in its traditional manner will help to ensure that the next harvest will be equally fruitful. These songs are usually sung by all of the members participating in the activity and they are not sung for an audience.

In each area and even within a single area, different social groups have their own individual songs whose origins are lost in antiquity. The songs are passed on from one generation to another and, in most of the cases the composers are unknown. Apart from folk songs, one also hears outdoor instrumental music in villages. The music is provided by an ensemble of varying size, which usually consists basically of a *Shehnai* in North India and *Nāgaswaram* in the South (an oboe type of instrument), and a variety of drums. These groups play at weddings, funerals, and religious processions. The musicians are professional or semi-professional. Such ensembles are found among the tribal as well as folk societies in villages and in cities.

Other kind of professional music is also found in the rural regions. Most areas are visited by religious mendicants, many of whom travel around the countryside singing devotional songs, along with a one-, two-, or three-stringed lute that generally provides only a drone or with a frame (tambourine-like) drum. They carry with them a small begging bowl and make them living entirely on what they receive in alms. (There are also itinerant magicians, snake charmers, acrobats, and storytellers who travel in the rural areas, often providing the only entertainment available in the villages.) Music is often involved in their acts, and the storyteller generally narrates the tales in the form of songs, which may be taken from the source of *Mahābhārata* and the *Rāmāyaṇa*, or from the *Purāṇas*, the legends that describe the adventures of the different incarnations of God as they rid the evil that beset world. Sometimes the narrative songs are concerned with historical characters which describe significant events of the wars that took place and the heroic deeds of the regional rulers. Some storytellers are specialized in narrating the tragic stories of romance and lovers.

During certain religious festivals, the villages might be visited by a traveling band of players who enact some of the mythological episodes connected with the festival. Such performances are accompanied by music and dances. During the festivals villagers may visit neighborhood shrines or temples, encountering religious mendicants singing devotional songs and perhaps watching elaborate enactments of the episodes connected with the festival. Thus, the villagers become familiar with the mythological and philosophical aspects of their religion.

In the modern times, rural areas are being influenced to a greater extent by the urban culture. The introduction of relatively less expensive transistorized radios, exerted profound influence and found their way into fairly remote villages. By the end of the twentieth century the television and its multi-channel coverage, has brought music of all ranges to the remote areas. In addition, the touring halls cinema set up quickly and easily in tents, have made their appearance in the rural areas for some years. As a result, the traditional rural forms of music and dance have undergone some change.

Classical Music

Classical music is based on two main elements, *rāga* and *tāla*. The word *rāga* is derived from a Sanskrit root which means "to colour", the underlying idea being that certain melodic shapes, involving specific intervals of the scale, produce a continuity of emotional experience and "colour" the mind. Since, neither the melodic shapes nor their sequence are fixed precisely, a *rāga* serves as a basis for composition and improvization. While a *rāga* is primarily a musical concept, specific *rāgas* have acquired, particularly in North Indian music, a number of extra musical elements which are associated with particular periods of the day, seasons of the year, colours, deities, and specific moods. The second element of Indian music, *tāla*, is at best described as time measure. It has two main constituents; the duration of the time measure in terms of time units that vary according to the tempo chosen; and the distribution of stress within the time measure. *Tāla,* like *rāga*, serves as a basis for composition and improvisation.

Small ensembles of not more than five or six musicians generally perform Indian classical music. Improvisation plays a major part in a performance, and great emphasis is laid on the creativity and sensitivity of the soloist. Performance of a *rāga* usually goes through well-defined stages, beginning with an *ālāpa* (improvised melodic prelude) that is followed by a composed piece set in a particular time measure. The composition is generally quite short and serves as a frame of reference to which the soloist returns at the conclusion of his improvisation. There is no set duration for the performance of a *rāga.* A characteristic feature of North Indian classical music is the gradual acceleration of tempo, which leads to a final climax. The South India *Carāntic* music is nothing but devotional music. Many saint composers like, *Purandaradāsa*, *Tyāgarāja*, *Śyāma Śāstri*, Muthuswāmi *Dikşitār* are venerated for their great contribution to the *Carnātic* music.

Non-classical Music of the Cities

Classical music creates interest only to the people a small

proportion, even in the cities. Since 1930, a new genre, associated with the cinema, achieved extraordinary widely acclaimed popularity. Most of the Indian films are similar to the Western musicals and generally include six or more songs. Film music derives its source of inspiration from both Indian and Western: classical, folk, and devotional music are the main Indian sources, while Western influence is seen most obviously in the use of large orchestras that employ both Western and Indian instruments. The influence of Western popular music, too, is very evident. In spite of the eclectic nature of Indian film music, most of the songs maintain an Indian feeling that arises largely from the vocal technique of the singers and the ornamentation of the melody line.

Apart from classical and film music, there are several other forms of urban music, some of which has similar resemblance with the music of the rural areas. In city streets one is likely to encounter with an outdoor announcement of a wedding or a funeral. Street musicians, religious mendicants, snake charmers, storytellers, and magicians perform at every available opportunity, and construction workers and other labourers are engaged in singing songs related to that work. In private homes still other forms of music are performed, ranging from religious chanting to traditional folk and devotional songs. In public places of entertainment, the listener may encounter, apart from classical and film music, theatrical music from one of the relatively modern forms of regional theatre; and in the lowbrow places of entertainment courtesans still sing and dance in traditional fashion. In the larger cities there are performances of Western chamber music and occasionally symphony concerts, as well as popular dance music, rock, and jazz in the nightclubs.

In India, music is a handmaid of religion, a vehicle for the expression of the pining of the soul for communion with the Absolute. Composers of music have achieved a rare blending of religion, art and science to a remarkable extent. The platform on which such achievement is realised is built with the sublimation of the emotional nature in the individual. The pursuit of perfection in art is but a path of divinity; every lamppost on this path is an outburst of creative exuberance. In music, this took the form of compositions.

During the post period of *Śankara*, with the rise of *Gorakhnāth* and the *Nāth Sampradāya*, there arose a line of Saints and Mystics who brought the wisdom of the ancients, the *Ṛiṣis* and the *Āchāryās*, to the common people in different part of the country. They adopted the local language for communication and used the medium of song in their mission. They were pilgrims, all the time moving among the people. They come from all classes and different strata of the society, which in itself was the outcome of the universal consciousness with the feeling of the basic oneness of men that they proclaimed. They might have risen in diverse schools of religion or philosophy, but all of them emphasized the fundamental truths and upheld the eternal values. With satire and sarcasm, and in local language with similes and symbols, they declaimed hypocrisy and corruption, empty forms and rituals and all kinds of sham. Their plea was for sincerity of faith, fellowship of beings and integration of the whole man.

With the fall of *Hindu* kingdoms the ideals and institutions of *Dharma* and *Bhakti*, which they cherished were in peril. The minstrels of upheld the morality of the people and preached the need for spiritual values and their significance over mundane pursuits. They revitalized the devotion and faith, the *Bhakti* and *Sraddha*, of different classes and the masses. With the advent of acculturation, confrontation was not the only outcome; but there was also a synthesis, which gave rise to bridge the gulf to the saints with the voice of integration.

Music and Devotion

Music occupies an important place in the context of spiritual *Sādhana* in India. In order to recognize the real meaning and spirit of music and thereby to experience truth in this art, practice of *Rāgas* is very important. Music in India is also very much involved in the correct representations of the *Rāgas*, where the musician would recognise the true emotional spirit of music. To achieve perfect happiness even in this mundane life through concentration and undivided meditation to experience the essence of truth in its depth in this world performance of music happens to be the only successful media.

The realization of *Rāgas* is very deep and meaningful irrespective of the pattern, character and colour: music touches the sentiments of all 'human beings. The musical tunes create the melodic pattern in the spirit of ascents and descents maintaining harmonious relations in the context of the spirit of *Mūrcchanās*, *Alankāras*, *Tānas* and ten essentials which tend to render music lively and vibrating with the new spirit.

The microtones are equipped with aesthetic tones, sentiments and spirit and make celestial forms of the *Rāgas* enriched with those qualities. Those who therefore come in contact with tunes of music, become absorbed in it and darkness enveloped in their mind become slowly dispelled by the bright rays emanating from it. Their heart' becomes elevated too. Thereby the self-effulgent light of the eternal *Ātman* gets kindled. In reality the realisation of the knowledge or the *Ātman* is indeed the principal object of all music artistes and music lovers and the knowledge of music does indeed elevate the mind of the genuine *Sādhaka* of music to achieve something sublime and great.

Music as the medium of a language, converges the feelings and sentiments of a man in remarkably an effective manner. The history of Indian music is covered in deep antiquity and was cultivated as necessary accomplishment of religion. The origin of music at the out set seems to have conveyed the idea of our passions to others. In course of time, when language had attained a certain degree of intelligibility, its use began to be restricted to the worship of the Supreme Being. Subsequently it was extended to the commemoration of great events, the celebration of praises of chieftains and heroes, and lastly to the alleviation of the sufferings of the society.

In the North, the compositions of the saint-poets of the 15th and 16th centuries, left an indelible mark on our cultural heritage: *Kabirdas* (1456); *Soordas* (1540); *Tulsidas* (1554); *Mirabai* (1560); *Raidas* (16th century); *Namdev* (15th century), *Tukaram* (16th century); *Nanakdev* (1469) and others.

In the South the evolution of the musical forms took place during the seventh century, the age in which the *Śaivite* saints *Appār, Sundarār* and others sang their devotional songs. These compositions were set in melody-forms, which were later, termed as *rāgas*. In the 12th centrury, *Jayadeva* in his immortal *Geetagovinda* wrote the *aṣṭapadis* set to the constraints of *rāga* and *tāla*. Later with the compostions of Annamācharya and others of *Tallapākkam* during the 15th century, the *devarnāmas* of *Purandaradāsa* during the 16th century

The *varṇas* of *Pallavi Gopālayyar* and *Pachimariyam Adiyapriah* built the strong structure of the musical forms set in developing sections in *rāga* and *tāla*. *Bhadrāchala Rāmadās, Gopālakrishna Bhārati, Swāti Tiruṇāl* and the musical *Trinity, Tyāgarāja, Śyāma Śāstri and Muthuswāmi Dikshitār stabilized* the form *Kṛiti* with its *angās* or parts, viz., *pallavi, anupallavi* and *charaṇa*, giving scope for improvisation. Thus the *Bhajana* or devotional form of music made its entry to the realms of scientific classical music, enriched by the great composers and eminent musicologists. The theme of classical compositions continued to be devotional.

Thus we find music, playing a significant role in the spiritual development of individuals and the society. In all religions, music has got to play a vital role in group worship, rituals and spiritual *sādhana*.

Commenting on the Indian music, its spirit and form, Sir Rabindranath Tagore rightly says, "Indian music has a transcendental significance, it disengages the spiritual from the happening of life; it sings of the relationship of the human soul with the soul of things beyond." The spirit of nationalism in its depth and religion shows itself in Indian music as much as in other things. It has a sacred purpose connected with the regeneration of the human heart.

The aesthetics of Indian music comprises of philosophical reflections on its origin, nature, power, purpose and value. It produces the beauty of harmony with the expression of emotion as its essential feature. The sounds so produced with musical compositions create a pleasant mood which consoles those in grief, comforts those in distress and alleviates those in suffering and take them to the heights of bliss.

South India has a rich heritage of classical music. The musical Trinity, *Tyāgarāja, Śyāma Śāstri* and *Muthuswāmi Dikshitār* had shone in all its glory, iived aesthetically and spiritually richly. They stand as lasting ideals for the countless generations known for their devotional dedication. The wealth of their compositions is so great that their creations are identified with Carnatic Music. Their each composition is complete in deep and profound devotion.

As Dr. V. Raghavan observes, "No one could be a votary of Carnatic Music without coming under the influence of the religious and spiritual message of the repertoire of that art; nor could one study the history of Indian music, or even of Indian literature, without having to study at the same time the devotional movements that had swept the country. The historical continuity and the country-wide sweep seen in the activities of these saints of the regional languages underline the great role of consolidation that they played, leading to renewals and re-affirmations, from time to time, of the moral, religious and spiritual values of the people."

S. Radhakrishnan while writing Foreword to the book entitled, *The Spiritual Heritage of Tyāgarāja* aptly puts out:

> "The poets, singers and saints with their passionate devotion to the ideals to the ideals of beauty, harmony, freedom and aspiration have had the strongest impact on society."

Worshipping God as the beloved was propagated by many saint composers who believed that the best way to worship God was to love Him as their own kith and kin. They categorized this love as *śānta* (ordinary), *dāsya* (as a servant), *sakhya* (as a friend), *vātsalya* (as a son), and *madhura* (as a beloved). In the passage of time, the popularity of *bhajans* and *kīrthanas* did not diminish. Even today they are being composed by poets, musicians and ascetics. These devotional compositions represent the loftiest ideals, the deepest feelings and the sweetest melodies. The story of their music reveals the story of the Supreme soul.

Bibliography

Ashok, D. Ranade, *Essays in Indian Ethnomusicology*, Munshiram Manoharlal Publishers, Pvt. Ltd. New Delhi, 1986.

Babu Nanak Prasad, *Indian Music - Scientific and Practical*, Sundeep Prakasham, New Delhi, 1986.

Bharati Shuddhanand, *Alvar Saints and Acharyas*, Sudhanand Library, Adyar, Madras, 1980.

_____, *The Grand Epic of Shaivism* (contents), South India Shaiva Siddhanta Works, Madras, 1980.

Bandopadhyaya. Tinkodi Sangīta Shatadala, Vol-1, Sri Aurobindo Ashram, Pondicherry, 1979.

Bhagyalekshmy. S., *Lakṣana Granthas*, C.B.H. Publications, 1991.

Bharatiya D.S., *Hinduism through the Ages*, Vidya Bhavan, Bombay, 1987.

Chakraborty. P.C., *The Cultural Heritage of India*, Ist Ed, Firma KLM Publishers, Calcutta, 1933.

Chandradhar Sharma, *A Critical Survey of Indian Philosophy*, Motilal Banarsidass, Delhi, 1987.

Das. A.C. *Rigvedic India*, Munshiram Manoharlal Publishers Pvt. Ltd., New Delhi, 1927

David L. Sills, *International Encyclopedia of the Social Sciences*, The Macmillan Company & The Free Press, New York, Vol-9, 1973.

De, S.K., *History of Sanskrit Poetics, Bengali Literature in the 19th Century*, Firma KLM Publishers, Calcutta, 1946.

Deshpande, Vamanrao, *Maharashtra's Contribution to Music*, Maharashtra Information Centre, New Delhi, 1970.

Devasenapathi. V.. .., *Nayanamars, Devotional Poets and Mystics*, Part-I, Publication Division, Ministry for Information and Broadcasting, Government of India, Delhi, 1978.

Dutt. B.N., *Dialectics of Hindu Ritualism*, Munshiram Manoharlal Publishers Pvt. Ltd., New Delhi, 1950.

Ganesh Vasudeo Tagore, *Bhāgavatha Purāṇa* 10.33.10, Translated and annotated, Motilal Banarsdidass, Delhi, 1979.

Gangoly. O.C., *Rāgās and Rāginis. A Pictorial & Iconographic Study of Indian Musical Modes Based on Original Sources*. Munishiram Manoharlal Publishers Pvt. Ltd, 1989.

Gautam M.R., *Evolution of Rāga and Tāla in Indian Music*, Munshiram Manoharlal Publishers Pvt. Ltd., New Delhi, 1989.

Gentleman, Monthly, Vol –20, No. 7, July, 2000.

Gonda. J., *Vedic Rituals*, Leiden, E.J.Brill, 1980.

Goswami. O., *The Story of Indian Music*, Asia Publishing, Bombay, p.14, 1979

Gouri Nath Sastri. *The Philosophy of Word and Meaning*. 1959.

Gowry Kuppuswamy and M. Hariharan, *Glimpses of Indian Music*, ed. Sundeep Prakashan, Delhi, 1982.

Gowry Kuppuswamy, *Index of South Indian Music*, B.R. Publishing Corporation, Delhi, 1981.

Herbert A. Popley, *The Music of India*, Y.M.C.A. Publishing House, New Delhi, 1966.

Herward. C., *Higher Physical Development*, Manoharlal Publishers, New Delhi, 1960.

Jampanakumaravarma, *Vārtha Telugu Daily*, Prabhathavartha Cultural, 24th June, 2006.

Jayantha R.A., *Tallapāka Annamācharya, Composers, Cultural Leaders of India*, Ed, Ministry of Information and Broadcasting, Government of India, Delhi, 1979.

Joad. C.E.M., *Philosophy for Our Times*, London, 1940.

John Woodroffe, *Principles of Tantra*, Part –II, Oxford University Press, London, 1957.

Josef Kuckertz, *Essays on Indian Music*, Indian Musical Society, Bombay & Baroda, 1999.

Krishna Warrier A.G., Brahman as Value in the Brahmavidya, *The Adyar Library Bulletin*, XXX, 1961.

Lakshman Swarup, *The Rgveda and Mohenjadaro*, Indian Culture, Vol. IV, 1937.

Lewis Rowell, *Music And Musical Thought In Early India*, Munshiram Manoharlal Publishers Pvt. Ltd, New Delhi, 1998

Macdonell. A.A., *The Vedic Grammar*, Oxford University Press, London, 1958.

Mangala Gowri. N., *The Divine Musical Heritage of Muthuswami Dikshitar*, Ph.D, Thesis, Andhra University, Visakhapatnam, 1999.

Mircea Eliade, *The Encyclopedia of Religion*, Editor in chief, Volume 10, 1987.

Mukherjee P.B., *The Metaphysics of Sound, An Appendix to Japasūtram*, 1961.

Mukhopadhyay. K.L., *History of Science and Technology in Ancient India*: The Beginnings, Firma KLM, Calcutta, 1986.

Nagaraja Sharma. R., *Glimpses of Indian Music*, Ed. Sundeep Prakashan, Delhi, 1982.

Pande. G.C., *The Down of Indian Civilization*, Centre for Studies in civilizations, Vol-1, Part-1, 1999.

Pandit M.P., *Sādhana in Sri Aurobindo's Yoga*, The Jupiter Press Pvt. Ltd. Madras, 1964..

Parthasarathi. T.S., *Sri Tyāgarāja Kṛitīs*, Higginbothams, Madras, 1973.

_____, *Glimpses of Indian Music*, Ed, Sundeep Prakashan, Delhi, 1982

Peggy Holroyde, *The Music of India*, Praeger Publishers, New York & Washington, 1972.

Philip P. Wiener, *Dictionary of the History of Ideas, Studies of Selected Pivotal Ideas*, Charles Scribner's sons, New York, 1973.

Popley. H.A., *The Music of India*. Y.M.C.A. Publishing House, New Delhi, 1966.

Rabindranath Tagore, *Gitanjali*, Bharatiya Samskriti Samsad Trust, Calcutta, 1973.

_____, *Creative Unity*, Macmillan India Ltd., reprint, New Delhi, 1995.

Raghavan. V., *The Great Integrators*, Patel Memorial Lectures, (Ed), Ministry of Information and Broadcasting, Government of India, Delhi, 1979..

_____, *Cultural Leaders of India, Devotional Poets and Mystics*, Part-I, (Ed) Publication Division, Ministry of Information and Broadcasting, Government of India, New Delhi, 1983.

_____, *Cultural Leaders of India, Composers*, (Ed), Publication Division, Ministry of Information and Broadcasting, Government of India, New Delhi, 1978.

_____, *Cultural Leaders of India, Devotional Poets and Mystics*, Part-II, (Ed) Publication Division, Ministry of Information and Broadcasting, Government of India, New Delhi, 1981.

_____, *Sangītā Sāmpradāya Pradarsini, Subba Rāma Dikshitār*, Music Academy, Madras, Vol-I, 1961.

Rāmānujachariar.C. Prof. V. Raghavan, *The Spiritual Heritage of Tyōgarāja*, Sri Ramakrishna Math, Madras, 1958

Ramakrishnamath *Bhajana Ratnākara*, Ramakrishnamath Press, Madras, 1972.

Ramnanathan .N. *Musical forms in Sangītā Ratnākāra*, Sampradaya Publications, Chennai, 1999

Ranga Rāmānuja Iyengar, *Kṛiti Mani Malai*. Vol iii, Sabarmati Publications, Madras, 1947.

Robert Leopold Simon, *Spiritual Aspects of Indian Music*, Sundeep Prakashan, Delhi, 1984.

Sabharatnam, K., *India's Spiritual Heritage*, Divya Jeevan Publications League, Nagpur, 1966.

Satyanarayana Nookala, *Sri Tyāgarāja Pancharatna Kirtanamulu*, Maruthi Publications, Madras, 1986.

Selina Thielemann, *Singing The Praises Divine: Music in the Hindu Tradition*, A.P.H Publishing Corporation, New Delhi, 2000.

_____, *The Spirituality of Music*, A.P.H Publishing Corporation, New Delhi, 2001.

_____, *Divine Service and the Performing Arts in India*, A.P.H Publishing Corporation, New Delhi, 2001.

_____, *The Music of South Asia*, A.P.H. Publishing Corporation, New Delhi, 1999.

Shantheela Sathianathan, *Saints of South India*, Kanishka Publishers Distributors, New Delhi, 1996.

Sharma. D.S., *Hinduism Through the Ages*, Bharatiya Vidya Bhavan , Bombay, 1996.

Shastri Neelkanth A. *History of South India*, Oxford University Press, London, 1966.

Sinha. J.N., *Indian Psychology*, II, *Emotion and Will*, Gyan Publishing House, New Delhi, 1961.

Sircar. D.C., *Studies in the Religious Life of Ancient and Medieval India*, Motilal Banarasidas, Delhi, 1971.

Srinivasan. R., *Facets of Indian Culture*, Bharathiya Vidya Bhavan, Bombay, 1980.

Srinivas Raghavan. A., *Alvars, Devotional Poets and Mystics*, part-I, Publications Division, Ministry of Information and Broadcasting, Government of India, New Delhi, 1978.

Subrahmanya Sastri, Sangīta Ratnākara of Śārańgadēva, with Kalānidhi of Kāllinātha and Sudhākara of Simhabhupāla, Ed, Sabarmati Publishers, Madras, Vol-I, 1947.

Sumati Mutatkar, *Bharathiya Samskriti*, Bharatiya Samskriti Samsad Trust, Calcutta, 1983.

Sundaram Iyer, *Dikshita Kṛiti Mani Malai*. National Book Trust India, New Delhi, Vol-XII, 1959

Suresh Chandra Dey, *The Quest For Music Divine*, Ashish Publishing House, New Delhi, 1990

S.V.Krishnamurthy, *The Hindu Speaks on Music*, Kasturi Sons Ltd. Chennai, Ed.1999.

Swami Chidbhavananda, *The Bhagavad Gīta*, Sri Ramakrishna Tapovanam, Tirupparaitturai, Madras, 1970.

Swami Hari Premananda Sarasvati. Yogatārāvali by Adi Śankarāchārya, (commentary), *Yoga Magazine of the Bihar School of Yoga*, Monghyr, August, 1977.

Swāmi Prajñānānanda, *A Historical Study of Indian Music*, Munshiram Manoharlal Publishers Pvt. Ltd, New Delhi, 1981,

_____, *Historical Development of Indian Music*, Firma K.L. Mukhopadhyay Publishers, Calcutta, 1960.

_____, *The Form and Function of Music, in Ancient India*, Ramakrishna Vedanta Math, Calcutta, 1989.

Tachur Brothers, *Gāyaka Pārijātha*, II Seiries, Vijayanagaram, 1927.

_____, *Gāyaka Lochanam*, IV series, Madras, 1902.

Telang.M..R., *Sangītā Makāranda of Nārada*, Ed. Oriental Institute, Baroda, 1920.

Vasudēvacharya .K, *A Comparative Study of Sri Tyāgarāja and other Vaggeya Kārās*, Coimbatore, Sri Purandradasa Souvenir, 1964.

Vasudeva Sastri, *The Science of Music*, Tanjore, 1954.

Vernn Arnold. E., *Vedic Meter in its Historical Development*, Cambridge University Press, Cambridge, 1905.

Vidyashankar, *Śyāma Śāstri*, National Book Trust India, New Delhi, 1980.

Vijay Lakshmi M., *A Critical Study of Sangītā Makaranda of Narada*, Gyan Publishing House, New Delhi, 1996.

Wayne Howard, *Sāmavedic Chant*, New Haven: Yale University Press, 1977.

_____, *Mātralakṣanam*, translation and ed, Indira Gandhi National Centre for the Arts, New Delhi, 1988.

William Pole, *The Philosophy of Music*, London, 1879.

Index

■■■